Copyright © 2010 by Do

Hank Aaron (86) d. Jan 24
715th HR for Atlanta Braves
8 April 1974
broke Ruths record · career 755
Barry Bonds · Giants 762

Pujols game! pg. 240

Sources

My primary source of information is retrosheet.com. I also used "The Fall Classic: A Definitive History" by Eric Enders and "The World Series: An Illustrated Encyclopedia of the Fall Classic" by Josh Leventhal.

Thanks

THANKS TO KEN DEESEN FOR HIS TECHNICAL EXPERTISE IN THE FORMATTING OF THIS BOOK, FOR ALWAYS BEING THERE FOR THE NEXT CHANGE, AND FOR STICKING WITH THE DETROIT TIGERS THROUGH THICK AND THIN.

Dear God, thanks for baseball!

Dad, thanks for passing the grand game on to me.

For Cecilia

Foreword

Why write a book about the World Series? I guess it beats lying on a couch and flipping channels! To a great extent that is the reason. But also, in all my travels, I've never happened upon a book that offers a "thorough" account of each and every World Series game. There are numerous books that provide overviews of an entire series, but if there is one that breaks down each and every individual game, I haven't seen it. So I set out to do exactly that. Along the way I discovered some very interesting—very vibrant characters—whose attitudes, actions, sensibilities seem so bizarre and foreign to my own that I can't help but wonder what it would be like to sit and talk with them, either back in their world or at the Starbucks down the street.

A good example would be fiery NY Giants skipper John McGraw who won the National League pennant in 1904 but flat out refused to play the American League representative, Boston Pilgrims, sighting them and the league they represented as an inferior minor league team. McGraw was backed by team owner John T. Brush and the World Series was cancelled. Then there's Grover Cleveland Alexander, a World War I veteran and chronic alcoholic who's pictures bespeak a man closer in appearance to our grandfathers then to our baseball heroes. Yet this chiseled gladiator has woven his name eternally into World Series lore with some of the most heroic—and catastrophic performances in Fall Classic history.

Let's not forget the lovely and cuddly Ty Cobb who, during the 1909 World Series, travelled separately from his team to avoid being arrested on stabbing charges. Or how about Roger Peckinpaugh whose World Series' record eighth error in the seventh game of the 1925 Fall Classic cost the Washington Senators a championship? Peckinpaugh appeared to have shaken the albatross from his neck with what would've been a World Series winning homer in the seventh game, only to commit his eighth and final error moments later to lose it.

And on and on it goes. From the turn of the century into the twenties, thirties, forties, fifties, etc., the World Series is chock full of screwball characters and straight laced ones as well—all who—at one time or another execute feats of the grandest brilliance on the grandest of stages or, conversely, hiccup incompetence at precisely the worst moment.

Throughout the book, when I discover some interesting tidbit— such as Detroit Tigers' catcher Charles "Boss" Schmidt who played the 1907 World Series with a broken throwing hand and, not surprisingly, set the record for stolen bases allowed by a catcher, I enter it in footnote format. Rather than store all these footnotes at the back of the book, I do my best to enter them at the bottom of the page wherever the player and his "moment" or the accompanying fact occurs—if allowable. This is entirely for the reader's convenience.

As I discovered more and more personalities, events, controversies, oddities, I felt a profound sense that the characters behind them were still very much alive. It was as if they were staring up at me from the pages of the books in which I found them, and as odd as it may sound I could hear them saying to me, somewhat sternly, "Get it straight, Bud. Don't make me look bad!" So it is in deference to these indomitable souls that I do my best to humanize them, to keep them alive, to honor them and to respect them.

Therefore, I cannot, for example, write about Fred Snodgrass's crucial error in the tenth inning of the deciding game of the 1912 World Series without telling you about the over the shoulder catch he made later in the inning to turn a run scoring triple into a long and exciting out.

Looking back, having now completed this "Ruthian" task—that being the completion of this book—I feel as though I have gained acceptance into an ancient and strange fraternity, where all that matters is our grand game—baseball. And in this fraternity men are not judged by the size of their shoe, nor the size of their bank account, but by what they did or didn't do when it was their turn to perform on the grandest of grand stages. And with this acceptance comes a new found awareness and appreciation of an intangible golden thread that ties all of its members—from "Brickyard" Kennedy to Madison Bumgarner— together. I now dare call myself a strand of that golden thread. - Douglas Mallon

1903

Boston Americans (5) - Pittsburgh Pirates (3)

In the very first World Series, the Boston Pilgrims, later to become the Red Sox, battled back from a three-games-to-one deficit to beat the Pittsburgh Pirates five-games—yep that's right—five games—to three!

Game 1	October 1, 1903
Huntington Avenue Grounds (Boston)	T: 1:55[1]
Pittsburgh 7 : Boston 3	A: 16,242

Cy Young was touched up for four runs in the very first inning as the Pirates trounced the Beantown nine. Tommy Leach had two triples and Jimmy Sebring walloped the first round tripper in World Series history to pace the Pittsburgh attack. "Deacon" Phillippe fanned ten Boston hitters and scattered six hits en route to a complete game victory.

Game 2	October 2, 1903
Huntington Avenue Grounds (Boston)	T: 1:47
Boston 3 : Pittsburgh 0	A: 9,415

Boston hurler Bill Dinneen struck out eleven and scattered three hits while blanking the Pirates to even the series. Patsy Dougherty sparked the Pilgrims' offense with an inside-the-park-homer in the first inning and an over-the-wall blast in the sixth. Sam Leever, who lasted just one inning, was saddled with the loss.

Game 3	October 3, 1903
Huntington Avenue Grounds (Boston)	T: 1:50
Pittsburgh 4 : Boston 2	A: 18,801

The Pirates touched up Pilgrims' starter Tom Hughes for three runs in just two-plus innings of work, which proved to be enough as "Deacon" Phillippe notched his second complete game victory of the series—on just one day's rest! Cy Young came on in relief of Hughes in the third and surrendered only one run on three hits over the next seven innings.

Game 4	October 6, 1903
Exposition Park (Pittsburgh)	T: 1:30
Pittsburgh 5 : Boston 4	A: 7,600

Ginger Beaumont had three hits and Tommy Leach knocked in three runs as the Pirates jumped out to a commanding lead in the series. This one didn't come without a scare. Pittsburgh took a four-run cushion into the ninth but Boston battled back to cut the lead to one. With the tying run in scoring position, "Deacon" Phillippe induced pinch-hitter Jack O'Brien to pop out to end the game. It was Phillippe's third complete game victory of the series. Bill Dinneen went the distance for Boston in a losing effort.

Game 5	October 7, 1903
Exposition Park (Pittsburgh)	T: 2:00
Boston 11 : Pittsburgh 2	A: 12,322

Cy Young put Boston back in the hunt with an impressive six-hit complete game victory. Young, who did not allow an earned run, got it done with the stick as well, recording two hits and knocking in three runs. Pittsburgh's "Brickyard" Kennedy, who surrendered ten runs on eleven hits in seven innings of work, suffered the loss.

Game 6	October 8, 1903
Exposition Park (Pittsburgh)	T: 2:02
Boston 6 : Pittsburgh 3	A: 11,556

Sam Leever was handed his second loss of the series as Boston walloped the Pirates. Bill Dinneen went the distance for his second win. Jimmy Collins, Chick Stahl and Hobe Ferris all had run scoring singles to pace the Pilgrim's attack. Ginger Beaumont went 4-for-5, scored a run and stole two bases in a losing effort.

Game 7	October 10, 1903
Exposition Park (Pittsburgh)	T: 1:45
Boston 7 : Pittsburgh 3	A: 17,038

Cy Young turned in a three-hit complete game victory. Boston backstop Lou Criger had two hits and knocked in three runs. "Deacon" Phillippe turned in his fourth complete game of the series, allowing seven runs on eleven hits in a losing effort.

Game 8	October 13, 1903
Huntington Avenue Grounds (Boston)	T: 1:35
Boston 3 : Pittsburgh 0	A: 7,455

Hobe Ferris went 2-for-4, knocking in all three runs and Bill Dinneen recorded his third victory and second shutout as Boston downed Pittsburgh to win the first World Series. "Deacon" Phillippe allowed just three runs on three hits in eight innings of work, but suffered the loss. It was his fifth decision of the series and his second defeat in three days.

1904
World Series Cancelled

The National League champion New York Giants refused to play the American League champion—and defending World Champion—Boston Pilgrims in what would have been the second World Series. Giants' owner, John T. Brush remarked, "We have gained all the glory there is to be acquired in baseball—winning the National League pennant." But Brush's truer motives might have been found in his contempt for American League president, Ban Johnson, who had placed an AL franchise—the New York Highlanders—(soon to become the Yankees) just a stone's throw away from the Polo Grounds. As the owner of a National League franchise it is not likely that Brush would be willing to do anything that would help legitimize the upstart new league, nor welcome the box office competition that was certain to come with it. The Giants' legendary manager, John McGraw[2], was equally as adamant about not playing the Pilgrims. "... Never while I am the manager of the New York Club and while this club holds the pennant will I consent to enter into a haphazard box-office game with Ban Johnson & Company." The general fans' sentiment was one of great disappointment. One New York newspaper generated a petition with the signatures of ten-thousand Giants' faithful asking that the World Series be played. The petition fell on deaf ears.

1905

NY Giants (4) - Philadelphia Athletics (1)

In the only World Series that featured a shutout in every contest, the Giants vanquished Philadelphia in five games. Christy Matthewson tossed three complete game shutouts, a record that still stands to this day.

Game 1	October 9, 1905
Columbia Park (Philadelphia)	T: 1:46
New York 3 : Philadelphia 0	A: 17,955

Christy Matthewson pitched a four-hit shutout and the Giants touched up Philadelphia hurler Eddie Plank—(staff ace Rube Waddell was injured in a scuffle with a teammate)—for two in the fifth on Mike Donlin's RBI base hit and Sam Mertes' run scoring double. Roger Bresnahan singled home a run in the ninth to close out the scoring.

Game 2	October 10, 1905

Polo Grounds (New York)	T: 1:55
Philadelphia 3 : New York 0	A: 24,992

The A's turned the tables on the Giants as Charles "Chief" Bender fanned ten while scattering four hits en route to a complete game shutout. Bris Lord had two run scoring singles and Topsy Hartsel added an RBI double. Joe "Iron Man" McGinnity, who did not allow a single earned run over eight innings, suffered the loss.

Game 3	October 12, 1905
Columbia Park (Philadelphia)	T: 1:55
New York 9 : Philadelphia 0	A: 10,991

Christy Matthewson came back on one day's rest and turned in the second of his three complete game shutouts, allowing just four hits and striking out eight as the Giants trounced the A's. Dan McGann had three hits and knocked in four runs to pace the New York attack. Andy Coakley went the distance for the A's, allowing nine runs on nine hits in a losing effort.

Game 4	October 13, 1905
Polo Grounds (New York)	T: 1:55
New York 1 : Philadelphia 0	A: 13,598

The Giants capitalized on two fourth inning errors to plate the only run of the game. "Iron Man" McGinnity hurled a five-hit complete game shutout. Eddie Plank suffered the loss despite not allowing an earned run in his eight innings of work.

Game 5	October 14, 1905
Polo Grounds (New York)	T: 1:35
New York 2 : Philadelphia 0	A: 24,187

The New York Giants captured their first World Series title as Christy Matthewson turned in the third of his aforementioned three complete game shutout victories. Matthewson scattered six hits and struck out four but did not walk a batter. Control was losing pitcher Chief Bender's undoing. He issued three walks—two of which led to New York runs.

1906

Chicago White Sox 4 - Chicago Cubs 2

In the only all-Chicago World Series in history the heavily favored (Tinker to Evers to Chance) Cubs, winners of a record 116 regular season games, are upended by their cross-town rival White Sox, a team the local press had dubbed "The Hitless Wonders".

Game 1	October 9, 1906
West Side Park (Cubs)	T: 1:45
White Sox 2 : Cubs 1	A: 12,693

In freezing temperatures and snow flurries the White Sox stunned the Cubs in the opener. Cubs' backstop Johnny Kling's two passed balls and one error led to both White Sox runs. Nick Altrock hurled a complete game for the win. Mordecai "Three Finger" Brown went the distance for the Cubs in a losing effort.

Game 2	October 10, 1906
Southside Park (White Sox)	T: 1:58
Cubs 7 : White Sox 1	A: 12,595

There were no Tinkers to Evers to Chance double plays in this one but the Cubs' tremendous trio did combine for six runs, four hits an RBI and five stolen bases. Ed Reulbach turned in a complete game one hit gem for the victory. Sox starter Doc White allowed four runs over three innings and was charged with the loss.

Game 3	October 11, 1906
Westside Park (Cubs)	T: 2:10
White Sox 3 : Cubs 0	A: 13,667

George Rohe drove in all three runs with his second triple of the series as the White Sox triumphed again. Sox starter Ed Walsh allowed only two hits—both in the first inning and struck out twelve en route to a complete game shutout. Jack Pfiester went the distance for the Cubs— fanning nine in a losing effort.

Game 4	October 12, 1906
Southside Park (White Sox)	T: 1:36
Cubs 1 : White Sox 0	A: 18,385

In a rematch of the opener, Mordecai "Three Finger" Brown bested Nick Altrock with a two hit shutout to even the series. The Cubs plated the only run of the game in the seventh when Frank Chance singled, Joe Tinker laid down a sacrifice bunt and Johnny Evers singled Chance home.

Game 5	October 13, 1906
Westside Park (Cubs)	T: 2:40
White Sox 8 : Cubs 6	A: 23,257

The White Sox, despite a Fall Classic record six errors, tamed the Cubs to move to within one win of a stunning World Series triumph. Frank Isbell clubbed four doubles, scored three runs and knocked in two to pace the Southsiders attack. Ed Walsh lasted six innings for the win. Jack Pfiester allowed four runs in one and a third innings of work and was charged with the loss. The Sox George Davis executed the first steal of home in World Series history.

Game 6	October 14, 1906
South Side Park (White Sox)	T: 1:55
White Sox 8 : Cubs 3	A: 19,249

Facing elimination, the Cubs sent their ace, Mordecai Brown, to the mound on just one day's rest. The move backfired as the White Sox jumped on "Three Finger" for three in the first and four in the second en route to a series clinching victory. Doc White went the distance for the win. The Sox Jiggs Donahue and George Davis combined for five hits and six RBI.

1907

Chicago Cubs (4) - Detroit Tigers (0) - (1 Tie)

Ty Cobb's rookie season ends in disappointment as the Cubs return to the Fall Classic to vanquish the Tigers in four straight games.

Game 1	October 8, 1907
West Side Park (Chicago)	T: 2:40
Detroit 3 : Chicago 3	A: 24,377

In the first tie game in World Series history Detroit was just one strike away from victory when "Wild Bill" Donovan fanned Del Howard for the final out, but catcher Charles "Boss" Schmidt[3] missed the ball, Howard took first and the tying run scored from third. The game was called due to darkness after twelve innings. "Wild Bill" pitched all twelve!

Game 2	October 9, 1907
West Side Park (Chicago)	T: 2:13
Chicago 3 : Detroit 1	A: 21,901

In the first inning Detroit 3rd baseman Bill Coughlin pulled the hidden ball trick on Chicago's Jimmy Slagle, for the first and only time in World Series history. But the Cubs got the last laugh as Slagle singled home Joe Tinker with what proved to be the game winning run in the fourth. Jack Pfiester went the distance for the win, scattering ten hits along the way. George Mullin also went the distance in a losing effort.

Game 3	October 10, 1907

West Side Park (Chicago)	T: 1:35
Chicago 5 : Detroit 1	A: 13,114

Johnny Evers had three hits including an RBI double and Ed Reulbach scattered six hits en route to a complete game victory as the Cubs tamed the Tigers. Detroit starter Ed Siever did not survive a three run fourth that featured four singles, a missed fly ball and two unearned runs. Ty Cobb managed one base hit in four trips to the plate.

Game 4	October 11, 1907
Bennett Park (Detroit)	T: 1:45
Chicago 6 : Detroit 1	A: 11,306

Ty Cobb tripled and scored to give the Tigers a short lived 1-0 lead in the fourth. But Cubs pitcher Orval Overall's two-run single in the fifth gave Chicago a lead they would not relinquish. Overall went the distance for the victory. "Wild Bill" Donovan also went the distance in a losing effort.

Game 5	October 12, 1907
Bennett Park (Detroit)	T: 1:42
Chicago 2 : Detroit 0	A: 7,370

The Cubs are champions! Jimmy Slagle scored what proved to be the game winning run in the very first inning and knocked in the second run later in the contest. "Three Finger" Brown turned in a seven hit complete game shutout to clinch it for Chicago. George Mullin suffered his second complete game loss of the series. Ty Cobb finished at .200, managing a triple and three singles in twenty trips to the plate.

1908

Chicago Cubs (4) - Detroit Tigers (1)

The Cubs and Tigers square off in the Fall Classic for the second straight year and when the dust finally settles the results are the same— Cubs Win! Cubs Win! Cubs Win!

Game 1	October 10, 1908
Bennett Park (Detroit)	T: 2:10
Chicago 10 : Detroit 6	A: 10,812:

Just as they had done the year before, the Tigers took the lead into the 9th inning of Game 1 only to see it slip away as the Cubs tallied five times in the final frame on the strength of six straight singles with a double-steal mixed in. "Three Finger" Brown, who came on in relief in the eighth was credited with the victory. Ed Summers was the loser in relief.

Game 2	October 11, 1908
West Side Park (Chicago)	T: 1:30
Chicago 6 : Detroit 1	A: 17,760

The Cubs exploded for six runs in the eighth on the strength of three singles, a double by Johnny Kling, a triple by Frank Schulte and a homer by Joe Tinker. Orval Overall went the distance for the win. "Wild Bill" Donovan, who took a shutout into the eighth, surrendered all six runs and was charged with the loss.

Game 3	October 12, 1908
West Side Park (Chicago)	T: 2:10
Detroit 8 : Chicago 3	A: 14,543

Ty Cobb had four hits and knocked in two runs as the Tigers beat the Cubs for the first time ever in the World Series. With the game seemingly out of reach in the ninth, Cobb stole second, then stole third and then was thrown out trying to steal home. George Mullin was the winner. Jack Pfiester was the loser. Both hurlers turned in complete game efforts.

Game 4	October 13, 1908

12

Bennett Park (Detroit)	T: 1:35
Chicago 3 : Detroit 0	A: 12,907

RBI singles by Harry Steinfeldt and Solly Hofman staked "Three Finger" Brown to a 2-0 lead. Brown turned in a four-hit complete game shutout for his second win of the series. The Cubs added an insurance run in the ninth when Ty Cobb muffed a fly ball in right field allowing Johnny Evers to score the final run of the game. Ed Summers was charged with his second loss of the series.

Game 5	October 14, 1908
Bennett Park (Detroit)	T: 1:25
Chicago 2 : Detroit 0	A: 6,210[4]

Johnny Evers singled and scored the game winning run in the first inning and later doubled home the second and final run of the contest as the Cubs defeated the Tigers in the World Series for the second year in a row. Orval Overall pitched a three-hit complete game shutout, striking out ten along the way to clinch it for Chicago. "Wild Bill" Donovan suffered his second complete game loss of the series.

1909

Pittsburgh Pirates (4) - Detroit Tigers (3)

In his third and final trip to the World Series, Ty Cobb is foiled again, this time in seven games, as Honus Wagner and the Pirates capture their first World Series title.

Game 1	October 8, 1909
Forbes Field (Pittsburgh)	T: 1:55
Pittsburgh 4 : Detroit 1	A: 29,264

The Tigers jumped out to a 1-0 lead in the first inning with Ty Cobb[5] scoring Detroit's lone run. But Fred Clarke belted a solo homer to tie it and George Gibson's RBI double an inning later plated what proved to be the winning run as Pittsburgh captured the opener. Despite a rocky start Pirates' rookie hurler Babe Adams notched a complete game victory. George Mullin pitched a complete game for the Tigers but was tagged with the loss.

Game 2	October 10, 1909
Forbes Field (Pittsburgh)	T: 1:45
Detroit 7 : Pittsburgh 2	A: 30,915

The Pirates scored two in the first off "Wild Bill" Donovan but it was all Tigers the rest of the way. "Boss" Schmidt had a single, a double and four RBI to pace Detroit's attack. Donovan went the distance for the win. Howie Camnitz was the loser. Ty Cobb stole home in the Tigers' three-run third inning.

Game 3	October 11, 1909
Bennett Park (Detroit)	T: 1:56
Pittsburgh 8 : Detroit 6	A: 18,277

Honus Wagner had three hits, scored a run, knocked in two more and stole three bases as the Pirates fended off the Tigers. Pittsburgh tallied five times in the opening frame but barely escaped with the victory. Nick Maddox scattered ten hits en route to a complete game win. Ed Summers lasted just one-third of an inning and was charged with the loss. Ty Cobb had two hits and knocked in two runs.

Game 4	October 12, 1909
Bennett Park (Detroit)	T: 1:57
Detroit 5 : Pittsburgh 0	A: 17,036

Tigers' backstop Oscar Stanage's second inning two-run single proved to be the game winning hit as battery-mate George Mullin scattered five hits and fanned ten en route to a complete game shutout. Ty Cobb added a two-run double later in the contest. The Pirates committed six errors, tying the World Series record. Lefty Leifield was the loser.

Game 5	October 13, 1909
Forbes Field (Pittsburgh)	T: 1:46
Pittsburgh 8 : Detroit 4	A: 21,706

Detroit's Davy Jones led off the game with a homer, the first time in World Series history that such a feat had been recorded. But the Pirates behind Fred Clarke's three-run round tripper in the seventh, prevailed. Babe Adams turned in his second complete game victory of the series. Ed Summers was tagged with his second loss of the series.

Game 6	October 14, 1909
Bennett Park (Detroit)	T: 2:00
Detroit 5 : Pittsburgh 4	A: 10,535

Honus Wagner doubled home two runs in Pittsburgh's three run first inning but George Mullin settled down and recorded his second complete game triumph of the series. Jimmy Delahanty's RBI double in the fifth put Detroit ahead for good. Ty Cobb added an RBI two-bagger an inning later. Vic Willis took the loss. Honus Wagner had a hit and knocked in two runs.

Game 7	October 16, 1909
Bennett Park (Detroit)	T: 2:10
Pittsburgh 8 : Detroit 0	A: 17,562

In the first ever seventh and deciding contest in World Series' history, Babe Adams recorded his third complete game victory as the Pirates clinched their first World Championship. Honus Wagner walked twice, tripled in two runs and scored while

Ty Cobb went 0-for-4. Though he would play for another nineteen seasons, Cobb would never again appear in a Fall Classic. "Wild Bill" Donovan lasted three innings and took the loss.

1910

Philadelphia Athletics (4) - Chicago Cubs (1)

Legendary manager Connie Mack[6] relied on just two pitchers, thirty-one game-winner Jack Coombs and "Chief" Bender to vanquish the heavily favored Cubs in five games.

Game 1	October 17, 1910
Shibe Park (Philadelphia)	T: 1:54
Philadelphia 4 : Chicago 1	A: 26,891

Frank "Homerun" Baker went 3-for-4, doubling twice, knocking in two runs and scoring one as well and "Chief" Bender went the distance, striking out eight and allowing only three hits as the Athletics stunned the Cubs in the opener. Orval Overall lasted just three frames and took the loss.

Game 2	October 18, 1910
Shibe Park (Philadelphia)	T: 2:25
Philadelphia 9 : Chicago 3	A: 24,597

Despite walking nine and surrendering eight hits, Jack Coombs picked up the first World Series win of his career and the Athletics made it two-straight over the heavily favored Cubs. Eddie Collins had three hits, scored two runs and knocked in one as well to pace the Philadelphia attack. "Three Finger" Brown, involved in an automobile accident on the way to the ballgame, allowed all nine A's runs on thirteen hits in a losing effort.

Game 3	October 20, 1910

West Side Park (Chicago)	T: 2:07
Philadelphia 12 : Chicago 5	A: 26,210

On just one day's rest, Jack Coombs earned his second straight complete game win—he also had three hits and knocked in three runs as the Athletics moved to within one victory of their first World Championship. Cubs' player-manager Frank Chance attacked a heckling fan before the game and, later that day, was ejected for arguing that the Athletics' Danny Murphy's three-run homer should have been ruled a ground rule double. It was the first ejection in World Series history.

Game 4	October 22, 1910
West Side Park (Chicago)	T: 2:14
Chicago 4 : Philadelphia 3 (10)	A: 19,150

The Cubs staved off elimination when player-manager Frank Chance tripled home the tying run in the bottom of the ninth and Jimmy Sheckard singled home the game winner in the bottom of the tenth. "Three Finger" Brown pitched two scoreless innings for the win. "Chief" Bender pitched the entire game for the A's, but was saddled with the loss.

Game 5	October 23, 1910
West Side Park (Chicago)	T: 2:06
Philadelphia 7 : Chicago 2	A: 27,374

The Athletics erupted for five runs in the eighth inning to blow it wide open and the stunning upset was complete. Jack Coombs turned in his third complete game victory in six days. Eddie Collins had three hits and knocked in two runs. "Home Run" Baker went hitless but did score a run. Cubs ace "Three Finger" Brown went the distance in a losing effort.

1911

Philadelphia Athletics (4) - NY Giants (2)

The Athletics capture their second straight World Championship in one of the most exciting and hotly contested Fall Classics of all time.

Game 1	October 14, 1911
Polo Grounds (New York)	T: 2:12
New York 2 : Philadelphia 1	A: 38,281

More than 38,000 crammed the newly rebuilt Polo Grounds to watch New York's ace Christy Matthewson square off against A's ace "Chief" Bender in the opener. Bender, who fanned eleven, lost the duel in the bottom of the seventh when Josh Devore doubled home what proved to be the game-winning run. Matthewson went the distance for the win.

Game 2	October 16, 1911
Shibe Park (Philadelphia)	T: 1:52
Philadelphia 3 : New York 1	A: 26,286

"Home Run" Baker's two-run blast in the sixth inning off Rube Marquard broke a 1-1 tie and gave the Athletics a series tying victory. Eddie Plank, who went the distance for Philadelphia, picked up the win.

Game 3	October 17, 1911
Polo Grounds (New York)	T: 2:25
Philadelphia 3 : New York 2 (11)	A: 37,216

"Home Run" Baker tied the game in the ninth inning with his second homer of the series, garnering the nickname that followed him into eternity. A pair of errors led to two Philadelphia runs in the eleventh and the Giants could only push one across in the bottom of the frame. Both starters, Jack Coombs for the A's and Christy Matthewson for NY, went the distance.

Game 4	October 24, 1911
Shibe Park (Philadelphia)	T: 1:49
Philadelphia 4 : New York 2	A: 24,355

After a six-day postponement due to rain, the Series resumed with Christy Matthewson and "Chief" Bender locking horns once again. Philadelphia's dynamic-duo—Eddie Collins and Frank "Homerun" Baker— were in the thick of things with Collins singling twice and Baker blasting a pair of doubles. Bender went the distance for the win. Matthewson allowed all four runs on ten hits over seven innings and was tagged with the loss.

Game 5	October 25, 1911
Polo Grounds (New York)	T: 2:33
New York 4 : Philadelphia 3	A: 33,228

The Giants lived to fight another day as Josh Devore's two-run single in the ninth tied it and Fred Merkle's sacrifice fly in the tenth won it. Though base runner Larry Doyle missed home plate, and never actually scored the winning run, the Athletics did not appeal and left the field leaving home plate umpire Bill Klem with no choice but to count the run. Doc Crandall picked up the win and Eddie Plank was the loser.

Game 6	October 26, 1911
Shibe Park (Philadelphia)	T: 2:12
Philadelphia 13 : Giants 2	A: 20,485

The Athletics clinched their second consecutive World Championship in decisive fashion, exploding—even by modern-day standards—for thirteen runs on thirteen hits including a four-run fourth and a seven-run seventh! "Chief" Bender registered his second complete game win to close it out. By series' end Frank "Homerun" Baker, who registered nine hits including two doubles and two homers, had become a national celebrity, a superstar, and the hero of every school boy in America.

1912

Boston Red Sox (4) - NY Giants (3) - (1 Tie)

In one of the most thrilling games in World Series history—Game 8!—two players—Fred Snodgrass and Fred Merkle would etch their names in infamy and the Red Sox would christen their brand new ballpark with a World Championship.

Game 1	October 8, 1912
Polo Grounds (New York)	T: 2:10
Boston 4 : New York 3	A: 35,730

Thirty-five game winner "Smokey" Joe Wood struck out eleven en route to a complete game victory in the series opener. Wood took a two-run lead into the bottom of the ninth but surrendered three straight singles. With the tying run on third and the go-ahead on first and just one out, Wood fanned the final two hitters to end it. Rookie Jeff Tesreau allowed all four Sox runs over seven innings of work and was tagged with the loss.

Game 2	October 9, 1912
Fenway Park (Boston)	T: 2:38
New York 6 : Boston 6 (11)	A: 30,148

The Red Sox scored three in the first inning but by the time the ninth rolled around the score was tied 5-5. The Giants scored a run in the top of the tenth and the Red Sox answered with one of their own in the bottom of the frame. The game was then called due to darkness. Christy Matthewson pitched all eleven innings for New York.

Game 3	October 10, 1912
Fenway Park (Boston)	T: 2:15
New York 2 : Boston 1	A: 34,624

Rube Marquard took a shutout into the bottom of the ninth and survived the scare of his life as the Sox cut the lead to one and had runners on second and third with two out. Then Hick Cady drilled one to the gap in right-center where Josh Devore ran it down for the final out of the game. Buck O'Brien allowed both NY runs over eight innings and took the loss.

Game 4	October 11, 1912
Polo Grounds (New York)	T: 2:06
Boston 3 : New York 1	A: 36,502

"Smokey" Joe Wood turned in his second complete game victory, scattering nine hits and fanning eight. Wood also had two hits and knocked in a run. Jeff Tesreau, owner of the league's lowest regular season ERA, lasted seven innings and surrendered two runs in a losing effort.

Game 5	October 12, 1912
Fenway Park, (Boston)	T: 1:58
Boston 2 : New York 1	A: 34,683

The Red Sox touched up Christy Matthewson for two runs in the second when Steve Yerkes and Harry Hooper hit back-to-back triples and Tris Speaker reached on an error. The Giants nearly tied it in the seventh when Bud Herzog singled and Art Fletcher doubled him home. Pinch hitter Moose McCormick followed with a base hit but Fletcher was nailed at the plate. Hugh Bedient posted a complete game victory.

Game 6	October 14, 1912
Polo Grounds (New York)	T: 1:58
New York 5 : Boston 2	A: 30,622

The Giants erupted for five runs in the opening frame on the strength of four singles, two doubles and a steal of home (by Art Herzog) and never looked back. The Red Sox answered with a pair in the second on Clyde "Hack" Engle's two-run double. Neither team scored the rest of the way. Rube Marquard scattered seven hits en route to his second complete game victory of the series. Buck O'Brien suffered his second loss.

Game 7	October 15, 1912
Fenway Park (Boston)	T: 2:21
New York 11 : Boston 4	A: 32,694

The Giants jumped all over "Smokey" Joe Wood, pummeling the Red Sox ace for six runs in the opening frame to force a series deciding eighth game. Wood lasted just one inning. Larry Doyle had three hits including a homerun to pace the New York attack. Jeff Tesreau went the distance for the win. Larry Gardner homered for Boston.

Game 8	October 16, 1912
Fenway Park (Boston)	T: 2:37
Boston 3 : New York 2 (10)	A: 17,034

In the bottom of the tenth inning sure handed centerfielder Fred Snodgrass dropped "Hack" Engle's fly ball for a two-base error. Then Tris Speaker lofted an easy pop-fly in foul territory near first base but first sacker Fred Merkle let it drop and Speaker promptly ripped a base hit to right field to tie the game. The winning run scored just two batters later and the "Red Sox" had their first World Championship. Both Snodgrass and Merkle would be vilified[7]—not only for the rest of their careers—but for the rest of their lives. Smokey Joe Wood got his third win of the series. Christy Matthewson allowed just two runs in 9.2 innings but took the loss.

1913

Philadelphia Athletics (4) - NY Giants (1)

Connie Mack's A's claim their third World Series title in four years, rolling over arch-nemesis John McGraw and the New York Giants in five games.

Game 1	October 7, 1913
Polo Grounds (New York)	T: 2:06
Philadelphia 6 : New York 4	A: 36,291

The opener was a slugfest with both teams combining for ten runs on twenty-two hits, (eleven each) but in the end it was "Homerun" Baker's two-run homer in the fifth that decided it. Baker had three hits on the day as did Eddie Collins. "Chief" Bender, who went the distance for the A's, picked up the W. Rube Marquard was the loser.

Game 2	October 8, 1913
Shibe Park (Philadelphia)	T: 2:22
New York 3 : Philadelphia 0 (10)	A: 20,563

In one of the greatest individual performances in World Series history, Christy Matthewson pitched ten shutout innings and broke a scoreless tie in the top of the final frame with a base hit as the Giants evened things up at one apiece. Art Fletcher added a two-run single later in the inning to cap the scoring. Eddie Plank, who pitched 9 1/3 scoreless innings before surrendering the three runs, suffered the loss.

Game 3	October 9, 1913
Polo Grounds (New York)	T: 2:11
Philadelphia 8 : New York 2	A: 36,896

23

Eddie Collins had three hits and drove in three runs and "Homerun" Baker added a pair of hits and two runs batted in as well as the A's pummeled the Giants. The A's battery was in the thick of it as backstop Wally Schang chipped in with a solo homer and starter Joe Bush earned the first World Series win of his career with a complete game victory. Jeff Tesreau was tagged with the loss.

Game 4	October 10, 1913
Shibe Park (Philadelphia)	T: 2:09
Philadelphia 6 : New York 5	A: 20,568

New York came storming back from a six-run deficit but came up a buck short as Philadelphia moved to within one victory of another title. Fred Merkle's three-run homer cut the lead in half in the seventh and the Giants came up with two more in the eighth, but "Chief" Bender weathered the storm to turn in his second complete game victory of the series. Wally Schang had two hits and knocked in two runs for Philadelphia. Al Demaree took the loss for the Giants.

Game 5	October 11, 1913
Polo Grounds (New York)	T: 1:39
Philadelphia 3 : New York 1	A: 36,632

Eddie Plank made it five-straight complete game performances for A's hurlers, allowing just one unearned run as Philadelphia claimed its third World Championship in four years. Frank "Homerun" Baker had two hits and knocked in three runs. Christy Mathewson went the distance but suffered the loss in what would be his final World Series appearance.

1914

Boston Braves (4) - Philadelphia A's (0)

The National Leagues' perennial doormat—the Boston Braves—lifted themselves off the scrapheap to capture the pennant and stun the heavily favored Philadelphia Athletics in four-straight.

Game 1	October 9, 1914
Shibe Park (Philadelphia)	T: 1:58
Boston 7 : Philadelphia 1	A: 20,562

Catcher Hank Gowdy hit a single, a double, a triple, drove in two runs and scored one as the Braves stunned the defending champs in the opener. Walter "Rabbit" Maranville had two hits and plated a pair as well. Dick Rudolph went the distance for the win. Chief Bender was the loser.

Game 2	October 10, 1914
Shibe Park (Philadelphia)	T: 1:56
Boston 1 : Philadelphia 0	A: 20,562

Spitballer Bill James pitched a two-hit shutout as Boston made it two straight. The Braves scored the only run of the game in the ninth when Charlie Deal doubled and Herbie Moran singled him home. The A's had two on with one gone in the bottom of the ninth but James induced right-fielder "Honest Eddie" Murphy to bounce to shortstop "Rabbit" Maranville who stepped on second and fired to first for the game-ending double-play. Eddie Plank allowed just one run over nine frames but took the loss.

Game 3	October 12, 1914
Fenway Park (Boston)	T: 3:06
Boston 5 : Philadelphia 4 (12)	A: 35,520

The A's scored two in the top of the tenth on "Homerun" Baker's two-run single. But in the bottom of the frame Hank Gowdy homered and Joe Connolly launched a sac-fly to tie it. Then in the twelfth, Gowdy doubled leading off and scored the winning run on Joe Bush's throwing error. Bush, who pitched the entire game, was charged with the loss. Bill James pitched two scoreless innings and picked up the win.

Game 4	October 13, 1914
Fenway Park (Boston)	T: 1:49
Boston 3 : Philadelphia 1	A: 34,365

Johnny Evers' two-out two-run single in the bottom of the fifth broke a 1-1 tie and Dick Rudolph slammed the door shut the rest of the way as the Braves completed their stunning sweep of the mighty Athletics. It was Rudolph's second complete game win. Bob Shawkey allowed all three Boston runs in five innings of work to garner the defeat.

1915

Boston Red Sox (4) - Philadelphia A's (1)

After five fiercely contested games, the Red Sox emerge as champions again. For the first time in World Series history the President of the United States (Woodrow Wilson) is in attendance and throws out the first ball. Babe Ruth makes his World Series debut.

Game 1	October 8, 1915
Baker Bowl (Philadelphia)	T: 1:58
Philadelphia 3 : Boston 1	A: 19,343

The Phillies broke a 1-1 tie with two runs in the bottom of the eighth to take the opener. Grover Cleveland Alexander went the distance for the win. Babe Ruth made his World Series debut, appearing as a pinch-hitter in the ninth inning and grounding out to first base. Ernie Shore took the loss.

Game 2	October 9, 1915
Baker Bowl (Philadelphia)	T: 2:05

| Boston 2 : Philadelphia 1 | A: 20,306 |

Sox centerfielder Harry Hooper stole home[8] in the first inning and winning pitcher Rube Walker added a game winning RBI single in the ninth—his third hit of the day—to even the series. Phillies centerfielder Dode Paskert nearly tied it with two out in the ninth, blasting what appeared to be a game-tying bomb over the centerfield fence. But Tris Speaker made a leaping snare of the drive to end the game. Erskine Mayer took the loss.

Game 3	October 11, 1915
Braves Field (Boston)	T: 1:48
Boston 2 : Philadelphia 1	A: 42,300

The Red Sox abandoned Fenway for the brand new and much more profitable Braves Field and its 42,000 seating capacity—the largest in baseball. Left fielder Duffy Lewis had three hits—including the game winner—an RBI single that plated Harry Hooper in the bottom of the ninth to end it. Lewis also made a sensational running catch to save two runs earlier in the contest. Dutch Leonard got the win for Boston and Grover Cleveland Alexander suffered the loss for the Phillies.

Game 4	October 12, 1915
Braves Field (Boston)	T: 2:05
Boston 2 : Philadelphia 1	A: 41,096

Red Sox left fielder Duffy Lewis was at it again; making two sensational catches and driving home the winning run—this time with a double in the sixth inning as Boston posted its third-straight 2-1 victory. Ernie Shore went the distance for the Sox, scattering seven hits and fanning four. George Chalmers also went the distance but was tagged with the loss.

Game 5	October 13, 1915

Baker Bowl (Philadelphia)	T: 2:15
Boston 5 : Philadelphia 4	A: 20,306

The Red Sox took a liking to the cozy confines of the Baker Bowl, launching three homers en route to a series clinching victory. Duffy Lewis was in the thick of things again, launching a game tying two-run blast in the eighth inning. Harry Hooper belted his second round tripper of the game to win it for Boston in the ninth. Rube Foster notched his second complete game win of the series. Eppa Rixey suffered the loss in relief.

1916

Boston Red Sox (4) - Brooklyn Robins (1)

The Red Sox make it two straight World Championships, conquering Brooklyn in five. Twenty-one-year-old southpaw Babe Ruth completes his season long coming out party with an epic fourteen inning masterpiece in Game 2.

Game 1	October 7, 1916
Braves Field (Boston)	T: 2:16
Boston 6 : Brooklyn 5	A: 36,117

Boston starter Ernie Shore took a five-run lead into the ninth but Brooklyn came storming back, posting four runs and loading the bases with two out. Carl Mays came on in relief and got the final out to end it. Casey Stengel had two hits and scored two runs for Brooklyn in a losing effort. Rube Marquard was saddled with the loss.

Game 2	October 8, 1916
Braves Field (Boston)	T: 2:32
Boston 2 : Brooklyn 1 (14)	A: 41,373

In the greatest pitching performance in World Series history and the greatest pitching duel as well, Babe Ruth surrendered one run—an inside-the-park homer to Hy Myers in the first inning—and then pitched 13.1 scoreless frames. The Red Sox finally claimed the prize when Del Gainer's pinch-hit single plated the winning run in the fourteenth. Ruth's RBI single in the third tied it. Sherry Smith pitched the entire game for Brooklyn but wound up with the loss.

Game 3	October 10, 1916
Ebbets Field (Brooklyn)	T: 2:01
Brooklyn 4 : Boston 3	A: 21,087

Brooklyn fended off Boston to capture the first World Series win in its history. Jack Coombs got the win and Jeff Pfeffer notched the save. Ivy Olson's fifth inning two-run triple proved to be the game winning blow. Larry Gardner's seventh inning homer cut the lead to one but that was as close as the Red Sox would get. Carl Mays was saddled with the loss.

Game 4	October 11, 1916
Ebbets Field (Brooklyn)	T: 2:30
Boston 6 : Brooklyn 2	A: 21,662

Larry Gardner's three-run inside-the-park homer in the second proved to be all the Red Sox would need as they moved to within one victory of back-to-back World Championships. Dutch Leonard went the distance for the win. Rube Marquard, who lasted just four innings, suffered the loss—his second of the series.

Game 5	October 12, 1916
Braves Field (Boston)	T: 1:43
Boston 4 : Brooklyn 1	A: 43,620

Ernie Shore cruised to his second win of the series, scattering three hits en route to a complete game victory as the Red Sox claimed their second consecutive World Championship. Brooklyn never recovered from shortstop Ivy Olson's double-error in the third inning. Olson mishandled what could have been an inning ending double play and then compounded the mistake with a throwing error. When the dust finally settled two runs scored and the Red Sox had a lead they would not relinquish. Jeff Pfeifer was saddled with the loss.

1917

Chicago White Sox (4) - NY Giants (2)

Superstars Eddie Collins and "Shoeless Joe" Jackson lead the White Sox to the World Series where stone-faced skipper John McGraw and a revamped New York Giants team awaits them. When the dust settles, it's Chicago in six!

Game 1	October 6, 1917
Comiskey Park (Chicago)	T: 1:48
Chicago 2 : New York 1	A: 32,000

Sox centerfielder Happy Felsch's solo homer in the bottom of the fourth proved to be the game winner as Eddie Cicotte scattered seven hits en route to a complete game victory in the opener. Shano Collins had a double, two singles and a run scored for Chicago. Slim Sallee went the distance for New York but earned the loss for his troubles.

Game 2	October 7, 1917
Comiskey Park (Chicago)	T: 2:13
Chicago 7 : New York 2	A: 32,000

The White Sox erupted for five runs in the bottom of the fourth and never looked back. Chicago's dynamic-duo of Eddie Collins and "Shoeless Joe" Jackson combined for five hits and three runs batted in. Shortstop Buck Weaver had three hits and knocked one in as well. Winning pitcher Urban Faber put the dunce cap on in the fifth when he stole third base only to discover it was already occupied.

Game 3	October 10, 1917
Polo Grounds (New York)	T: 1:55
New York 2 : Chicago 0	A: 33,616

"Rube" Benton baffled the White Sox hitters all night long, scattering five hits en route to a shutout victory. The Giants touched up losing pitcher Eddie Cicotte for the only two runs of the ballgame in the second inning when Walter Holke doubled home a run and scored on George Burns' RBI single.

Game 4	October 11, 1917
Polo Grounds (New York)	T: 2:09
New York 5 : Chicago 0	A: 27,746

Ferdie Schupp notched New York's second straight shutout as the Giants evened the series and extended Chicago's scoreless innings streak to twenty-two. Centerfielder Benny Kauff took care of things on the offensive side, slamming two homers and knocking in three runs. Urban Faber took the loss for the White Sox.

Game 5	October 13, 1917
Comiskey Park (Chicago)	T: 2:37
Chicago 8 : New York 5	A: 27,323

Home cooking made all the difference as the White Sox rallied from a three-run deficit to post the victory. Eddie Collins and "Shoeless Joe" Jackson each had three hits and scored two runs apiece. Urban Faber pitched two scoreless innings in relief and was credited with the win. Slim Sallee, who allowed seven runs on thirteen hits, suffered his second loss of the series.

Game 6	October 15, 1917
Polo Grounds (New York)	T: 2:18
Chicago 4 : New York 2	A: 33,969

Two Giants' errors plus a botched run-down play led to three unearned runs in the fourth inning—all the White Sox would need as Urban Faber went the distance to collect his third victory of the series and the first World Championship in White Sox history. Chick Gandil had two hits and knocked in two runs to pace the Chicago attack. Rube Benton was the loser.

1918

Boston Red Sox (4) - Chicago Cubs (2)

Babe Ruth establishes the record for consecutive scoreless innings in the World Series...the players go on strike—for an hour!—and when play is resumed it's the Red Sox in 6!

Game 1	October 5, 1918
Comiskey Park (Chicago)	T: 1:50
Boston 1 : Chicago 0	A: 19,274

The Red Sox took the opener as Babe Ruth hurled a complete game shutout. The only run of the game was scored in the fourth when Hippo Vaughn walked Dave Shean leading off and later in the inning Stuffy McInnis singled him home. Vaughn went the distance in a losing effort.

Game 2	October 6, 1918
Comiskey Park (Chicago)	T: 1:58
Chicago 3 : Boston 1	A: 20,040

Lefty Tyler evened things up for the Cubs, going the distance for the victory. Tyler also singled home two runs in the second—the inning that saw Chicago plate all three of its runs. Boston broke through with a run in the ninth and had the tying runs aboard but Tyler retired the last two batters to end it. Joe Bush went the distance but suffered the loss for Boston.

Game 3	October 7, 1918

Comiskey Park (Chicago)	T: 1:57
Boston 2 : Chicago 1	A: 27,054

Due to wartime travel restrictions the third game was played in Chicago. The Red Sox tallied twice in the fourth—all the runs they would need as Carl Mays bested Hippo Vaughn. Both hurlers went the distance. The game ended in dramatic fashion when Chicago's Charlie Pick tried to score from second base on a passed ball but got nailed at the plate to end it.

Game 4	October 9, 1918
Fenway Park (Boston)	T: 1:50
Boston 3 : Chicago 2	A: 22,183

Despite injuring his throwing hand in a scuffle with teammate Walt Kinney, Babe Ruth notched his second win of the series. The Babe ran into trouble in the ninth allowing the first two Cubs hitters to reach. But Joe Bush came on in relief and after an unsuccessful sacrifice bunt for the first out; he got pinch-hitter Turner Barber to bounce into a game-ending 6-4-3 double play. Ruth[9] also tripled and knocked in two runs.

Game 5	October 10, 1918
Fenway Park (Boston)	T: 1:42
Chicago 3 : Boston 0	A: 24,694

Hippo Vaughn entered the winner's circle with a complete game shutout to keep the Cubs hopes alive. Les Mann doubled home the game winning run in the third and Dode Paskert doubled home two more in the eighth. "Sad" Sam Jones suffered the loss for the Red Sox.[10]

Game 6	October 11, 1918

Fenway Park (Boston)	T: 1:46
Boston 2 : Chicago 1	A: 15,238

The Red Sox tallied two unearned runs in the third inning when, with two out and two aboard, Cubs right fielder Max Flack dropped George Whiteman's line drive allowing both runners to score. Carl Mays scattered just three hits en route to a series clinching complete game victory. Lefty Tyler was charged with the loss.

1919

Cincinnati Reds (5) Chicago White Sox (3)

Baseball sustains the greatest crisis in its history as the notorious Arnold Rothstein conspires with members of the heavily favored White Sox to throw the World Series. The affair is dubbed "The Black Sox Scandal".

Game 1	October 1, 1919
Crosley Field (Cincinnati)	T: 1:42
Cincinnati 9 : Chicago 1	A: 30,511

White Sox pitcher Eddie Cicotte hits Reds' leadoff hitter Morrie Rath signaling that the fix is on. Cicotte, the AL's best pitcher, allows six runs on seven hits in just 3.2 innings of work. The Reds win a laugher.

Game 2	October 2, 1919
Crosley Field (Cincinnati)	T: 1:42
Cincinnati 4 : Chicago 2	A: 29,690

Chicago starter Claude Williams' pinpoint control "mysteriously" vanishes in the fourth inning as he walks three batters and then serves up a three-run triple to Larry Kopf—all the runs the Reds will need as the White Sox roll over again.

34

Game 3	October 3, 1919
Comiskey Park (Chicago)	T: 1:30
Chicago 3 : Cincinnati 0	A: 29,126

Rothstein fails to hold up his end of the bargain, paying only part of what he'd promised. So the fix is off...for now. Rookie left hander Dickie Kerr hurls a three-hit shutout and ringleader Arnold "Chick" Gandil singles home two runs as the White Sox send the Rothstein syndicate a message with a dominating victory.

Game 4	October 4, 1919
Comiskey Park (Chicago)	T: 1:37
Cincinnati 2 : Chicago 0	A: 34,363

Rothstein comes through with $20,000 and Cicotte goes to work in the fifth, committing two throwing errors and cutting off a throw to the plate that would've nailed the runner. The Reds tally two unearned runs in the frame—the only two runs of the ballgame—to win it.

Game 5	October 6, 1919
Comiskey Park (Chicago)	T: 1:45
Cincinnati 5 : Chicago 0	A: 34,379

Claude Williams keeps up appearances, blanking the Reds over the first five frames. But the White Sox get down to business in the sixth. Williams serves up a double, a single, a walk and a triple while "Happy" Felsch and "Shoeless" Joe Jackson chip in with a couple of missed fly balls to hand Cincinnati four of their five runs. Meanwhile the offense extends its scoreless innings streak to twenty-two.

Game 6	October 7, 1919
Crosley Field (Cincinnati)	T: 2:06
Chicago 5 : Cincinnati 4	A: 32,006

Rothstein's bill is past due so the White Sox turn the fix light off with a hard-fought extra inning victory. Ringleader Gandil wins it in the tenth with an RBI single. Dickie Kerr won it. Jimmy Ring was the loser.

Game 7	October 8, 1919
Crosley Field (Cincinnati)	T: 1:47
Chicago 4 : Cincinnati 1	A: 13,923

Cicotte, pitching to win for the first time in the series, scatters seven hits en route to a complete game victory. Co-conspirators Felsch and Jackson supply the offense—each of them collecting two hits and knocking in two runs.

Game 8	October 9, 1919
Crosley Field (Cincinnati)	T: 2:27
Cincinnati 10 : Chicago 5	A: 32,930

With the fix now in doubt Rothstein threatens the life of Game Eight starter Williams' wife. Williams lasts just one-third of an inning, surrendering four runs before being lifted. The Reds pound out sixteen hits en route to the series clinching victory and "The Black Sox Scandal" is complete.

1920

Cleveland Indians (5) - Brooklyn Dodgers (2)

The Indians survive the only in-game death of a player in Major League Baseball history, Ray Chapman,[11] and go on to win their first World Series in honor of their fallen teammate.

Game 1	October 5, 1920
Ebbets Field (Brooklyn)	T: 1:41
Cleveland 3 : Brooklyn 1	A: 23,573

Stan Coveleski cruised to a complete game victory as Cleveland scored two unearned runs in the second off Brooklyn hurler Rube Marquard and never looked back. Tribe backstop Steve O'Neill had two hits and knocked in a pair as well. Rube Marquard was tagged with the loss.

Game 2	October 6, 1920
Ebbets Field (Brooklyn)	T: 1:55
Brooklyn 3 : Cleveland 0	A: 22,559

The Dodgers evened things up as Burleigh Grimes shut out the Indians and their ace Jim Bagby. Brooklyn's Tommy Griffith got it done at the plate with a double, a single and two runs batted in. Grimes also singled and scored a run.

Game 3	October 7, 1920
Ebbets Field (Brooklyn)	T: 1:47
Brooklyn 2 : Cleveland 1	A: 25,088

The Dodgers chased Indians' starter Ray Caldwell in the first inning, tallying twice and putting runners on first and second with just one out. Player-Manager Tris Speaker called on Walter "Duster" Mails who retired the next two hitters to end the threat. But Brooklyn starter Sherry Smith turned in a complete game gem, allowing just one run on three hits, to cement the Brooklyn victory.

Game 4	October 9, 1920
League Park (Cleveland)	T: 1:54
Cleveland 5 : Brooklyn 1	A: 25,734

Dodgers' pitcher Rube Marquard was arrested for scalping World Series tickets before the game. It didn't get any better from there as the Indians pasted Brooklyn pitching for five runs on twelve hits en route to a series tying triumph. Tris Speaker had two hits and scored what proved to be the winning run in the second inning. Stan Coveleski posted his second complete game victory of the series.

37

Game 5	October 10, 1920
League Park (Cleveland)	T: 1:49
Cleveland 8 : Brooklyn 1	A: 26,884

Cleveland's Elmer Smith hit the first grand slam in World Series history and the Indians never looked back. Tribe 2nd baseman Bill Wambsganss executed the first—and still only—unassisted triple-play in the history of the Fall Classic when he snared a line drive off the bat of Clarence Mitchell, stepped on second to retire Pete Kilduff and then tagged a dumbfounded Otto Miller to complete the historic trifecta.

Game 6	October 11, 1920
League Park (Cleveland)	T: 1:34
Cleveland 1 : Brooklyn 0	A: 27,194

George Burns doubled home Tris Speaker with the only run of the contest as Cleveland moved to within one game of its first World Series title. "Duster" Mails went the distance for the win, allowing just three hits. Sherry Smith lasted eight and suffered the loss for Brooklyn.

Game 7	October 12, 1920
League Park (Cleveland)	T: 1:55
Cleveland 3 : Brooklyn 0	A: 27,525

Stan Coveleski notched his third win of the series—a complete game shutout—and the Indians captured their first World Series title. Burleigh Grimes, who allowed three runs on seven hits, suffered the loss. Coveleski, and mound-mates Jim Bagby and "Duster" Mails limited Brooklyn to just two runs over the last forty-four innings of play. Tris Speaker tripled and drove in a run to pace the Indians' attack.

1921

New York Giants (5) - New York Yankees (3)

In their World Series debut the New York Yankees take on the New York Giants in the first ever "subway series". With Yankee Stadium under construction, the entire series is played in the same park—The Polo Grounds.

Game 1	October 5, 1921
Polo Grounds (New York)	T: 1:38
NY Yankees 3 : NY Giants 0	A: 30,203

The Yankees captured the opener behind Carl Mays' masterful five-hit shutout. Babe Ruth posted the first World Series RBI in Yankee history when he singled home Elmer Miller in the top of the first. Mike McNally singled, doubled and stole home for the Bronx Bombers. Frankie Frisch had four hits for the Giants. Phil Douglas was the loser.

Game 2	October 6, 1921
Polo Ground (New York)	T: 1:55
NY Yankees 3 : NY Giants 0	A: 34,939

It was Déjà vu all over again as the Yankees won it 3-0 and executed a steal of home along the way. Waite Hoyt tossed the shutout and Bob Meusel swiped the dish. The game winning run crossed the plate when Hoyt bounced into a double play in the fourth. Art Nehf took the loss.

Game 3	October 7, 1921
Polo Grounds (New York)	T: 2:40
NY Giants 13 : NY Yankees 5	A: 36,509

The Giants rallied to clobber the Yankees in their "return" home to the Polo Grounds. The Bronx Bombers plated four in the top of the third but the Giants scored four in the bottom of the frame to tie it and then erupted for eight in the seventh to put it out of reach. George Burns and Frank Snyder each had four hits to pace the orange and blacks' twenty-hit attack. Ross Youngs chipped in with four RBI. Jesse Barnes won it in relief.

Game 4	October 9, 1921
Polo Grounds (New York)	T: 1:38
NY Giants 4 : NY Yankees 2	A: 36,372

The Giants evened the series as Phil Douglas bested Carl Mays. Mays carried a no-hitter into the sixth but it was broken up by George Burns with two out in the frame. Burns' two-run double in the eighth spoiled Mays' shutout bid and turned out to be the game deciding blow. Babe Ruth blasted the first World Series homer of his career in the ninth.

Game 5	October 10, 1921
Polo Grounds (New York)	T: 1:52
NY Yankees 3 : NY Giants 1	A: 35,758

Babe Ruth ignited the Yankees attack with a bunt single to open the fourth inning and scored moments later when Bob Meusel doubled him home. The Bronx Bombers added an insurance run later in the frame and never looked back as Waite Hoyt posted his second complete game victory of the series. Art Nehf suffered his second defeat of the series.

Game 6	October 11, 1921
Polo Grounds (New York)	T: 2:31
NY Giants 8 NY Yankees 5	A: 34,283

The Yankees received devastating news before the start of the game—Babe Ruth would be unavailable for the rest of the series due to nagging injuries. "Irish" Meusel and Frank Snyder each homered and George Kelly added three hits as the Giants outslugged the Yankees to even things up at three apiece.

Game 7	October 12, 1921

Polo Grounds (New York)	T: 1:40
NY Giants 2 NY Yankees 1	A: 36,503

Phil Douglas bested Carl Mays for the second time in as many outings and the Giants moved a step closer to the ultimate triumph. McGraw's men plated the winning run in the bottom of the seventh when Frank Snyder doubled home Johnny Rawlings. Frank "Homerun" Baker and Roger Peckinpaugh each had two hits for the Yankees. George Burns smacked a pair of doubles for the Giants.

Game 8	October 13, 1921
Polo Grounds (New York)	T: 1:57
NY Giants 1 : NY Yankees 0	A: 25,410

Art Nehf pitched a four-hit complete game shutout and the Giants were champions. The only run of the game was plated in the first inning on the strength of two walks and an error. Waite Hoyt, who allowed one unearned run over nine frames, was charged with the loss.

1922

New York Giants (5) - New York Yankees (3)

After three consecutive years of a best-five-out-of-nine matchup, the World Series returned to a best-four-out-of-seven format with the two New York teams, the Giants and the Yankees, squaring off for the second consecutive year.

Game 1	October 4, 1922
Polo Grounds (New York)	T: 2:08
NY Giants 3 : NY Yankees 2	A: 36,514

Joe Bush took a shutout into the eighth inning but Irish Meusel's two-run single tied it and Ross Youngs' sacrifice fly pushed the winning run across. Rosy Ryan won it in relief. Babe

Ruth went 1-for-4, with an RBI. He also struck out twice and was caught stealing. Bush took the loss. Heine Groh had three hits and Frankie Frisch two hits for the Giants.

Game 2	October 5, 1922
Polo Grounds (New York)	T: 2:40
NY Giants 3 : NY Yankees 3 (10)	A: 37,020

With the score tied at three after three innings, umpire George Hildebrand called the game due to darkness. The crowd rained down boos on Hildebrand—and on Commissioner "Kennisaw Mountain" Landis who was in attendance. The field became covered in debris. Speculation was that profit motivated the ruling as an extra game would generate additional revenue. To quell the fans' ire Landis ruled that the proceeds from the tie game would be donated to a worthy cause.

Game 3	October 6, 1922
Polo Grounds (New York)	T: 1:48
NY Giants 3 : NY Yankees 0	A: 37,630

Journeyman pitcher Jack Scott hurled a complete game four-hit shutout while his teammates collected twelve safeties—all singles—en route to the win. Frankie Frisch's sacrifice fly in the third proved to be the game winning run. Frisch and Heine Groh both had two hits for the Giants. Babe Ruth's hard slide into third base nearly triggered a bench-clearing brawl but order was restored before anything came of the incident.

Game 4	October 7, 1922
Polo Grounds (New York)	T: 1:41
NY Giants 4 : NY Yankees 3	A: 36,242

Dave Bancroft singled home two runs in a four-run fifth inning and Hugh McQuillan went the distance for the win as the Giants moved to within one game of a second consecutive World

Championship. Carl Mays also went the distance but was saddled with the loss.

Game 5	October 8, 1922
Polo Grounds (New York)	T: 2:00
NY Giants 5 : NY Yankees 3	A: 38,551

The Giants rallied for three runs in the bottom of the eighth inning to capture their second straight World Championship. George Kelly's two run single highlighted the uprising. Art Nehf went the distance for the win in the clincher just as he had done the year before. Babe Ruth was 0-for3 on the day and finished the series hitting just .118. Frankie Frisch and Heine Groh each had two hits for the Giants. Joe Bush took the loss.

1923

New York Yankees (4) - New York Giants (2)

The Yankees, facing the Giants in the World Series for the third consecutive year, christen brand new Yankee Stadium with the first World Championship in their storied history.

Game 1	October 10, 1923
Yankee Stadium (New York)	T: 2:05
NY Giants 5 : NY Yankees 4	A: 55,307

Casey Stengel's ninth inning inside-the-park homerun broke a 4-4 tie as the Giants captured the opener. It was the first World Series homer in Yankee Stadium history. Stengel's shoe fell off as he raced around the bases. Heine Groh and Frankie Frisch each had two. Rosy Ryan won it in relief. Joe Bush was the loser.

Game 2	October 11, 1923
Polo Grounds (New York)	T: 2:08
NY Yankees 4 : NY Giants 2	A: 40,402

Babe Ruth homered twice and Herb Pennock scattered nine hits as the Yankees evened the series. Aaron Ward also homered for the Yankees and "Irish" Meusel blasted one over the wall for the Giants. Hugh McQuillan took the loss.

Game 3	October 12, 1923
Yankee Stadium (New York)	T: 2:05
NY Giants 1 : NY Yankees 0	A: 62,430

Casey Stengel's homer in the top of the seventh proved to be the only run of the game. Stengel thumbed his nose at the Yankees dugout as he circled the bases and was fined $50 by Commissioner Landis. Frankie Frisch had two hits for the Giants. Art Nehf pitched a six-hit shutout to collect the victory. Sam Jones allowed just one run over eight frames but was saddled with the loss.

Game 4	October 13, 1923
Polo Grounds (New York)	T: 2:32
NY Yankees 8 : NY Giants 4	A: 46,302

The Yankees erupted for six runs in the second and never looked back. Bob Meusel tripled home a pair to highlight the uprising. Whitey Witt had three hits while Wally Pipp, Aaron Ward and Everett Scott collected two apiece to power the Bronx Bombers' attack. Ross Youngs smacked an inside-the-park-homer in the ninth for the Giants. Frankie Frisch added two hits. Bob Shawkey won it and Jake Scott was the loser.

Game 5	October 14, 1923
Yankee Stadium (New York)	T: 1:55
NY Yankees 8 : NY Giants 1	A: 62,817

The Yankees jumped all over the Giants, tallying three times in the first and four times in the second. Joe Dugan had three hits including a three-run inside-the-park homer. Bob Meusel also had three hits and knocked in three runs. Joe Bush went the distance for the win. Jack Bentley was the loser.

Game 6	October 15, 1923
Polo Grounds (New York)	T: 2:05
NY Yankees 6 : NY Giants 4	A: 34,172

The Yankees captured their first World Championship with a thrilling come from behind victory. Trailing by three in the eighth, the Bronx Bombers scored five times on two bases loaded walks and a three-run single off the bat of Bob Meusel to win it. Herb Pennock picked up the victory. Babe Ruth hit his third homer of the series in the first inning. Art Nehf suffered the loss. Frank Snyder homered and Frankie Frisch had three hits in a losing effort.

1924

Washington Senators (4) - NY Giants (3)

In a thrilling seven-game series Walter "Big Train" Johnson leads the lowly Senators to their first World Series and their only World Championship. The outcome is finally decided in the twelfth inning of the final game.

Game 1	October 4, 1924
Griffith Stadium (Washington, D.C.)	T: 3:07
New York 4 : Washington 3 (12)	A: 35,760

Art Nehf scattered ten hits en route to a twelve inning complete game victory. The Senators tied it in the bottom of the ninth on solo homers by George Kelly and Bill Terry only to lose it in "overtime". Walter Johnson allowed just four runs on fourteen hits and fanned a record tying twelve batters in his twelve frame stint. But the "Big Train" was handed the loss for his efforts.

Game 2	October 5, 1924

45

Griffith Stadium (Washington, D.C.)	T: 1:58
Washington 4 : New York 3	A: 35,922

"Goose" Goslin belted a two-run homer in the bottom of the first— the first of three homeruns he would hit in the series—as the Senators evened things up at one game apiece. Hack Wilson's RBI single tied the game with two outs in the ninth but Roger Peckinpaugh doubled home the game winner in the bottom of the frame to win it. Firpo Marberry pitched just one-third of an inning for the win. Tom Zachary recorded twenty-six outs but was saddled with the loss.

Game 3	October 6, 1924
Polo Grounds (New York)	T: 2:25
New York 6 : Washington 4	A: 47,608

Eighteen-year-old Freddie Lindstrom—the youngest player in World Series history—belted a sixth inning RBI double that plated what proved to be the game winning run as the Giants fended off the Senators. Hugh McQuillan picked up the win. Rosy Ryan homered and Frankie Frisch had two hits to pace the NY attack. Firpo Marberry suffered the loss.

Game 4	October 7, 1924
Polo Grounds (New York)	T: 2:10
Washington 7 : New York 4	A: 47,608

"Goose" Goslin had a career day on the grand stage, belting his second homer of the series—a three-run job—and finishing the day with four hits and four RBI as Washington evened things up at two games apiece. George McBride won it and Virgil Barnes was the loser.

Game 5	October 8, 1924
Polo Grounds (New York)	T: 2:30
New York 6 : Washington 2	A: 49,211

Freddie Lindstrom had four hits and knocked in two runs as New York handed Walter Johnson his second loss of the series and moved to within one win of another championship. Jack Bentley, who pitched into the eighth for the win, chipped in at the plate as well with two hits and two RBI. Goose Goslin homered and Joe Judge had three hits for the Senators.

Game 6	October 9, 1924
Griffith Stadium (Washington DC)	T: 1:57
Washington 2 : New York 1	A: 34,254

Player-Manager Bucky Harris' two-run single in the bottom of the fifth proved to be enough as the Senators sent the series to a seventh and deciding game. Tom Zachary went the distance for the win and Art Nehf suffered the loss. Frankie Frisch smacked two doubles for the Giants.

Game 7	October 10, 1924
Griffith Stadium (Washington DC)	T: 3:00
Washington 4 : New York 3	A: 31,667

The Senators tied it in the eighth when Bucky Harris' grounder took a wicked hop over third baseman Freddie Lindstrom's head, scoring two runs. Then, in the bottom of the twelfth, Earl McNeely's grounder to Lindstrom did the exact same thing and "Muddy" Ruel came home with the game winning—and series clinching run. Walter Johnson pitched four scoreless innings in relief for the vindicating victory. Jack Bentley was tagged with his second defeat. Frankie Frisch had two hits.

1925

Pittsburgh Pirates (4) - Washington Senators (3)

Senators' shortstop Roger Peckinpaugh's series record eight errors are too much to overcome and the Pittsburgh Pirates are champions after a hard fought seven game series.

Game 1	October 7, 1925
Forbes Field (Pittsburgh)	T: 1:57
Washington 4 : Pittsburgh 1	A: 41,723

Walter Johnson scattered five hits and fanned ten en route to a complete game victory in the opener. Joe Harris belted a solo homer and Sam Rice had two hits and knocked in two runs as well. Pie Traynor homered accounting for the Pirates lone run. Lee Meadows was the loser.

Game 2	October 8, 1925
Forbes Field (Pittsburgh)	T: 2:04
Pittsburgh 3 : Washington 2	A: 43,364

The Pirates capitalized on Roger Peckinpaugh's error in the top of the eighth as Kiki Cuyler followed with a two-run homer to break a 1-1 tie. The Senators came roaring back in the ninth, loading the bases with nobody out, but they could only manage one run and finished a buck short. Vic Aldridge held on for the complete game victory.   Glenn Wright also homered for the Pirates. Stan Coveleski was saddled with the loss.

Game 3	October 10, 1925
Griffith Stadium (Washington DC)	T: 2:10
Washington 4 : Pittsburgh 3	A: 36,495

With Washington leading 4-3 in the eighth inning, one of the most controversial plays in World Series history unfolded. Pittsburgh's Earl Smith launched a long fly ball to right field, outfielder Grantfield Rice leaped over the wall in pursuit, and (after what Pirates' fans viewed a small eternity) reemerged, ball-in-hand. Umpire Cy Rigler ruled the play an out and 4-3 turned out to be the final. Pittsburgh fans bombarded the commissioner's office with letters of protest but the ruling stood. Alex Ferguson won it and Ray Kremer was the loser.

Game 4	October 11, 1925
Griffith Stadium (Washington DC)	T: 2:00
Washington 4 : Pittsburgh 0	A: 38,701

Walter Johnson's complete game shutout left the Senators just one win shy of their second consecutive World Championship. Washington scored all four runs in the third when Goose Goslin belted a three-run homer and the very next batter, Joe Harris, launched a solo blast. Emil Yde did not survive Pittsburgh's third frame uprising and was saddled with the loss.

Game 5	October 12, 1925
Griffith Stadium (Washington DC)	T: 2:26
Pittsburgh 6 : Washington 3	A: 35,899

Facing elimination Pittsburgh pounded Washington pitchers for six runs on thirteen safeties with five of the starting nine notching multiple hit games. Pirates' starter Vic Aldridge went the distance, scattering eight hits en route to the victory. Max Carey, Kiki Cuyler, Clyde Barnhart, Glenn Wright and Earl Smith all had two hits—Barnhart knocked in two runs. Stan Coveleski was tagged with his second loss of the series.

Game 6	October 13, 1925
Forbes Field (Pittsburgh)	T: 1:57
Pittsburgh 3 : Washington 2	A: 43,810

Eddie Moore's solo blast in the bottom of the fifth proved to be the game winning run as the Pirates averted elimination for the second day in a row. Rey Kremer went the distance for the win. Washington's Goose Goslin homered marking the second straight year that he'd belted three round-trippers in World Series play. Alex Ferguson suffered the loss.

Game 7	October 15, 1925

| Forbes Field (Pittsburgh) | T: 2:31 |
| Pittsburgh 9 : Washington 7 | A: 42,856 |

The Pirates became the first team in World Series history to come back from a three-games-to-one deficit to claim the ultimate prize. The game was tied going into the eighth inning when Roger Peckinpaugh homered to put the Senators back in front. It looked like Peckinpaugh, despite a horrendous defensive series at shortstop, would emerge the hero after all. But in the bottom of the eighth he committed his eighth error of the series[12] and the Pirates made the most of his miscues, tallying three times to win it. Ray Kremer won it and Walter Johnson was tagged with the loss in his final World Series appearance.

1926

St. Louis Cardinals (4) - New York Yankees (3)

Player-Manager Rogers Hornsby leads the Cardinals to their first World Series where they vanquish Miller Huggins' Yankees in seven games.

Game 1	October 2, 1926
Yankee Stadium (New York)	T: 1:48
New York 2 : St. Louis 1	A: 61,658

Lou Gehrig knocked in both Yankee runs and Herb Pennock pitched a three-hit shutout as the Yankees caged the Cardinals in the opener. Bill Sherdel allowed just two runs over seven innings but was charged with the defeat.

Game 2	October 3, 1926
Yankee Stadium (New York)	T: 1:57

St. Louis 6 : New York 2	A: 63,600

The Cardinals pounded out twelve hits including a three-run homer by Billy Southworth and a solo round tripper of the inside-the-park variety by Tommy Thevenow. Southworth and Thevenow each collected three hits on the day. Thirty-nine-year-old epileptic alcoholic Grover Cleveland Alexander allowed just two runs on four hits, fanning ten along the way, for the victory. Urban Shocker suffered the loss.

Game 3	October 5, 1926
Sportsman's Park (St. Louis)	T: 1:41
St. Louis 4 : New York 0	A: 37,708

St. Louis knuckleballer Jesse Haines had the game of his life as he not only shut the Yankees out, but added a two-run homer as well. Dutch Ruether suffered the loss.

Game 4	October 6, 1926
Sportsman's Park (St. Louis)	T: 2:38
New York 10 : St. Louis 5	A: 38,825

Babe Ruth hit three homeruns—two of which left the stadium—as the Yankees pummeled five Cardinals' pitchers for ten runs on fourteen hits. Waite Hoyt who "scattered" fourteen hits and struck out eight, pitched a complete game for the win. Art Reinhart was the loser. Billy Southworth posted his third straight multi-hit game for St. Louis.

Game 5	October 7, 1926
Sportsman's Park (St. Louis)	T: 2:28
New York 3 : St. Louis 2 (10)	A: 39,552

The Yankees tied it in the ninth on a leadoff double by Lou Gehrig and a run scoring pinch-hit single by Ben Paschal and they won it in the tenth when Tony Lazzeri's sacrifice fly scored Mark Koenig. Herb Pennock pitched all ten frames and notched his second victory of the series. Bill Sherdel also went the distance but was charged with the defeat.

Game 6	October 9, 1926
Yankee Stadium (New York)	T: 2:05
St. Louis 10 : New York 2	A: 48,615

Les Bell singled home two runs in the top of the first and added a two-run round-tripper in the seventh as the Cardinals clobbered the Yankees to force a seventh and deciding game. Rogers Hornsby chipped in with a single, a run scored and three knocked in as well. Grover Cleveland Alexander struck out six and scattered eight hits en route to his second complete game victory of the series.

Game 7	October 10, 1926
Yankee Stadium (New York)	T: 2:15
St. Louis 3 : New York 2	A: 38,093

For the second year in a row, the seventh and deciding game was played in the rain. In the top of the fourth, errors by shortstop Mark Koenig and left fielder Bob Musial led to three unearned Cardinal runs. The Yankees cut the lead to one and had the bases loaded with two outs in the seventh when Rogers Hornsby called on Grover Cleveland Alexander who'd pitched nine innings the day before. Alexander fanned Tony Lazzeri to end the inning and then pitched a scoreless eighth and ninth and the Cardinals were champions. Jesse Haines was credited with the victory. Waite Hoyt was tagged with the loss. Babe Ruth homered for New York.

1927

New York Yankees (4) - Pittsburgh Pirates (0)

Considered to be the greatest team of all time, the 1927 Yankees, aka "Murderer's Row", make short work of the Pittsburgh Pirates, sweeping them in four straight.

Game 1	October 5, 1927
Forbes Field, Pittsburgh	T: 2:04
New York 5 : Pittsburgh 4	A: 41,467

Lou Gehrig's sacrifice fly in the top of the fifth proved to be the game winning run as the Yankees beat a tenacious Pirates team in the opener. Gehrig also tripled home a run in the first. Babe Ruth had three singles. Waite Hoyt posted the victory for New York. Ray Kremer was the loser. Paul Waner had three hits for the Pirates.

Game 2	October 6, 1927
Forbes Field (Pittsburgh)	T: 2:20
New York 6 : Pittsburgh 2	A: 41,634

The Yankees got all the offense they would need in a three run third inning. Mark Koenig singled home a run and scored on Babe Ruth's sacrifice fly and later in the frame Tony Lazzeri's sac fly plated Lou Gehrig. Koenig had three hits and two RBI on the day. George Pipgras went the distance for the win. Vic Aldridge was the loser.

Game 3	October 7, 1927
Yankee Stadium (New York)	T: 2:04
New York 8 : Pittsburgh 1	A: 60,695

Babe Ruth belted a three-run homer and Lou Gehrig added a two-run triple as the Yankees moved to within one win of a clean sweep. Herb Pennock retired the first twenty-two batters he faced en route to a complete game victory. Earle Combs and Mark Koenig each had two hits and knocked in two runs. Lee Meadows was handed the defeat.

Game 4	October 8, 1927

Yankee Stadium, (New York)	T: 2:15
New York 4 : Pittsburgh 3	A: 57,909

Babe Ruth knocked in three runs with a two-run homer and an RBI single but it was a wild-pitch by Pittsburgh reliever Johnny Miljus in the bottom of the ninth that plated Earle Combs with the tie-breaking, game-winning and series-clinching run, marking the only time that a World Series has ended on a wild-pitch. Wilcy Moore won it and Miljus was the loser. Lloyd Waner had three hits for the Pirates.

1928

NY Yankees (4) - St. Louis Cardinals (0)

The Yankees become the first team in history to sweep two World Series' in a row as they clip the wings of the St. Louis Cardinals.

Game 1	October 4, 1928
Yankee Stadium (New York)	T: 1:49
New York 4 : St. Louis 1	A: 61,425

Bob Meusel's two-run homer in the fourth inning proved to be the game winner as the Yankees rolled to victory in the opener. Lou Gehrig singled, doubled and knocked in two runs as well. Waite Hoyt pitched a three-hitter for the win. Jim Bottomley belted a solo homer to account for St. Louis's only run of the ballgame. Bill Sherdel suffered the loss.

Game 2	October 5, 1928
Yankee Stadium (New York)	T: 2:04
New York 9 : St. Louis 3	A: 60,714

Lou Gehrig belted a three-run homer in the bottom of the first and Bob Meusel's two-run double highlighted a four-run third inning as the Yankees crushed the Cardinals. George Pipgras posted a complete game four-hit victory. Grover Cleveland Alexander[13] allowed eight runs before the third frame was completed and was saddled with the loss.

Game 3	October 7, 1928
Sportsman's Park, (St. Louis)	T: 2:09
New York 7 : St. Louis 3	A: 39,602

Lou Gehrig belted two homeruns—one of them an inside-the-parker as the Yankees moved to within one game of their second consecutive four-game sweep of the World Series. Gehrig knocked in three runs. Bob Meusel stole home to become the first player ever to swipe the dish twice in the Fall Classic. Tom Zachary got the win. Jessie Haines was the loser.

Game 4	October 9, 1928
Sportsman's Park (St. Louis)	T: 2:25
New York 7 : St. Louis 3	A: 37,331

Babe Ruth belted three homers—with two of them leaving the stadium as the Yankees completed their second consecutive four game sweep of the World Series. The Babe flashed the leather as well, reaching over the wall to snare Frankie Frisch's drive with two out in the ninth to end it. Lou Gehrig also homered and Waite Hoyt scattered eleven hits en route to a complete game victory—his second of the series. Bill Sherdel took his second loss. Andy High and Earle Smith both had three hits for St. Louis.

1929

Philadelphia Athletics (4) - Chicago Cubs (1)

In a rematch of the 1910 affair it's the Athletics and the Cubs—with Connie Mack still at the A's helm and age-old nemesis

---

John McGraw now piloting the Cubs. The results are the same as Philadelphia takes it in five.

Game 1	October 8, 1929
Wrigley Field (Chicago)	T: 2:03
Philadelphia 3 : Chicago 1	A: 50,740

Veteran hurler Howard Ehmke who earlier in the year convinced Connie Mack not to release him, scouted the Cubs for two weeks and then pitched a masterpiece—striking out a World Series record thirteen batters as Philadelphia caged Chicago in the opener. Jimmie Foxx homered for the A's. Charlie Root lasted seven innings and was charged with the loss.

Game 2	October 9, 1929
Wrigley Field, (Chicago)	T: 2:29
Philadelphia 9 : Chicago 3	A: 49,987

The Athletics played long ball as Jimmie Foxx belted a three-run homer and Al Simmons added a two-run blast in Philadelphia's nine-run, twelve-hit demolition of Chicago pitching. Lefty Grove won it in relief. Pat Malone started and lost it for the Cubs.

Game 3	October 11, 1929
Shibe Park (Philadelphia)	T: 2:09
Chicago 3 : Philadelphia 1	A: 29,921

Kiki Cuyler's two-run single in the sixth turned out to be the game winning hit as the Cubs climbed back into the series. Rogers Hornsby and Hack Wilson each had two hits. Guy Bush went the distance for the win. George Earnshaw went the distance as well, but was charged with the loss.

Game 4	October 12, 1929
Shibe Park (Philadelphia)	T: 2:12
Philadelphia 10 : Chicago 8	A: 29,921

Trailing by eight in the bottom of the seventh, the Athletics erupted for ten runs on ten hits with a walk and a hit batsman mixed in between to complete the greatest rally in World Series history. Al Simmons and Mule Haas homered—Haas' blast was a three-run inside-the-parker that Hack Wilson lost in the sun. Simmons, Jimmie Foxx and Jimmie Dykes all had two hits in the record setting frame. Eddie Rommel pitched one inning for the win. Sherriff Blake allowed just two of the ten runs but suffered the loss.

Game 5	October 14, 1929
Shibe Park (Philadelphia)	T: 1:42
Philadelphia 3 : Chicago 2	A: 29,921

Trailing by two runs in the bottom of the ninth, the Athletics scored three on the strength of a two-run homer by Mule Haas and a game winning and series clinching walk-off RBI double by Bing Miller. Rube Walberg got the win in relief and Pat Malone, who finished just one out shy of a complete game victory, suffered his second loss of the series.

1930

Philadelphia A's (4) - St. Louis Cardinals (2)

Connie Mack leads his Athletics back to the Fall Classic where they capture their second consecutive championship, drubbing St. Louis in five.

Game 1	October 1, 1930
Shibe Park (Philadelphia)	T: 1:48
Philadelphia 5 : St. Louis 2	A: 32,295

In what was becoming a common theme in the World Series, the Athletics engineered a come-from-behind victory as Al Simmons homered to tie it and Mickey Cochrane's long ball put it out of reach. Lefty Grove, making his first career start in the Fall

Classic, went the distance for the win while chiseled October veteran Burleigh Grimes suffered the loss.

Game 2	October 2, 1930
Shibe Park (Philadelphia)	T: 1:47
Philadelphia 6 : St. Louis 1	A: 32,295

Mickey Cochrane homered to open the scoring in the first and later scored on a double by Al Simmons as the A's cruised to their second straight victory. Jimmy Foxx also doubled home a run and Jimmie Dykes added a two-run two-bagger. George Earnshaw fanned eight and went the distance for the win. Flint Rhem lasted just 3.1 innings in a losing effort.

Game 3	October 3, 1930
Sportsman's Park (St. Louis)	T: 1:55
St. Louis 5 : Philadelphia 0	A: 36,944

It was all St. Louis in this one as "Wild Bill" Hallahan turned in a complete game shutout. Taylor Douthit's fourth inning solo homer proved to be the game winning blow. Jimmy Wilson added a two-run single and Chick Hafey an RBI double. Rube Walberg was the loser.

Game 4	October 5, 1930
Sportsman's Park (St. Louis)	T: 1:41
St. Louis 3 : Philadelphia 1	A: 39,946

A's third-sacker Jimmy Dykes' fourth inning error led to two runs as the Cardinals snatched the lead and flew away with a victory. Jesse Haines held baseball's most feared attack to just one run on four hits en route to a complete game victory. Lefty Grove allowed just one earned run over eight frames but was charged with the loss.

Game 5	October 6, 1930
Sportsman's Park (St. Louis)	T: 1:58

| Philadelphia 2 : St. Louis 0 | A: 38,844 |

Jimmy Foxx's two-run homer in the top of the ninth plated the only runs of the ballgame as the A's moved to within one win of their second consecutive World Championship. Lefty Grove pitched two scoreless innings for the win. Burleigh Grimes went the distance and suffered the heart breaking loss.

Game 6	October 8, 1930
Shibe Park (Philadelphia)	T: 1:46
Philadelphia 7 : St. Louis 1	A: 32,295

Al Simmons hit a solo homer and Jimmy Dykes added a two-run blast as the Athletics demolished St. Louis pitching to close out the series with an explanation point. George Earnshaw went the distance for his second complete game victory of the series. "Wild Bill" Hallahan was the loser. All seven Philadelphia hits were for extra-bases.

1931

St. Louis Cardinals (4) - Philadelphia A's (3)

It's a rematch of last year's Fall Classic with Philadelphia—winners of 107 regular season games—the prohibitive favorites. But this time the underdog Cardinals—winners of a mere 101—topple the defending champs in seven.

Game 1	October 1, 1931
Sportsman's Park (St. Louis)	T: 1:55
Philadelphia 6 : St. Louis 2	A: 38,529

Jimmie Foxx singled home two runs in Philadelphia's four-run third inning and Al Simmons launched a two-run blast in the seventh as the A's caged the Cardinals in the opener. Redbirds rookie Pepper Martin[14] had three hits and stole a base in his World

Series debut. Lefty Grove won it and rookie Paul Derringer was saddled with the loss.

Game 2	October 2, 1931
Sportsman's Park (St. Louis)	T: 1:49
St. Louis 2 : Philadelphia 0	A: 35,947

"Wild Bill" Hallahan tossed a three-hit shutout as the Cardinals evened the series. Pepper Martin had two hits and scored both St. Louis runs. George Earnshaw went the distance but was saddled with the loss.

Game 3	October 5, 1931
Shibe Park (Philadelphia)	T: 2:10
St. Louis 5 : Philadelphia 2	A: 32,925

It was all Cardinals as Burleigh Grimes took a no-hitter into the eighth and a shutout into the ninth. Bing Miller's single ended the no-no and Al Simmons' two-run homer ended the shutout. Grimes, who allowed just two hits on the day, did it at the plate as well, collecting two singles and two runs batted in. Lefty Grove went the distance but was charged with the loss.

Game 4	October 6, 1931
Shibe Park (Philadelphia)	T: 1:58
Philadelphia 3 : St. Louis 0	A: 32,295

Philadelphia evened the series as George Earnshaw turned in a two-hit eight-strikeout masterpiece. Al Simmons' run-scoring double in the bottom of the first proved to be the game-winning run. Jimmie Foxx added a solo homer and Jimmie Dykes an RBI single. Pepper Martin had both St. Louis hits. Syl Johnson was the loser.

Game 5	October 7, 1931
Shibe Park (Philadelphia)	T: 1:56
St. Louis 5 : Philadelphia 1	A: 32,295

Pepper Martin had three hits, one of them a "Ruthian" homer to left that garnered a standing ovation from the Philadelphia crowd. The St. Louis speedster knocked in four of St. Louis' five runs as the Cardinals moved to within one victory of a World Championship. "Wild Bill" Hallahan went the distance for the win. Waite Hoyt suffered the loss.

Game 6	October 9, 1931
Sportsman's Park (St. Louis)	T: 1:57
Philadelphia 8 : St. Louis 1	A: 39,401

The Athletics posted four in the fifth and four in the seventh en route to a decisive, series tying victory. Jimmy Foxx had two hits and scored two runs and Al Simmons scored a run and knocked in two to pace the Athletics' attack. Lefty Grove scattered five hits and struck out seven for his second win of the series. Paul Derringer suffered his second loss of the series.

Game 7	October 10, 1931
Sportsman's Park (St. Louis)	T: 1:57
St. Louis 4 : Philadelphia 2	A: 20,805

An error, a wild pitch and a passed ball led to two St. Louis runs in the very first inning as the Cardinals completed their stunning upset of the Athletics. George Watkins' two-run homer in the third proved to be the game winning blow. The A's made some noise in the ninth, tallying twice and sending the go-ahead run to the plate in the person of Max Bishop. But Pepper Martin's lunging grab of Bishop's two-out liner to center snuffed out the rally and the Cardinals were champs. Burleigh Grimes won it and George Earnshaw was the loser.

1932

New York Yankees (4) - Chicago Cubs (0)

Babe Ruth blasts the most famous homerun in baseball history as the Yankees sweep the Cubs four straight.

Game 1	Sept 28, 1932
Yankee Stadium (New York)	T: 2:31
New York 12 : Chicago 6	A: 41,459

The Yankees pounded Cubs pitching for twelve runs on just eight hits and took the opener going away. Lou Gehrig belted a two run homer. Earle Combs had two hits and knocked in two runs as well. Red Ruffing picked up the win in his first World Series appearance. Guy Bush was the loser.

Game 2	Sept 29, 1932
Yankee Stadium (New York)	T: 1:46
New York 5 : Chicago 2	A: 50,709

The Yankees played small ball—converting ten singles and four walks into five runs and Lefty Gomez scattered nine hits while striking out eight en route to a complete game. Lou Gehrig had three hits and an RBI. Bill Dickey had two hits and knocked in two as well. Lon Warneke was the loser.

Game 3	October 1, 1932
Wrigley Field (Chicago)	T: 2:11
New York 7 : Chicago 5	A: 49,986

Babe Ruth hit a three-run homer in the top of the first and returned to the plate in the fifth to blast the "called-shot" homer that will forever live in the lore of baseball history. Lou Gehrig followed the Babe's bravado with a homer of his own—his second of the game. Kiki Cuyler and Gabby Hartnett each homered for the Cubs. George Pipgras got the win for New York. Charlie Root surrendered all four homers, took the loss, and lent his name to a trivia question for the ages.

Game 4	October 2, 1932

Wrigley Field (Chicago)	T: 2:27
New York 13 : Chicago 6	A: 49,844

The Yankees left no doubt as to who was the better team as they pounded out thirteen runs on nineteen hits to complete their sweep of Chicago. Earl Combs and Tony Lazzeri homered to power the New York attack. Lazzeri knocked in four runs on the day. Lou Gehrig chipped in with two hits and three runs batted in. Babe Ruth went 1-for-5 with an RBI in his final World Series contest. Wilcy Moore won it in relief and Jakie May was the loser.

1933

NY Giants (4) - Washington Senators (1)

A new look New York Giants team returns to the Fall Classic to face a new look Washington Senators club. The Giants avenge their 1924 defeat—besting the Senators in five.

Game 1	October 3, 1933
Polo Grounds (New York)	T: 2:07
New York 4 : Washington 2	A: 46,672

Ace lefty Carl Hubbell struck out ten and allowed just two unearned runs on five hits as New York captured the opener. Mel Ott went 4-for-4 with a two-run homer and three runs batted it in to power the Giants' attack. Lefty Stewart lasted just two innings and was charged with the defeat.

Game 2	October 4, 1933
Polo Grounds (New York)	T: 2:09
New York 6 : Washington 1	A: 35,461

Goose Goslin's third inning homer looked like it might hold up but the Giants exploded for six runs in the sixth. Lefty O'Doul's two-run pinch-hit single opened the floodgates and put New York ahead to stay. The Senators managed just one base hit the rest of the way. Rookie Hal Schumacher went the distance for the win. Alvin "General" Crowder was the loser.

Game 3	October 5, 1933
Griffith Stadium (Washington DC)	T: 1:55
Washington 4 : New York 0	A: 25,727

With President Franklin Delano Roosevelt in attendance to throw out the first ball, the Senators notched their lone victory of the series as Earl Whitehill tossed a complete game shutout. Buddy Myer had two hits and knocked in three runs to power the Washington attack. Freddie Fitzsimmons allowed all four runs and was ticketed with the loss.

Game 4	October 6, 1933
Griffith Stadium (Washington DC)	T: 2:59
New York 2 : Washington 1 (11)	A: 26,762

Carl Hubbell turned in his second complete game victory of the series—allowing just one run over eleven innings as the Giants moved to within one victory of their fourth World Series title. Senators' fans pelted the field with debris in the sixth when Heinie Manush was ejected for arguing a call. The Giants took the lead in the eleventh on an RBI single by Blondy Ryan. The Senators came storming back in their half of the frame, loading the bases with just one out. But pinch-hitter Cliff Bolton bounced into a 6-4-3 double play to end the game. Monte Weaver pitched into the eleventh only to be saddled with a loss at the end of the marathon.

Game 5	October 7, 1933
Griffith Stadium (Washington DC)	T: 2:38
New York 4 : Washington 3 (10)	A: 28,454

Washington's Fred Schulte belted a game tying three-run homer in the bottom of the sixth. Then in the tenth inning, one of the most controversial plays in World Series history unfolded when Mel Ott's drive to centerfield was originally ruled a ground-rule double. But after a long conference between the umpires, that ruling was overturned and Ott was awarded a homerun, plating what proved to be the winning run.

Dolf Luque won it in relief and Jack Russell lost it in the same capacity.

1934

St. Louis Cardinals (4) - Detroit Tigers (3)

In one of the most fiercely contested Fall Classics of all time the Dean brothers (Dizzy and Paul) account for all four wins as St. Louis's Gas House Gang takes Detroit in seven.

Game 1	October 3, 1934
Navin Field[15] (Detroit)	T: 2:13
St. Louis 8 : Detroit 3	A: 42,505

Ducky Medwick paced a thirteen hit attack, collecting four— including a solo homer—as the Cardinals cruised to victory in the opener. Dizzy Dean, likely the game's most colorful character, went the distance for the win. Alvin "General" Crowder suffered the loss. Hank Greenberg homered for Detroit and Charlie Gehringer added two hits and an RBI in a losing effort.

Game 2	October 4, 1934
Navin Field (Detroit)	T: 2:49
Detroit 3 : St. Louis 2 (12 innings)	A: 43,451

Schoolboy Rowe pitched a twelve inning complete game as the Tigers evened the series. Detroit trailed by a run in the bottom of the ninth but a missed pop-up gave Gee Walker new life and he promptly singled home the tying run. Goose Goslin plated

Charlie Gehringer with a base hit in the twelfth to win it. Bill Walker took the loss in relief.

Game 3	October 5, 1934
Sportsman's Park (St. Louis)	T: 2:07
St. Louis 4 : Detroit 1	A: 34,073

Pepper Martin paced the Redbird attack with a double, a triple and two runs scored and Ripper Collins chipped in with two hits as the Cardinals tamed the Tigers. Paul Dean tossed eight scoreless innings before finally surrendering a run in the ninth. Tommy Bridges surrendered all four St. Louis runs in just four innings of work.

Game 4	October 6, 1934
Sportsman's Park (St. Louis)	T: 2:43
Detroit 10 : St. Louis 4	A: 37,492

Hank Greenberg had four hits and knocked in four runs as the Tigers evened the series. Tragedy nearly struck in the fourth when pinch-runner Dizzy Dean was hit in the head and knocked unconscious by shortstop Billy Rogell's return throw during a double-play attempt. Dean was rushed to the hospital and the next day's headline which read: "X-RAYS OF DEAN'S HEAD SHOW NOTHING" was instantly woven into baseball lore. Eldon Aulker went the distance for the win. Bill Walker suffered his second loss.

Game 5	October 7, 1934
Sportsman's Park (St. Louis)	T: 1:58
Detroit 4 : St. Louis 1	A: 38,536

Dizzy Dean, just one day removed from being carried off the field, pitched eight solid innings but the Cardinals came up short as Tommy Bridges struck out seven en route to a complete game victory that moved Detroit to within one win of a World Championship. Charlie Gehringer homered for the Tigers. Bill DeLancey homered for the Cardinals.

Game 6	October 8, 1934
Navin Field (Detroit)	T: 1:58
St. Louis 4 : Detroit 3	A: 44,551

Paul Dean—who notched his second win of the series with a complete game victory—also singled home Leo Durocher with what proved to be the winning run as the Cardinals forced a seventh and deciding game. Durocher had three hits on the day. Schoolboy Rowe went the distance as well but suffered the loss. Mickey Cochrane had three hits for Detroit.

Game 7	October 9, 1934
Navin Field (Detroit)	T: 2:19
St. Louis 11 : Detroit 0	A: 40,902

St. Louis pounded out seventeen hits in a series deciding drubbing of Detroit. With the game well out of reach in the sixth, Ducky Medwick's hard slide into third nearly precipitated a benches clearing brawl. When Medwick returned to left field he was pelted with debris by a disgusted Detroit crowd. Commissioner Landis ultimately ordered Ducky off the field for his own safety. Dizzy Dean went the distance for the win and chipped in offensively as well with a single and a double in the Redbirds' seven-run third. Ripper Collins had four hits for St. Louis. Eldon Auker, who did not survive the aforementioned third frame, took the loss.

1935

Detroit Tigers (4) - Chicago Cubs (2)

Player-Manager Mickey Cochrane leads the Tigers back to the World Series where they square off with the Cubs for the third time. Despite losing their star player (Hank Greenberg) in the second game, the Tigers prevail in six.

Game 1	October 2, 1935

Navin Field (Detroit)	T: 1:51
Chicago 3 : Detroit 0	A: 47,931

The Cubs got two in the first on an error and an RBI single by Gabby Hartnett. Frank Demaree homered in the ninth to close out the scoring. Hartnett and Demaree both had two hits on the day. Lon Warneke pitched a complete game shutout. Schoolboy Rowe went the distance as well in a losing effort.

Game 2	October 3, 1935
Navin Field (Detroit)	T: 1:59
Detroit 8 : Chicago 3	A: 46,742

The Tigers evened things up but the price was costly as Hank Greenberg was hit on the wrist by a Charlie Root pitch and then collided with Cubs backstop Gabby Hartnett at the plate, worsening the injury. X-rays revealed the wrist was broken and Greenberg was sidelined for the rest of the series. Greenberg belted a two-run homer in a four-run first that sent Root to the showers before he'd retired a single batter. Tommy Bridges went the distance for the win.

Game 3	October 4, 1935
Wrigley Field (Chicago)	T: 2:27
Detroit 6 : Chicago 5	A: 45,532

Cubs' pinch hitter Ken O'Dea's two-run single in the bottom of the ninth sent the game into extra innings but the Tigers pushed the game winning run across in the top of the eleventh on Jo-Jo White's RBI single. Schoolboy Rowe won it in relief. Larry French was the loser. Goose Goslin had two hits and knocked in two runs for Detroit. Frank Demaree belted his second homer of the series for the Cubs.

Game 4	October 5, 1935
Wrigley Field (Chicago)	T: 2:28

| Detroit 2 : Chicago 1 | A: 49,350 |

Consecutive errors by left fielder Augie Galan and shortstop Billy Jurges led to the game winning run in the sixth inning as the Tigers moved to within one victory of their first World Championship. Alvin "General" Crowder went the distance for the win. Charlie Gehringer had two hits and knocked in a run for Detroit. Tex Carleton was the loser. Gabby Hartnett homered for the Cubs.

Game 5	October 6, 1935
Wrigley Field (Chicago)	T: 1:49
Chicago 3 : Detroit 1	A: 49,327

Chuck Klein's two-run homer in the bottom of the third was the game winning blow as the Cubs forced the series back to Detroit. The Tigers managed three straight singles in the ninth, tallying once and bringing the go-ahead run to the plate but that was as close as they would get. Lon Warneke picked up his second win of the series while Schoolboy Rowe suffered his second loss.

Game 6	October 7, 1935
Navin Field (Detroit)	T: 1:57
Detroit 4 : Chicago 3	A: 48,420

Stan Hack led off the top of the ninth with a triple and it looked like the Cubs were about to break a 3-3 tie and force a seventh game. But Tommy Bridges, who'd "scattered" twelve hits on the day, bore down and retired the next three hitters, stranding Hack. Then, in the bottom of the ninth, Goose Goslin singled home Mickey Cochrane with the game winning run and the Tigers were World Champions for the first time in their history. Bridges got the win. Larry French hurled all nine in a losing effort.

1936

NY Yankees (4) - NY Giants (2)

The Yankees return to the World Series for the first time without Babe Ruth. But Lou Gehrig is still around and so is a rookie centerfielder named Joe DiMaggio. When the dust settles it's the Bronx Bombers in six.

Game 1	Sept 30, 1936
Polo Grounds (New York)	T: 2:40
NY Giants 6 : NY Yankees 1	A: 39,419

Carl Hubbell struck out eight en route to a complete game victory and he "pitched" in from the plate as well; singling twice and driving in a run. Dick Bartell homered for the Giants. Red Ruffing suffered the loss. George Selkirk homered for the Yankees. Joe DiMaggio was 1-for-4 in his World Series debut.

Game 2	October 2, 1936
Polo Grounds (New York)	T: 2:49
NY Yankees 18 : NY Giants 4	A: 43,543

Tony Lazzeri's grand slam in the Yankees' seven-run third inning turned a close game into a blowout as the Bronx Bombers pounded out seventeen hits with each of the starting nine collecting at least one hit and run scored. Lazzeri finished with five runs batted in as did Bill Dickey whose three-run homer in the ninth closed out the scoring. Lefty Gomez hurled a complete game for the win. Hal Schumacher was the loser.

Game 3	October 3, 1936
Yankee Stadium (New York)	T: 2:01
NY Yankees 2 : NY Giants 1	A: 64,842

Lou Gehrig's second inning solo homer held up until the Giants' Jimmy Ripple homered to tie it in the fifth. Frank Crosetti singled home the game winning run with two outs in the bottom of the eighth to win it. Bump Hadley allowed just one run over eight innings for the win. Freddie Fitzsimmons allowed just four hits but suffered the loss.

Game 4	October 4, 1936
Yankee Stadium (New York)	T: 2:12
NY Yankees 5 : NY Giants 2	A: 66,669

Lou Gehrig doubled, homered and knocked in two runs as the Yankees bested Giants' ace Carl Hubbell. George Selkirk, Red Rolfe and Jake Powell chipped in with RBI singles. Monte Pearson went the distance for the win.

Game 5	October 5, 1936
Yankee Stadium (New York)	T: 2:45
NY Giants 5 : NY Yankees 4 (10)	A: 50,024

The Giants averted elimination as Bill Terry's sacrifice fly in the tenth inning plated the game winning run. Hal Schumacher pitched all ten innings for the victory. Pat Malone suffered the loss. George Selkirk homered for the Yankees. Joe DiMaggio belted a two-bagger as well.

Game 6	October 6, 1936
Polo Grounds (New York)	T: 2:50
NY Yankees 13 : NY Giants 5	A: 38,427

The Yankees captured their fifth World Championship with a seven-run ninth that turned a nip-and-tuck game into a blowout. Red Rolfe, Joe DiMaggio, Tony Lazzeri and Jake Powell each had three hits on the day. Powell homered and knocked in four runs. Lefty Gomez notched his second win of the series. Mel Ott and Jo-Jo Moore homered for the Giants. Freddie Fitzsimmons was saddled with the loss.

1937

NY Yankees (4) - NY Giants (1)

The Yankees and Giants square off in the Fall Classic for the second straight year with the Bronx's emerging dynasty making quick work of their Manhattan rival.

Game 1	October 6, 1937
Yankee Stadium (New York)	T: 2:20
NY Yankees 8 : NY Giants 1	A: 60,573

Joe DiMaggio and George Selkirk each singled home two runs in a seven-run sixth inning that chased Giants ace Carl Hubbell and put the game out of reach for good. Tony Lazzeri closed out the scoring with a homerun in the eighth. Lefty Gomez got the win and Hubbell was the loser.

Game 2	October 7, 1937
Yankee Stadium (New York)	T: 2:11
NY Yankees 8 : NY Giants 1	A: 57,675

Different day—same score! Joe DiMaggio, Bill Dickey, George Selkirk and Tony Lazzeri each had two hits as the Yankees pummeled the Giants for the second straight day. Selkirk knocked in three runs. Red Ruffing—who collected two hits and knocked in three as well—fanned eight and went the distance for the win. Cliff Melton was the loser.

Game 3	October 8, 1937
Polo Grounds (New York)	T: 2:07
NY Yankees 5 : NY Giants 1	A: 37,385

The Yankees moved to within one win of a clean sweep, scoring in five of the first six frames and cruising to an easy victory. Bill Dickey tripled home a run and Tony Lazzeri and Myril Hoag had RBI singles to pace the Bronx Bombers attack. Monte Pearson got the win and Hal Schumacher suffered the loss.

Game 4	October 9, 1937
Polo Grounds (New York)	T: 1:57
NY Giants 7 : NY Yankees 3	A: 44,293

The Giants erupted for six runs in the second inning and Carl Hubbell made it stand up, going the distance as the team from Manhattan stayed alive for just one more day. Harry Danning and Hank Leiber combined for five hits and five RBI. Bump Hadley suffered the loss for the Bronx Bombers. Lou Gehrig touched up Hubbell for a homer in the ninth.

Game 5	October 10, 1937
Polo Grounds (New York)	T: 2:06
NY Yankees 4 : NY Giants 2	A: 38,216

The Bronx Bombers captured their second consecutive World Championship as Lefty Gomez posted a ten-hit complete game victory and even chipped in with the bat—singling home Tony Lazzeri with what proved to be the winning run in the fifth inning. Joe DiMaggio and Myril Hoag homered for the Yankees. Cliff Melton was tagged with his second loss of the series. Mel Ott's two-run homer accounted for both Giants' runs.

1938

New York Yankees (4) - Chicago Cubs (0)

The Yankees become the first team to win three consecutive World Series', sweeping the Cubs in four straight and staking their claim to the title of greatest team ever.

Game 1	October 5, 1938
Wrigley Field (Chicago)	T: 1:53
New York 3 : Chicago 1	A: 43,642

Bill Dickey went 4-for-4 and Tommy Henrich and rookie Joe Gordon chipped in with two hits apiece as the Yankees

73

captured the opener. Red Ruffing went the distance for the win and Bill Lee suffered the loss.

Game 2	October 6, 1938
Wrigley Field (Chicago)	T: 1:53
New York 6 : Chicago 3	A: 42,108

Frank Crosetti and Joe DiMaggio each had two-run homers and hot-hitting rookie Joe Gordon doubled home two as well as New York doubled up on Chicago. Lefty Gomez got the win for the Yankees and Dizzy Dean was the loser. Joe Marty had three hits and knocked in all three Cubs runs.

Game 3	October 8, 1936
Yankee Stadium (New York)	T: 1:57
New York 5 : Chicago 2	A: 55,236

Joe Gordon homered and singled in two runs and Bill Dickey added a solo round tripper as the Yankees moved to within one victory of a sweep of the Cubs and a third straight World Series title. Monte Pearson went the distance for the win, striking out nine along the way. Clay Bryant, who took a no-hitter into the fifth, suffered the loss. Joe Marty had three hits for the second straight game—one of them a homerun.

Game 4	October 9, 1938
Yankee Stadium (New York)	T: 2:11
New York 8 : Chicago 3	A: 59,847

Frank Crosetti paced the Yankees attack with a triple a double and four runs batted in as New York clobbered Chicago to close out the four-game sweep. Red Ruffing posted his second complete game victory while Bill Lee suffered his second defeat of the series. Tommy Henrich homered for the Yanks. Ken O'Dea homered for Chicago. Lou Gehrig went 1-for-4 (a single) in his final World Series game.

1939

New York Yankees (4) - Cincinnati Reds (0)

The invincible New York Yankees cement their legacy with an unprecedented fourth consecutive World Series title—and second consecutive sweep. This year's fodder is the Cincinnati Reds and their "twin-aces", Bucky Walters and Paul Derringer.

Game 1	October 4, 1939
Yankee Stadium (New York)	T: 1:33
New York 2 : Cincinnati 1	A: 58,541

Starters Red Ruffing and Paul Derringer allowed just one run apiece over the first eight frames but Derringer ran into trouble in the ninth when rookie Charlie Keller tripled and scored the winning run on Bill Dickey's RBI single. Ruffing retired the final fourteen hitters en route to the victory.

Game 2	October 5, 1939
Yankee Stadium (New York)	T: 1:27
New York 4 : Cincinnati 0	A: 59,791

Monte Pearson pitched a two-hit shutout while the Yankees touched up Bucky Walters for four runs on nine hits—including a three run third inning that put it out of reach. Charlie Keller doubled home a run and Bill Dickey added an RBI single in the game deciding frame. Babe Dahlgren homered later in the contest to close out the scoring.

Game 3	October 7, 1939
Crosley Field (Cincinnati)	T: 2:01
New York 7 : Cincinnati 3	A: 32,723

Charlie Keller had two two-run homers, Joe DiMaggio had one two-run homer and Bill Dickey had one one-run homer as the Yankee juggernaut demolished Reds hurler Junior Thompson to move to within one victory of a fourth consecutive World Championship. Bump Hadley pitched eight solid innings for the win.

Game 4	October 8, 1939
Crosley Field (Cincinnati)	T: 2:04
New York 7 : Cincinnati 4 (10)	A: 32,794

The Yankees capitalized on Red's shortstop Bill Myers ninth inning error to send it into extra innings. Myers committed another miscue in the tenth and Joe DiMaggio promptly singled the go-ahead run home and raced all the way around the bases when Charlie Keller collided with backstop Ernie Lombardi. Three runs scored on the play. The Reds made some noise in the bottom of the tenth but could not push a run across and the Yankees had their fourth consecutive World Series title. Johnny Murphy got the win in relief. Keller and Bill Dickey homered for New York. Bucky Walters, pitching in relief, was handed his second loss of the series.

1940

Cincinnati Reds (4) - Detroit Tigers (3)

The Reds post 100 wins and return to the Fall Classic where Hank Greenberg, Charlie Gehringer and the rest of the Tigers are waiting. After a bitterly contested seven-game series, the Queen City wears the crown.

Game 1	October 2, 1940
Crosley Field (Cincinnati)	T: 2:09
Detroit 7 : Cincinnati 2	A: 31,793

The Tigers took the opener in a laugher as journeyman hurler Bobo Newsom went the distance, scattering eight hits along the way. Five singles, a walk and an error led to five runs in the second and Detroit never looked back. Bruce Campbell had two hits—including a two-run homer. Dick Bartell chipped in with two hits and two runs batted in as well to pace the Tigers attack. Paul Derringer did not survive Detroit's second inning outburst and was saddled with the loss.

Game 2	October 3, 1940
Crosley Field (Cincinnati)	T: 1:54
Cincinnati 5 : Detroit 3	A: 30,640

Reds' ace Bucky Walters (they had two aces!)[16] survived a shaky first inning to finish with a three-hit complete game victory. Jimmy Ripple's two-run homer in the third proved to be the game winning blow. Schoolboy Rowe suffered the loss.

Game 3	October 4, 1940
Navin Field (Detroit)	T: 2:08
Detroit 7 : Cincinnati 4	A: 52,877

Two two-run homers in the bottom of the seventh—one by Rudy York and the other by Pinky Higgins—were too much for the Reds to overcome as Detroit jumped out to a 2-1 series lead. Bruce Campbell had three hits and Mike Higgins knocked in three runs to pace the Tigers' attack. Tommy Bridges scattered ten hits en route to a complete game victory. Jim Turner was the loser.

Game 4	October 5, 1940
Navin Field (Detroit)	T: 2:06
Cincinnati 5 : Detroit 2	A: 54,093

Paul Derringer avenged his opening game defeat with a five-hit complete game victory. The Reds pounded out eleven hits on the day. Ival Goodman had two of them, scored twice and knocked in two as well to pace the Cincinnati attack. Dizzy Trout lasted two innings and suffered the loss.

Game 5	October 6, 1940

Navin Field (Detroit)	T: 2:26
Detroit 8 : Cincinnati 0	A: 55,189

Bobo Newsom posted his second victory of the series—this time a three-hit shutout—as the Tigers pushed the Reds to the brink of elimination. Junior Thompson[17] suffered the loss . Hank Greenberg had three hits, including a three-run homer to finish the day with four runs batted in. Teammate Bruce Campbell chipped in with three hits and two knocked in as well.

Game 6	October 7, 1940
Crosley Field (Cincinnati)	T: 2:01
Cincinnati 4 : Detroit 0	A: 30,481

Bucky Walters posted a five-hit shutout—his second victory of the series—to set up a seventh and deciding game. Walters also blasted a solo homer. Ival Goodman and Jimmy Ripple chipped in with two hits and a run batted in apiece. Detroit starter Schoolboy Rowe, who didn't make it out of the first inning, suffered his second loss of the series.

Game 7	October 8, 1940
Crosley Field (Cincinnati)	T: 1:47
Cincinnati 2 : Detroit 1	A: 26,854

The Reds captured their first World Series title since 1919 with a thrilling come from behind victory. Trailing 1-0 in the seventh, Jimmy Ripple doubled home Frank McCormick and one out later scored the winning run on a sac-fly off the bat of last year's World Series goat, Billy Myers. Paul Derringer went the distance for the win and Bobo Newsom, who also pitched a complete game, suffered the loss. Detroit's Charlie Gehringer had two hits in the final Fall Classic appearance of his career.

1941

NY Yankees (4) - Brooklyn Dodgers (1)

Leo Durocher pilots "Dem Bums" to their first World Series under his command but the resurgent Yankees will not be turned away.

Game 1	October 1, 1941
Yankee Stadium (New York)	T: 2:08
New York 3 : Brooklyn 2	A: 68,540

Joe Gordon homered, singled and knocked in two runs and Bill Dickey added an RBI double as the Yankees, behind Red Ruffing, captured the opener. Dodger rookie Pee Wee Reese had three hits and scored a run in his World Series debut. Ruffing went the distance. Curt Davis was tagged with the loss.

Game 2	October 2, 1941
Yankee Stadium (New York)	T: 2:31
Brooklyn 3 : New York 2	A: 66,248

The Dodgers snapped the Yankees World Series winning streak at ten as Dolph Camilli singled home Dixie Walker with what proved to be the game winner in the sixth. Whit Wyatt hurled all nine for the win. Joe "Ducky" Medwick had three hits for Brooklyn. Spud Chandler suffered the loss.

Game 3	October 4, 1941
Ebbets Field (Brooklyn)	T: 2:22
New York 2 : Brooklyn 1	A: 33,100

New York broke a scoreless tie in the eighth, plating two runs on consecutive singles by Red Rolfe, Tommy Henrich, Joe DiMaggio and Charlie Keller. Brooklyn managed one run in the bottom of the frame but finished a buck short. Marius Russo pitched a complete game for the victory. Hugh Casey, who lasted just one-third of an inning in relief, suffered the loss.

Game 4	October 5, 1941
Ebbets Field (Brooklyn)	T: 2:54
New York 7 : Brooklyn 4	A: 33,813

When Tommy Henrich struck out with two gone in the ninth it appeared that the Dodgers had evened the series with a one-run victory. But backstop Mickey Owens' passed ball allowed Henrich to reach first. After Joe DiMaggio singled, Charlie Keller's two-run double gave the Yankees the lead. Then Bill Dickey walked and Joe Gordon doubled home two insurance runs. Johnny Murphy got the win in relief and Hugh Casey suffered the loss in the same capacity.

Game 5	October 6, 1941
Ebbets Field (Brooklyn)	T: 2:13
New York 3 : Brooklyn 1	A: 34,072

Tiny Bonham posted the only World Series win of his career—a complete game victory—as the Yankees captured their ninth championship. New York tallied twice in the second on a wild pitch and an RBI single by Joe Gordon. Tommy Henrich homered later in the ballgame. Pete Reiser's third inning sacrifice fly accounted for Brooklyn's lone run. Whit Wyatt suffered the loss despite a nine-strikeout complete game effort.

1942

St. Louis Cardinals (4) NY Yankees (1)

Enos "Country" Slaughter and Stan "The Man" Musial lead St. Louis to a stunning upset of New York.

Game 1	Sept 30, 1942
Sportsman's Park (St. Louis)	T: 2:35

New York 7 : St. Louis 4	A: 34,769

Red Ruffing took a no-hitter into the eighth and a one-hitter into the ninth and the Yankees appeared to be cruising to an easy victory. But Marty Marion's two-run triple highlighted a four-run ninth that brought Stan "The Man" Musial to the plate with the bases loaded. Spud Chandler came on in relief of Ruffing and retired Musial on a grounder to end it. Mort Cooper suffered the loss for the Redbirds.

Game 2	October 1, 1942
Sportsman's Park (St. Louis)	T: 1:57
St. Louis 4 : New York 3	A: 34,255

Joe DiMaggio's RBI single and Charlie Keller's two-run homer tied the game in the eighth but the Cardinals jumped back in front in the bottom of the frame when Enos "Country" Slaughter doubled and Stan "The Man" Musial singled him home to win it. Rookie Johnny Beazley went the distance for the win. Tiny Bonham was the loser.

Game 3	October 3, 1942
Yankee Stadium (New York)	T: 2:30
St. Louis 2 : New York 0	A: 69,123

The Cardinals used pitching and defense to defeat the mighty Yankees. Ernie White pitched a complete game shutout in the only World Series appearance of his career and Stan Musial and Enos Slaughter robbed Joe Gordon and Charlie Keller of homeruns on back-to-back plays in the seventh to protect the two-run advantage. Marty Marion scored both Redbird runs on RBI singles by Ken O'Dea and Terry Moore. Spud Chandler suffered the loss for New York.

Game 4	October 4, 1942
Yankee Stadium (New York)	T: 2:28
St. Louis 9 : New York 6	A: 69,902

The Cardinals scored six runs in the fourth and took a five-run lead into the sixth but the Yankees posted five to tie it. The Cardinals came right back with two in the seventh and an insurance run in the ninth to win it. Charlie Keller's three-run homer was the big blow in New York's sixth inning uprising. Stan Musial had two hits, walked and scored twice and knocked in a run. Max Lanier won it in relief. Atley Donald was the loser.

Game 5	October 5, 1942
Yankee Stadium (New York)	T: 1:58
St. Louis 4 : New York 2	A: 69,052

The Cardinals completed their decisive upset of New York in dramatic fashion as rookie Whitey Kurowski launched a game-winning two-run homer in the ninth to win it. The Yankees put the first two men aboard in the bottom of the frame but winner Johnny Beazley picked Joe Gordon off second base and then retired the next two hitters to end it. Red Ruffing was the loser. Enos Slaughter also homered for St. Louis. Phil Rizzuto homered for New York.

1943

NY Yankees (4) - St. Louis Cardinals (1)

In a rematch of last year's Fall Classic, the Yankees turn the tables on the Redbirds—this time it's New York in five games.

Game 1	October 5, 1943
Yankee Stadium (New York)	T: 2:07
New York 4 : St. Louis 2	A: 68,676

Joe Gordon belted a mammoth homer and Spud Chandler posted a complete game victory as the Yankees captured the opener. A double play grounder, a wild pitch and an RBI single by Bill Dickey accounted for New York's remaining runs. Max Lanier was the loser.

Game 2	October 6, 1943

Yankee Stadium (New York)	T: 2:08
St. Louis 4 : New York 3	A: 68,578

Despite learning of the death of their father that morning, Mort and Walker Cooper—the the only brother battery in World Series history—led the Cards to their only win in of the series. Mort went the distance for the win and Walker chipped in with a base hit. Marty Marion and Ray Sanders homered for St. Louis. Tiny Bonham suffered the loss for New York.

Game 3	October 7, 1943
Yankee Stadium (New York)	T: 2:10
New York 6 : St. Louis 2	A: 69,990

Trailing by one in the eighth, the Yankees confiscated the game with a five run uprising. Billy Johnson's three-run triple was the big blow. Hank Borowy got the win and Al Brazle was the loser.

Game 4	October 10, 1943
Sportsman's Park (St. Louis)	T: 2:06
New York 2 : St. Louis 1	A: 36,196

Yankee southpaw Marius Russo turned in a complete game gem as the Yankees moved to within one victory of their tenth World Series title. Russo, who did not allow an earned run, also walked, singled, doubled and scored what proved to be the winning run on Frank Crosetti's sacrifice fly in the eighth. Cards' reliever Harry Brecheen suffered the loss.

Game 5	October 11, 1943
Sportsman's Park (St. Louis)	T: 2:24
New York 2 : St. Louis 0	A: 33,872

Spud Chandler scattered ten hits en route to a complete game shutout as the Yankees caged the Cardinals and claimed their tenth World Series title. St. Louis starter Mort Cooper, who fanned the first five batters he faced, surrendered a two-run homer to Bill Dickey in the sixth to account for the only runs of the game.

1944

St. Louis Cardinals (4) - St. Louis Browns (2)

With World War II raging in Europe, many of the game's greatest players are unavailable. Under these auspices a lackluster Browns team claims the first pennant in its history. But in the end the cross-town rival Cardinals fly away with their fifth World Series title.

Game 1	October 4, 1944
Sportsman's Park (St. Louis)	T: 2:05
Browns 2 : Cardinals 1	A: 33,242

George McQuinn's two-run homer off Mort Cooper was all the offense the Browns would need in capturing the opener. Cooper was the loser and Denny Galehouse the winner.

Game 2	October 5, 1944
Sportsman's Park (St. Louis)	T: 2:32
Cardinals 3 : Browns 2 (11)	A: 35,076

Ken O'Dea's single in the eleventh plated Ray Sanders with the game winning run. Blix Donnelly won it in relief and Bob Muncrief was as the loser.

Game 3	October 6, 1944
Sportsman's Park (St. Louis)	T: 2:19
Browns 6 : Cardinals 2	A: 34,737

The Browns strung together four runs on five singles—all after two were out in the fourth—and never looked back. Jack Kramer went the distance for the win, fanning ten along the way. Sig Jakucki took the loss.

Game 4	October 7, 1944
Sportsman's Park (St. Louis)	T: 2:22
Cardinals 5 : Browns 1	A: 35,455

Stan Musial had three hits including a two-run homer in the first inning as the Cardinals drubbed the Browns to even the series. Harry Brecheen got the win. Sig Jakucki suffered his second loss in as many days.

Game 5	October 8, 1944
Sportsman's Park (St. Louis)	T: 2:04
Cardinals 2 : Browns 0	A: 36,568

Mort Cooper hurled a seven-hit shutout and solo homers by Danny Litwhiler and Ray Sanders accounted for all the offense the Cardinals would need to move to within one victory of their fifth World Championship.

Game 6	October 9, 1944
Sportsman's Park (St. Louis)	T: 2:06
Cardinals 3 : Browns 1	A: 31,630

A walk an error and three singles led to three Cardinals runs—all the Redbirds would need to settle the matter once and for all. Max Lanier was the winner and Nels Potter suffered the loss.

1945

Detroit Tigers (4) - Chicago Cubs (2)

With the war now over the stars of the game return in time for October baseball and the Tigers best the Cubs in seven.

Game 1	October 3, 1945
Briggs Stadium (Detroit)	T: 2:10
Chicago 9 : Detroit 0	A: 54,637

The Cubs mauled Tigers' ace Hal Newhouser for seven runs in less than three innings of work in the opener. Phil Cavarretta and Andy Pafko paced the Chicago attack with three hits and three runs each—Cavarretta homered and Pafko doubled and stole a base as well. Hank Borowy scattered six hits en route to a shutout victory.

Game 2	October 4, 1945
Briggs Stadium (Detroit)	T: 1:47
Detroit 4 : Chicago 1	A: 53,636

Hank Greenberg belted a three-run homer in a four-run fourth and Virgil Trucks scattered seven hits en route to a series tying victory. Doc Cramer had three hits and knocked in a run for the Tigers. Hank Wyse was charged with the loss. Stan Hack and Peanuts Lowrey combined for five Cubs' hits.

Game 3	October 5, 1945
Briggs Stadium (Detroit)[18]	T: 1:55
Chicago 3 : Detroit 0	A: 55,500

Claude Passeau tossed a one-hit shutout in his World Series debut. Bill Nicholson and Roy Hughes had RBI singles and Passeau added a sacrifice fly to close out the scoring. The Tigers' lone safety came off the bat of Rudy York in the second inning. Stubby Overmire was the loser.

Game 4	October 6, 1945
Wrigley Field (Chicago)	T: 2:00

| Detroit 4 : Chicago 1 | A: 42,293 |

The Tigers touched up Cubs starter Ray Prim for four runs in the fourth and Dizzy Trout did the rest, allowing just one unearned run on five hits en route to a complete game victory. Before the game William "Billy Goat" Sianis bought box seats for himself and his pet goat but ushers would not allow "Murphy" into the stadium. Sianis led his pet away in a huff and placed a hex on the Cubbies who would go on to lose the series and never (at least up until the time of this writing) return to it.

Game 5	October 7, 1945
Wrigley Field (Chicago)	T: 2:18
Detroit 8 : Chicago 4	A: 43,463

Hank Greenberg's three doubles paced the Tigers' attack as Detroit "doubled up" on Chicago. Hal Newhouser avenged his loss in the opener with a nine-strikeout complete game victory. Hank Borowy was the loser.

Game 6	October 8, 1945
Wrigley Field (Chicago)	T: 3:28
Chicago 8 : Detroit 7 (12)	A: 41,708

Trailing 7-3 in the bottom of the eighth, the Tigers tallied four times with the tying run coming on a homer by Hank Greenberg. But things went haywire for "Hankus Pankus" (Greenberg) in the bottom of the twelfth when Stan Hack's routine single took a wicked hop over his head allowing Bill Schuster to race home with the winning run, forcing a seventh and deciding game. It was Hack's fourth hit and third RBI of the contest. Hank Borowy posted his second win and Dizzy Trout was the loser.

Game 7	October 10, 1945
Wrigley Field (Chicago)	T: 2:31
Detroit 9 : Chicago 3	A: 41,590

Hank Borowy, pitching for the third consecutive day, surrendered five first-inning runs with the big blow coming on Paul Richards' three-run double as Detroit rolled to its second World Series title. Paul Richards had two doubles and knocked in four runs for the Tigers. Hal Newhouser went the distance for his second win of the series. Borowy suffered his second loss. It was his fourth decision of the series. Phil Cavarretta had three hits and Peanuts Lowrey added two for the Cubs in a losing cause.

1946

St. Louis Cardinals (4) - Boston Red Sox (3)

"Country" Slaughter's Mad Dash Home caps off the Cardinals thrilling come back from a three-games-to-one deficit. Ted Williams is turned away in the only World Series of his career.

Game 1	October 6, 1946
Sportsman's Park (St. Louis)	T: 2:39
Boston 3 : St. Louis 2	A: 36,218

With the Red Sox down to their last strike, Tom McBride singled to tie the game and Rudy York homered in the tenth to win it. Earl Johnson pitched two scoreless innings for the win and Howie Pollett—who pitched all ten frames for St. Louis—was the loser. Ted Williams had one hit and walked twice in his World Series debut.

Game 2	October 7, 1946
Sportsman's Park (St. Louis)	T: 1:56
St. Louis 3 : Boston 0	A: 35,815

Southpaw Harry Brecheen tossed a four-hit shutout to even things up for St. Louis. Brecheen also singled home what proved to be the winning run in the third and scored the Cards final run later in the ballgame. Mickey Harris was ticketed with the loss for the Red Sox. Ted Williams went hitless in four at-bats.

Game 3	October 9, 1946
Fenway Park (Boston)	T: 1:54
Boston 4 : St. Louis 0	A: 34,500

Rudy York launched a three-run homer in the bottom of the first and the Red Sox never looked back. Johnny Pesky had two hits and Dom DiMaggio and Bobby Doerr both doubled. Ted Williams singled once and walked twice. Boo Ferriss tossed a complete game shutout. Murry Dickson suffered the loss.

Game 4	October 10, 1946
Fenway Park (Boston)	T: 2:31
St. Louis 12 : Boston 3	A: 35,645

The Cardinals battered six Boston hurlers for twelve runs on twenty hits to even the series at two apiece. Enos Slaughter homered, doubled and scored four runs to pace the Redbird's attack. Joe Garagiola had four hits and knocked in three runs. Red Munger went the distance for the win. Wally Moses had four hits for the Red Sox. Ted Williams singled, walked and scored a run. Tex Hughson lasted two innings and was saddled with the loss.

Game 5	October 11, 1946
Fenway Park (Boston)	T: 2:23
Boston 6 : St. Louis 3	A: 35,982

Joe Dobson allowed just four hits and surrendered three runs—two of them unearned—as the Red Sox moved to within one win of their sixth World Series title. Ted Williams knocked in a run in the first inning—the only RBI of his postseason career. Al Brazle was the loser.

Game 6	October 13, 1946
Sportsman's Park (St. Louis)	T: 1:56

St. Louis 4 : Boston 1	A: 35,768

Harry Brecheen posted his second win of the series, scattering seven hits and fanning six as the Cardinals staved off elimination and forced a seventh and deciding game. The Cards' got three in the third on a sacrifice fly by Terry Moore and RBI singles by Whitey Kurowski and Stan Musial. Marty Marion doubled home a run in the eighth to close out the scoring. Mickey Harris lasted 2.3 innings and was saddled with the loss. Ted Williams singled and walked.

Game 7	October 15, 1946
Sportsman's Park (St. Louis)	T: 2:17
St. Louis 4 : Boston 3	A: 36,143

Enos Slaughter's "Mad Dash Home" from first base plated the game winning run in the bottom of the eighth inning. Slaughter singled leading off and scored two outs later on Harry Walker's drive (it was actually ruled a double) to centerfield. Legend has it that Johnny Pesky hesitated momentarily before firing the relay home, giving Slaughter the extra-split-second he needed to score. This hesitation—whether real or imagined—has long since been woven into the tapestry of baseball lore. Harry Brecheen, pitching in relief, posted his third win of the series. Bob Klinger took the loss. Ted Williams was hitless in four trips to the plate.

1947

NY Yankees (4) - Brooklyn Dodgers (3)

The World Series sees its color barrier broken as Jackie Robinson leads the Brooklyn Dodgers to the World Series where they fall in seven games to the New York Yankees.

Game 1	Sept 30, 1947
Yankee Stadium (New York)	T: 2:20

| New York 5 : Brooklyn 3 | A: 73,365 |

In the first televised World Series game, the Yankees busted open a scoreless tie with a five-run fifth inning. Johnny Lindell and Tommy Henrich both had two-run singles to highlight the uprising. Spec Shea won it for the Yankees and Ralph Branca suffered the loss for Brooklyn. Jackie Robinson walked twice, stole a base and scored a run in his World Series debut.

Game 2	October 1, 1947
Yankee Stadium (New York)	T: 2:36
New York 10 : Brooklyn 3	A: 69,865

The Yankees touched up four Brooklyn hurlers for ten runs on fifteen hits in the only blowout of the series. Allie Reynolds notched a complete game victory. Tommy Henrich homered for the Yankees and Johnny Lindell had two hits and knocked in three runs. Vic Lombardi suffered the loss. Dixie Walker homered for Brooklyn. Pee Wee Reese and Jackie Robinson both had two hits in a losing effort.

Game 3	October 2, 1947
Ebbets Field (Brooklyn)	T: 3:05
Brooklyn 9 : New York 8	A: 33,098

Eddie Stanky and Carl Furrillo belted two-run doubles in a six-run second inning as the Dodgers fended off the Yankees to climb back into the series. Hugh Casey won it in relief and Bobo Newsom was the loser. Yogi Berra and Joe DiMaggio homered for New York. Berra's blast was of the pinch hit variety—the first in World Series history.

Game 4	October 3, 1947
Ebbets Field (Brooklyn)	T: 2:20
Brooklyn 3 : New York 2	A: 33,443

Yankee hurler Bill Bevens took a no-hitter into the ninth and lost it—and the game—on the same pitch. Bevens, who had walked ten and allowed one run up until that point, surrendered a two-run double to pinch hitter Cookie Lavagetto who drilled the first pitch he saw off the right field wall scoring Al Gionfriddo and Eddie Miksis to win it for Brooklyn. Hugh Casey pitched two-thirds of an inning and walked away with a win.

Game 5	October 4, 1947
Ebbets Field (Brooklyn)	T: 2:46
New York 2 : Brooklyn 1	A: 34,379

Spec Shea posted his second win of the series, allowing just four hits and striking out seven en route to a complete game victory. Shea also plated the first run of the game with an RBI single in the fourth. Joe DiMaggio's solo homer in the fifth proved to be the game winning run. Jackie Robinson singled home Brooklyn's lone tally in the sixth. Rex Barney was the loser.

Game 6	October 5, 1947
Yankee Stadium (New York)	T: 3:19
Brooklyn 8 : New York 6	A: 74,065

With a World Series record 74,065 in attendance, the Dodgers outlasted the Yankees in a back-and-forth slugfest that saw both teams combine for fourteen runs on twenty-seven hits. The game yielded one of the most famous plays in the history of the Fall Classic when Al Gionfriddo robbed Joe DiMaggio of what would have been a game-tying three-run homer. Gionfriddo raced to the bullpen fence and made a reaching one hand grab of the "Yankee Clipper's" drive some 415 feet from home plate. DiMaggio's ire was captured on tape when he kicked the dirt in disgust.

Game 7	October 6, 1947
Yankee Stadium (New York)	T: 2:19
New York 5 : Brooklyn 2	A: 71,548

The Dodgers touched up Spec Shea for two runs in the second inning, but relievers Bill Bevens and Joe Page blanked "Dem Bums" the rest of the way as the Yankees battled back to claim their eleventh World Series title. Phil Rizzuto scored what proved to the winning run on an RBI single by Tommy Henrich in the fourth inning. Page was credited with the victory. Dodger starter Hal Gregg was the loser. Rizzuto had two hits, scored twice, knocked in a run and stole a base as well.

1948

Cleveland Indians (4) - Boston Braves (2)

In a World Series featuring standout hurlers such as Warren Spahn, Johnny Sain, Bob Feller, Bob Lemon and Satchel Paige, Cleveland takes Boston in six—to date the last World Series title for the Indians.

Game 1	October 6, 1948
Braves Field (Boston)	T: 1:42
Boston 1 : Cleveland 0	A: 40,135

Johnny Sain bested Bob Feller with the game's only run scoring in the bottom of the eighth. In that fateful frame it appeared that Phil Masi had been picked off second base but umpire Bill Stewart ruled the runner safe. After Cleveland's vehement argument, Tommy Holmes singled Masi home to win it. Feller allowed just two hits on the day.

Game 2	October 7, 1948
Braves Field (Boston)	T: 2:14
Cleveland 4 : Boston 1	A: 39,633

Bob Lemon bested legendary lefty Warren Spahn and the Indians evened the series. Player-manager Lou Boudreau had two hits and knocked in a run as did Tribe rookie Larry Doby—the first

African American in A.L. history.[19]   Lemon went the distance, scattering eight hits along the way.

Game 3	October 8, 1948
Municipal Stadium (Cleveland)	T: 1:36
Cleveland 2 : Boston 0	A: 70,306

In a game pitting lesser known hurlers, Gene Bearden pitched a five-hit shutout and Vern Bickford didn't make it out of the fourth inning. Bearden also doubled and scored the first run of the game on Larry Doby's grounder. Jim Hegan's RBI single accounted for Cleveland's second run.

Game 4	October 9, 1948
Municipal Stadium (Cleveland)	T: 1:31
Cleveland 2 : Boston 1	A: 81,897

Lou Boudreau doubled home a run and Larry Doby connected for a solo homer—all the Tribe would need as former infielder Steve Gromek turned in a complete game victory. Johnny Sain went the distance as well, but suffered the loss. The Red Sox lone run came on Marv Rickert's homer.

Game 5	October 10, 1948
Municipal Stadium (Cleveland)	T: 2:39
Boston 11 : Cleveland 5	A: 86,288

Bob Elliott got it going for the Braves with a three-run homer in the opening frame to push the series back to Boston. Warren Spahn was the winner in relief and Bob Feller suffered the loss. Elliott finished the day with two homers, three runs scored and four batted in. Satchel Paige retired both batters he faced in the seventh inning, the lone World Series appearance of his career.

Game 6	October 11, 1948

Braves Field (Boston)	T: 2:16
Cleveland 4 : Boston 3	A: 40,103

The Braves battled valiantly but came up a buck short as the Indians closed it out with a hard-fought victory. Bob Feller scattered eight hits en route to his second win of the series. Former Bronx Bomber Joe Gordon homered for the Indians. Bill Voiselle was the loser.

1949

NY Yankees (4) - Brooklyn Dodgers (1)

The Dodgers vaunted offense—featuring Pee Wee Reese, Roy Campanella, Gil Hodges, Carl Furillo and Jackie Robinson— still can't make it by the Yankees—who win the series in five.

Game 1	October 5, 1949
Yankee Stadium (New York)	T: 2:24
New York 1 : Brooklyn 0	A: 66,224

Allie Reynolds fanned nine and surrendered just two hits en route to a complete game shutout in the opener. Tommy Henrich's solo homer in the bottom of the ninth plated the only run of the game. Dodger rookie Don Newcombe, who struck out eleven, suffered the loss.

Game 2	October 6, 1949
Yankee Stadium (New York)	T: 2:30
Brooklyn 1 : New York 0	A: 70,053

The Dodgers turned the tables on the Yankees as Preacher Roe baffled the Bronx Bombers all day long en route to a six-hit shutout. Jackie Robinson scored the only run of the game on a base hit by Gil Hodges in the second inning. Vic Raschi allowed just one run over eight innings but was ticketed with the loss.

Game 3	October 7, 1949
Ebbets Field (Brooklyn)	T: 2:30
New York 4 : Brooklyn 3	A: 32,788

The Yankees broke a 1-1 tie in the ninth on a pinch-hit two-run single by Johnny Mize and an RBI single by Jerry Coleman. But solo homers by Luis Olmo and Roy Campanella in the bottom of the frame made it a one-run game before Joe Page fanned Bruce Edwards to end it. Page was credited with the win. Ralph Branca was the loser. Pee Wee Reese also homered for Brooklyn.

Game 4	October 8, 1949
Ebbets Field (Brooklyn)	T: 2:42
New York 6 : Brooklyn 4	A: 33,934

Bobby Brown's three-run triple in the fifth proved to be the game winning blow as the Yankees moved to within one win of their twelfth World Series title. Eddie Lopat won it and Don Newcombe, pitching on two days' rest, was the loser. Brooklyn scored all four of their runs on RBI singles by Jackie Robinson, Luis Olmo, Roy Campanella and Gene Hermanski in the sixth inning.

Game 5	October 9, 1949
Ebbets Field (Brooklyn)	T: 3:04
New York 10 : Brooklyn 6	A: 33,711

The Yankees punished six Brooklyn pitchers for ten runs on eleven hits to close out the series in decisive fashion. Joe DiMaggio homered for the Yankees and Bobby Brown added three hits and three knocked in as well. Jerry Coleman also knocked in three runs for the Bronx Bombers. Gil Hodges launched a three-run blast for Brooklyn. Vic Raschi picked up the win and Rex Barney was the loser.

1950

NY Yankees (4) - Philadelphia Athletics (0)

Philadelphia's "Whiz Kids" swipe the pennant on the final day of the season but the Yankees are waiting with brooms in hands.

Game 1	October 4, 1950
Shibe Park (Philadelphia)	T: 2:17
New York 1 : Philadelphia 0	A: 30,746

Vic Raschi outdueled[20] Jim Konstanty as the Yankees captured the opener. Bobby Brown doubled in the third and scored the only run of the game two outs later. Raschi allowed just two hits en route to the shutout victory.

Game 2	October 5, 1950
Shibe Park (Philadelphia)	T: 3:06
New York 2 : Philadelphia 1	A: 32,660

Joe DiMaggio's tenth inning solo homer plated the game winning run. Allie Reynolds got the win. Robin Roberts, who'd scattered ten hits on the day, was the loser. Both hurlers went the distance. Richie Ashburn had two hits and knocked in Philadelphia's only run.

Game 3	October 6, 1950
Yankee Stadium (New York)	T: 2:35
New York 3 : Philadelphia 2	A: 64,505

The Yankees got one in the eighth—on three consecutive walks and an error by Granny Hamner to tie it—and one in the ninth on a two out RBI single by Jerry Coleman to win it. It was Coleman's third hit of the day and second RBI. Tom Ferrick posted the victory and Russ Meyer was the loser. Hamner had three hits on the day.

Game 4	October 7, 1950
Yankee Stadium (New York)	T: 2:05
New York 5 : Philadelphia 2	A: 68,098

Two rookie hurlers, Whitey Ford and Bob Miller, locked horns in this one. Miller retired just one batter and Ford left just one batter to be retired as the Yankees closed it out with little difficulty. The Phillies posted two unearned runs in the ninth when Gene Woodling muffed a fly ball to spoil Ford's shutout bid. Allie Reynolds came in to fan the final batter. Joe DiMaggio had two hits and knocked in a run. Yogi Berra homered and knocked in two.

1951

New York Yankees (4) - New York Giants (2)

Bobby Thompson's "Shot-Heard-Round-The-World" propels the Giants into the World Series where the machine that is the New York Yankees awaits them. When the dust settles the Yankees are champions for the third consecutive year.

Game 1	October 4, 1951
Yankee Stadium (New York)	T: 2:58
NY Giants 5 : NY Yankees 1	A: 65,673

The Giants captured the opener in convincing fashion. Whitey Lockman had an RBI double, Monte Irvin had four hits and stole home and Alvin Dark hit a three-run homer. Dave Koslo got the win. Allie Reynolds was the loser. Jerry Coleman singled home the Yankees only run.

Game 2	October 5, 1951
Yankee Stadium (New York)	T: 2:05

| NY Yankees 3 : NY Giants 1 | A: 66,018 |

Eddie Lopat scattered five hits en route to a complete-game victory, but the price was high for the Yankees. Rookie Mickey Mantle, chasing a fly ball off the bat of Willie Mays, got his foot caught in a drainage hole and was carried off the field. "The Mick" missed the rest of the series. Larry Jansen suffered the loss.

Game 3	October 6, 1951
Polo Grounds (New York)	T: 2:42
NY Giants 6 : NY Yankees 2	A: 52,035

Whitey Lockman's three-run homer in the Giants' five-run fifth inning settled the issue. Willie Mays had two hits and knocked in a run. Jim Hearn won it and Vic Raschi was saddled with the loss. Gene Woodling homered for the Yankees.

Game 4	October 8, 1951
Polo Grounds (New York)	T: 2:57
NY Yankees 6 : NY Giants 2	A: 49,010

Joe DiMaggio belted what would prove to be the final homerun of his career—a two-run blast off Sal "The Barber" Maglie to pace the Bronx Bombers attack. Allie Reynolds went the distance for the win and chipped in with the bat as well, singling home a run in the fourth. Maglie suffered the loss. Alvin Dark had three doubles for the Giants.

Game 5	October 9, 1951
Polo Grounds (New York)	T: 2:31
NY Yankees 13 : NY Giants 1	A: 47,530

The Yankees moved to within one win of their third consecutive World Series title—and the fourteenth in their storied history. AL Rookie of the Year Gil McDougald blasted a grand slam homer and Phil "The Scooter" Rizzuto added a two-run round tripper as well and finished the day with three runs batted in. He also scored three runs. Eddie Lopat went the distance for the win and Larry Jansen suffered the loss.

Game 6	October 10, 1951
Yankee Stadium (New York)	T: 2:59
NY Yankees 4 : NY Giants 3	A: 61,711

The Yankees carried a three-run lead into the ninth on the strength of Hank Bauer's sixth-inning bases loaded triple. But the Giants jammed the bases with nobody out in the final frame. In came reliever Bob Kuzava who surrendered two run scoring flies before retiring pinch hitter Sal Yvars to end it. Vic Raschi was the winner and Dave Koslo suffered the loss.

1952

NY Yankees (4) - Brooklyn Dodgers (3)
The Yankees and Dodgers square off in the World Series for the fourth time but the results are the usual and the Yanks are champs for the fourth straight year!

Game 1	October 1, 1952
Ebbets Field (Brooklyn)	T: 2:21
Brooklyn 4 : New York 2	A: 34,861

Joe Black scattered six hits and fanned six hitters en route to a complete game victory to become the first African-American pitcher to win a World Series game. Jackie Robinson, Duke Snider and Pee Wee Reese all homered for Brooklyn. Allie Reynolds was ticketed with the loss. Gil McDougald homered for New York.

Game 2	October 2, 1952
Ebbets Field (Brooklyn)	T: 2:47
New York 7 : Brooklyn 1	A: 33,792

Billy Martin's sixth inning three-run homer was the big blow of the ballgame as the Yankees evened the series. Martin knocked in four runs on the day. Mickey Mantle added three hits and scored two runs. Vic Raschi went the distance for the win. Carl Erskine suffered the loss.

Game 3	October 3, 1952
Yankee Stadium (New York)	T: 2:56
Brooklyn 5 : New York 3	A: 66,698

With the score tied in the ninth Jackie Robinson and Pee Wee Reese pulled off a double-steal and scored one out later on a passed ball by Yogi Berra. Johnny Mize homered in the bottom of the frame but the Yankees finished a buck short. Preacher Roe got the win and Eddie Lopat was the loser. Berra had three hits on the day including a solo homer.

Game 4	October 4, 1952
Yankee Stadium (New York)	T: 2:33
New York 2 : Brooklyn 0	A: 71,787

Allie Reynolds pitched a four-hit complete game shutout to even the series at two apiece. Reynolds fanned ten. Joe Black, who allowed just one run on three hits over seven innings, was the loser. Johnny Mize's fourth inning solo homer proved to be the game deciding blow.

Game 5	October 5, 1952
Yankee Stadium (New York)	T: 3:00
Brooklyn 6 : New York 5 (11)	A: 70,536

Duke Snider belted a three-run homer in the fifth to give the Dodgers a 4-0 lead but the Yankees posted five in the bottom of the frame with Johnny Mize blasting a three-run job of his own—his third homer in as many games. Snider tied the game in the seventh with an RBI single and won it in the eleventh with an RBI double. Billy Cox added three hits for the Dodgers. Carl Erskine

101

pitched all eleven innings for the win and retired the last nineteen batters he faced. Johnny Sain was the loser in relief.

Game 6	October 6, 1952
Ebbets Field (Brooklyn)	T: 2:56
New York 3 : Brooklyn 2	A: 30,037

Yogi Berra and Mickey Mantle both hit solo homers and Vic Raschi chipped in with an RBI single as the Yankees edged the Dodgers. Duke Snider homered for Brooklyn and Billy Cox had two hits. Raschi, who fanned nine hitters, posted his second win of the series. Billy Loes pitched 8.1 innings in a losing effort.

Game 7	October 7, 1952
Ebbets Field (Brooklyn)	T: 2:54
New York 4 : Brooklyn 2	A: 33,195

Reliever Bob Kuzava pitched out of a bases-loaded-nobody out jam in the seventh and closed the door in the final two frames to secure the victory. Allie Reynolds got the win in relief and Joe Black, starting on two days' rest for the second time in the series, was the loser. Mickey Mantle and Gene Woodling both homered for New York. Roy Campanella and Billy Cox each had two hits for Brooklyn.

1953

New York Yankees (4) - Brooklyn Dodgers (2)

Brooklyn sends its greatest team ever (105 wins) back to the Fall Classic for a rematch with the Yankees—but the results are the same and the Yankees are champions—again!

Game 1	Sept 30, 1953
Yankee Stadium (New York)	T: 3:10

New York 9 : Brooklyn 5	A: 69,374

Billy Martin's bases loaded triple highlighted a four-run first inning as the Yankees outlasted the Dodgers in a slugfest. Yogi Berra and Joe Collins homered later in the contest for New York. Jim Gilliam, Gil Hodges and George Shuba all belted round trippers for Brooklyn. Winning pitcher Johnny Sain—who doubled home two runs—won it in relief. Clem Labine suffered the loss in the same capacity.

Game 2	October 1, 1953
Yankee Stadium (New York)	T: 2:42
New York 4 : Brooklyn 2	A: 66,786

Billy Martin tied it with a solo-homer in the seventh and Mickey Mantle's two-run blast plated the final two runs of the game in the eighth to win it. Eddie Lopat was the winner and Preacher Roe was the loser. Both hurlers went the distance. The Dodgers scored their only two runs in the fourth on a two-run double by Billy Cox.

Game 3	October 2, 1953
Ebbets Field (Brooklyn)	T: 3:00
Brooklyn 3 : New York 2	A: 35,270

Carl Erskine, who lasted just one inning in Game 1, struck out a World Series record fourteen hitters—including Mickey Mantle four times—en route to a complete game win for Brooklyn. Roy Campanella, who sustained a broken finger in Game 1, broke a 2-2 tie with a solo homer in the eight to win it. Jackie Robinson had three hits for the Dodgers. Vic Raschi went the distance for the Yankees in a losing effort.

Game 4	October 3, 1953
Ebbets Field (Brooklyn)	T: 2:46
Brooklyn 7 : New York 3	A: 36,775

Duke Snider homered, doubled twice and knocked in four runs as Brooklyn defeated New York. Jackie Robinson, playing in left field, thwarted New York's ninth inning rally when he threw Billy Martin out at home plate to end the game. Jim Gilliam had three hits and knocked in two runs. Billy Loes fanned eight and pitched a complete game to win it. Whitey Ford did not survive Brooklyn's three-run first inning and was saddled with the loss.

Game 5	October 4, 1953
Ebbets Field (Brooklyn)	T: 3:02
New York 11 : Brooklyn 7	A: 36,775

If you love the long ball this was your game. Gene Woodling homered leading off the bottom of the first and Mickey Mantle belted a grand slam. Billy Martin and Gil McDougald also homered for New York. Billy Cox and Jim Gillian homered for Brooklyn. When the dust settled the Yankees were within one win of their sixteenth World Series title. Jim McDonald won it and Johnny Podres was the loser.

Game 6	October 5, 1953
Yankee Stadium (New York)	T: 2:55
New York 4 : Brooklyn 3	A: 62,370

Trailing by two in the top of the ninth, Brooklyn's Carl Furillo smacked a game-tying two-run homer but Billy Martin singled home Hank Bauer with the winning run in the bottom of the frame and the Yankees were champions for the fourth straight year. New York pounded out fourteen hits on the day. Gene Woodling, Yogi Berra, Martin and Phil Rizzuto all had multi-hit games. Allie Reynolds won it in relief and Clem Labine, also pitching in relief, suffered the loss.

1954

New York Giants (4) - Cleveland Indians (0)

The Indians post an AL record 111 win-season but are swept by the underdog Giants. The series features the greatest catch in baseball history: Willie Mays' over the shoulder basket catch to save the opener.

Game 1	Sept 29, 1954
Polo Grounds (New York)	T: 3:11
New York 5 : Cleveland 2	A: 52,751

With the score tied 2-2 in the top of the eighth, two on and nobody out, Vic Wertz blasted one to straight away centerfield (estimated at 450 ft.) and it looked like Cleveland was in business. But Willie Mays made "The Catch" which not only saved two runs, but seemed to take the wind out of Cleveland's sails. Pinch hitter Dusty Rhodes won it for New York with a three-run homer in the bottom of the tenth. Bob Lemon, who went the distance for the Tribe, was the loser and Marv Grissom won it in relief. Wertz had four hits on the day and knocked in two runs.

Game 2	Sept 30, 1954
Polo Grounds (New York)	T: 2:50
New York 3 : Cleveland 1	A: 49,099

Dusty Rhodes' pinch-hit single in the fifth tied it and his solo homer leading off the seventh won it. Giants' ace lefty, Johnny Antonelli went the distance for the win, fanning nine along the way. Early Wynn was the loser. Cleveland's only highlight came in the first when Al Smith led off the game with a homerun.

Game 3	October 1, 1954
Municipal Stadium (Cleveland)	T: 2:28
New York 6 : Cleveland 2	A: 71,555

Dusty Rhodes continued his story book series with a two-run pinch hit single as the Giants moved to within one game of knocking off the heavily favored Indians. Willie Mays had three hits and knocked in two runs. Ruben Gomez won it and Mike Garcia suffered the loss. Vic Wertz homered for Cleveland.

Game 4	October 2, 1954
Municipal Stadium (Cleveland)	T: 2:52
New York 7 : Cleveland 4	A: 78,102

Alvin Dark had three hits and Monte Irvin added two—including a two-run single as the Giants completed their stunning upset sweep of the Indians. Willie Mays doubled home a run and scored one as well. Cleveland pinch hitter Hank Majeski belted a three-run homer in the fifth and the Tribe added another run in the seventh, but that was as close as they would get. Don Liddle won it and Bob Lemon was the loser.

1955

Brooklyn Dodgers (4) - NY Yankees (3)
MVP: Johnny Podres

In the sixth October showdown between the Dodgers and Yankees, Brooklyn finally gets past New York and captures the only World Series title in its storied history.

Game 1:	Sept 28, 1955[21]
Yankee Stadium (New York)	T: 2:31
Brooklyn 6 : New York 5	A: 63,869

The Dodgers and Yankees went toe-to-toe with both sides homering five times collectively, (Duke Snider, Carl Furillo for Brooklyn; Elston Howard, Joe Collins (2) for New York) but the results were the usual—the Yankees won! The game yielded one of baseball's most memorable plays when Jackie Robinson stole home in the eighth. Catcher Yogi Berra argued the call vehemently and still insists—more than half a century later—that Robinson was out. Whitey Ford won it and Don Newcombe was the loser.

Game 2	Sept 29, 1955
Yankee Stadium (New York)	T: 2:28
New York 4 : Brooklyn 2	A: 64,707

Southpaw Tommy Byrne tossed a five-hitter and chipped in with the bat as well, doubling home two in a four-run fourth that saw the Yankees plate all the runs they would score. Billy Loes suffered the loss. Duke Snider and Jim Gilliam had RBI singles accounting for Brooklyn's runs.

Game 3	Sept 30, 1955
Ebbets Field (Brooklyn)	T: 2:20
Brooklyn 8 : New York 3	A: 34,209

Southpaw Johnny Podres, pitching on his twenty-third birthday, posted a complete game victory to put Brooklyn back in the series. Roy Campanella belted a two-run homer for the Dodgers—the Brooklyn backstop had three hits and knocked in three runs on the day. Mickey Mantle launched a solo round tripper for New York. Bob Turley lasted just 1.2 innings and was charged with the loss.

Game 4	October 1, 1955
Ebbets Field (Brooklyn)	T: 2:57
Brooklyn 8 : New York 5	A: 36,242

Roy Campanella hit a solo-homer, Gil Hodges added a two-run blast and Duke Snyder belted a three-run job as the Dodgers evened the series at two apiece. Brooklyn collected fourteen hits on the day.

Clem Labine won it in relief and Don Larsen, who started and lasted four innings, was the loser. Gil McDougald homered for New York.

Game 5	October 2, 1955
Ebbets Field (Brooklyn)	T: 2:40
Brooklyn 5 : New York 3	A: 36,796

Duke Snider homered twice to become the first player ever to belt four homers in two different World Series. Sandy Amoros also homered for Brooklyn. The Dodgers moved to within one win of their first World Series title with the win. Roger Craig posted the victory and Bob Grim suffered the loss. Bob Cerv and Yogi Berra homered for the Yankees.

Game 6	October 3, 1955
Yankee Stadium (New York)	T: 2:34
New York 5 : Brooklyn 1	A: 64,022

The Yankees scored five times in the very first inning and never looked back. Bill Skowron's three-run homer highlighted the uprising. Whitey Ford went the distance, striking out eight and allowing just four hits along the way. Karl Spooner, who lasted just one-third of an inning, suffered the loss.

Game 7	October 4, 1955
Yankee Stadium (New York)	T: 2:44
Brooklyn 2 : New York 0	A: 62,465

The Dodgers took a fragile 2-0 lead into the sixth when Yogi Berra launched a slicing line drive down the left field line for what looked like a game tying two-run double. But Sandy Amoros[22] — who'd just entered the game as a defensive replacement— entered World Series immortality as well when he raced to the left field wall to make the catch and then turned and fired to Pee Wee

Reese who relayed back to Gil Hodges at first base to double off Gil McDougald. Podres held the Yankees scoreless the rest of the way and "Dem Bums" were finally champs. Hodges drove home both Brooklyn runs with a single and a sacrifice fly. Johnny Podres posted his second complete game victory of the series. Tommy Byrne was the loser in relief.

1956
NY Yankees (4) - Brooklyn Dodgers (3)
MVP: Don Larsen

Don Larsen's perfect game highlights another intense October showdown between the Yankees and Dodgers in Brooklyn's final World Series. When the dust settles it's the Yankees in seven.

Game 1	Sept 28, 1956
Ebbets Field (Brooklyn)	T: 2:32
New York 3 : Brooklyn 6	A: 34,479

Gil Hodges three-run homer in the bottom of the second proved to be the game winning blow as the Dodgers captured the opener. Sal Maglie went the distance for the win, fanning ten along the way. Jackie Robinson also homered for Brooklyn. Mickey Mantle homered for New York. Whitey Ford lasted just three innings and was saddled with the loss.

Game 2	October 5, 1956
Ebbets Field (Brooklyn)	T: 3:26
Brooklyn 13 : New York 8	A: 36,217

Yogi Berra's grand slam homer off Don Newcombe capped a five run second inning for New York but the Dodgers posted six in the bottom of the frame with Duke Snider's three-run blast causing half the damage. Gil Hodges added two two-run doubles later in the game and when the dust settled Brooklyn had their second straight win. Don Bessent won it in relief and Tom Morgan was the loser. Don Larsen started for New York but didn't make it out of the Dodgers' six-run second.

Game 3	October 6, 1956
Yankee Stadium (New York)	T: 2:17
New York 5 : Brooklyn 3	A: 73,977

Whitey Ford scattered eight hits and fanned seven en route to a complete game victory that put the Yankees back in the series. Former Cardinals' star Enos Slaughter belted a three-run homer to put New York ahead for good in the sixth. Billy Martin added a solo blast as well. Roger Craig suffered the loss.

Game 4	October 7, 1956
Yankee Stadium (New York)	T: 2:43
New York 6 : Brooklyn 2	A: 69,705

The Yankees evened things up at two apiece and they used the long ball to do it as Mickey Mantle hit a solo homer and Hank Bauer added a two-run blast to put it out of reach. Tom Sturdivant went the distance for the win and Carl Erskine was the loser.

Game 5	October 8, 1956
Yankee Stadium (New York)	T: 2:06
New York 2 : Brooklyn 0	A: 64,519

Don Larsen performed a feat that likely will never be matched—a perfect game[23] in the World Series. But the legendary perfecto was very nearly extinguished in the second inning when Jackie Robinson blasted one off third baseman Andy Carey's glove. Shortstop Gil McDougald alertly picked up the ball and fired to first just in time to get Jackie. In the fifth Gil Hodges blasted one to deep left-center field but Mickey Mantle made a sensational one-hand grab for the out. The very next batter, Sandy Amoros, ripped what looked like a homer down the right field line, but the ball hooked foul by inches. Amoros then grounded out. In the ninth, Carl Furillo skied to right and Roy Campanella bounced to second. That left just one man—Dale Mitchell—standing between Larsen and immortality. Larsen fanned Mitchell on a check swing to end it—his seventh strikeout of the game—and the greatest pitching feat in World Series history was complete. Mickey Mantle's solo homer in the bottom of the fourth proved to be the game winning hit. Sal Maglie, who went the distance for Brooklyn, suffered the loss.

Game 6	October 9, 1956
Ebbets Field (Brooklyn)	T: 2:37
Brooklyn 1 : New York 0 (10)	A: 33,224

Jackie Robinson's game winning tenth inning RBI single broke a scoreless tie and forced a seventh game. Clem Labine pitched ten scoreless innings for the win and Bob Turley, who fanned eleven batters and called his performance, "the best game of my career" was the loser.

Game 7	October 10, 1956
Ebbets Field (Brooklyn)	T: 2:19
New York 9 : Brooklyn 0	A: 33,782

In an anti-climactic ending to an otherwise thrilling World Series, the Yankees clobbered the Dodgers to claim their sixteenth championship. Elston Howard hit a solo homer, Yogi Berra hit two two-run blasts and Moose Skowron hit a grand slam in New York's demolition of Brooklyn pitching. Johnny Kucks turned in a fine three-hit shutout performance for the victory. Don Newcombe, who allowed five runs in just three innings of work, was the loser.

Bill 'Moose' Skowron

1957

Milwaukee Braves (4) - NY Yankees (3)
MVP: Lew Burdette

In just their fourth year in Milwaukee, the Braves not only bring a World Series to their adoring fans, but vanquish the defending champion Yankees in seven games.

Game 1	October 2, 1957
Yankee Stadium (New York)	T: 2:10
New York 3 : Milwaukee 1	A: 69,476

The opener pitted two of the all-time greatest lefties—Warren Spahn for Milwaukee and Whitey Ford for New York—so to no one's surprise runs were scarce. The Yankees scored one in the fifth on Hank Bauer's double and added two more in the sixth on an RBI single by Andy Carey and a successfully executed suicide squeeze by Jerry Coleman. Red Schoendienst singled home a run in the seventh for Milwaukee. Ford went the distance for the win and Spahn was the loser.

Game 2	October 3, 1957
Yankee Stadium (New York)	T: 2:26
Milwaukee 4 : New York 2	A: 65,202

Henry Aaron tripled and scored the Braves first run and Johnny Logan homered for their second tally. But it was Wes Covington's two run single in the top of the fourth that broke a 2-2 tie and proved to be the game winning hit. Covington, playing in left field, also made a sensational catch of a blast off the bat of Gil McDougald that saved two runs. Lew Burdette slammed the door shut the rest of the way to post the victory. Bobby Shantz suffered the loss. Hank Bauer homered for New York.

Game 3	October 5, 1957
County Stadium (Milwaukee)	T: 3:18

112

New York 12 : Milwaukee 3	A: 45,804

The World Series made its debut in Milwaukee but the results were not what the city's Braves crazed fans were hoping for as New York's rookie shortstop, (Milwaukee native) Tony Kubek homered twice and knocked in four runs in the Yankees lopsided victory. Mickey Mantle chipped in with a two-run round tripper as well. Don Larsen got the win in relief and Bob Buhl, who didn't make it out of the first inning, was the loser. Henry Aaron launched a two-run homerun for the Braves.

Game 4	October 6, 1957
County Stadium (Milwaukee)	T: 2:31
Milwaukee 7 : New York 5 (10)	A: 45,804

Warren Spahn was just one strike away from a complete game victory when he surrendered a three-run homer to Elston Howard that tied the score and sent the contest into extra innings. The Yankees took the lead in the tenth on Hank Bauer's RBI triple but the Braves won it in the bottom of the frame when Johnny Logan's RBI double tied it and Eddie Mathews two-run homer ended it. Spahn was credited with a complete game victory. Henry Aaron had a three-run homer earlier in the game and Frank Torre launched a solo blast as well.

Game 5	October 7, 1957
County Stadium (Milwaukee)	T: 2:20
Milwaukee 1 : New York 0	A: 45,811

Lew Burdette outdueled Whitey Ford to post his second victory of the series—a complete game shutout. Milwaukee plated the only run of the game when Joe Adcock singled home Eddie Mathews in the sixth.

Game 6	October 9, 1957
Yankee Stadium (New York)	T: 2:09
New York 3 : Milwaukee 2	A: 61,408

Homeruns were the order of the day in this one. Yogi Berra got it started with a two-run blast in the third but solo homers by Frank Torre in the fifth and Henry Aaron in the seventh tied it. Hank Bauer decided the issue with a drive off the left field foul pole in the bottom of the seventh. Bob Turley went the distance for the win, allowing just two runs on four hits and striking out eight along the way. Ernie Johnson was the loser.

Game 7	October 10, 1957
Yankee Stadium (New York)	T: 2:34
Milwaukee 5 : New York 0	A: 61,207

Lew Burdette—pitching on just two days' rest—posted his third complete game victory of the series as the Braves brought Milwaukee its first ever World Championship. The Braves tallied four times in the fourth inning and never looked back. Eddie Mathews two-run double highlighted the uprising. Henry Aaron chipped in with a run scoring single and Frank Torre's fielder's choice plated a run as well. Del Crandall added a solo homer in the eighth. Don Larsen was the loser.

1958

NY Yankees (4) - Milwaukee Braves (3)
MVP: Bob Turley

To borrow a line from Yogi Berra, "It's déjà vu all over again" as the Braves and Yankees meet in the Fall Classic for the second straight year. This time it's the Yankees in seven.

Game 1	October 1, 1958
County Stadium (Milwaukee)	T: 3:09
Milwaukee 4 : New York 3 (10)	A: 46,367

Whitey Ford and Warren Spahn locked horns in the opener for the second straight year but this time Spahn and the Braves came out on top. Ford took a one-run lead into the eighth but Wes

Covington's sacrifice fly tied the game. Ryne Duren surrendered the winning run in the tenth when Billy Bruton's two-out single plated Joe Adcock to end it. Spahn went the distance for the win. Moose Skowron and Hank Bauer homered for New York.

Game 2	October 2, 1958
County Stadium (Milwaukee)	T: 2:43
Milwaukee 13 : New York 5	A: 46,367

The Yankees plated a run in the top of the first but the Braves went on the warpath for seven in the bottom of the frame and never looked back. Billy Burton's leadoff homer ignited the attack and winning pitcher Lew Burdette connected for a three-run blast. New York's Bob Turley didn't make it out of the first inning, retiring just one batter. Burdette went the distance for the victory. Mickey Mantle hit a pair of homers and Hank Bauer added one as well for the Yankees.

Game 3	October 4, 1958
Yankee Stadium (New York)	T: 2:42
New York 4 : Milwaukee 0	A: 71,599

Don Larsen and Ryne Duren pitched a combined six-hit shutout as the Yankees climbed back in to the series. Larsen fanned eight in his seven innings of work. Duren took over in the eighth and despite walking two, did not allow a hit or a run the rest of the way. Hank Bauer knocked in all four runs for New York with a two-run single in the fifth and a two-run homer in the seventh. Bob Rush suffered the loss for the Braves.

Game 4	October 5, 1958
Yankee Stadium (New York)	T: 2:17
Milwaukee 3 : New York 0	A: 71,563

Warren Spahn bested Whitey Ford for the second time in the series—this time turning in a two-hit shutout and moving the Braves to within one win of their second consecutive World Series triumph over the Yankees. Ford, who allowed all three runs in his seven innings of work, was charged with the loss.

Game 5	October 6, 1958
Yankee Stadium (New York)	T: 2:19
New York 7 : Milwaukee 0	A: 65,279

Bob Turley returned to regular season form, striking out ten en route to a five-hit shutout. Gil McDougald's third inning homer accounted for the only run of the game until the sixth when he belted a two-run double and Turley hit a two-run single sending Lew Burdette to the showers.

Game 6	October 8, 1958
County Stadium (Milwaukee)	T: 3:07
New York 4 : Milwaukee 3 (10)	A: 46,367

Gil McDougald broke a 2-2 tie with a leadoff homer in the top of the tenth and Moose Skowron added an RBI single later in the inning to give New York a 4-2 lead. Henry Aaron's RBI single in the bottom of the frame cut the lead to one but Bob Turley retired Frank Torre on a line drive to second base to end the game. Ryne Duran won it in relief. Warren Spahn went the distance for the Braves but suffered the loss.

Game 7	October 9, 1958
County Stadium (Milwaukee)	T: 2:31
New York 6 : Milwaukee 2	A: 46,367

Elston Howard singled home the go ahead run in the top of the eighth inning and Moose Skowron connected for a three-run homer later in the frame as the Yankees completed their astonishing comeback from a three-games-to-one deficit to win the World Series. Bob Turley got the win in relief of Don Larsen. Lew

Burdette,[24] pitching on just two days' rest, lasted eight innings but suffered the loss.

1959

L.A. Dodgers (4) - Chicago White Sox (2)
MVP: Larry Sherry

In just their second season in Los Angeles, the Dodgers deliver a World Championship to the City of Angels, vanquishing the "Go-Go Sox" in six.

Game 1	October 1, 1959
Comiskey Park (Chicago)	T: 2:35
Chicago 11 : Los Angeles 0	A: 48,013

Ted Kluszewski belted a pair of two-run homers and Early Wynn hurled seven scoreless innings as the White Sox captured the opener in decisive fashion. Kluszewski knocked in five runs on the day. Dodger starter Roger Craig lasted just 3.1 innings and was charged with the loss.

Game 2	October 2, 1959
Comiskey Park (Chicago)	T: 2:21
Los Angeles 4 : Chicago 3	A: 47,368

A pinch-hit homer by Chuck Essegian tied it in the seventh and later in the inning light-hitting second baseman Charlie Neal's second round-tripper of the game won it for LA. Johnny Podres went six innings for the win and rookie reliever Larry Sherry allowed just one run over the final three frames for the save. Bob Shaw was saddled with the loss.

Game 3	October 4, 1959

Memorial Coliseum (Los Angeles)	T: 2:33
Los Angeles 3 : Chicago 1	A: 92,394

Before a record World Series crowd of 92,394,[25] Don Drysdale allowed just one run in seven innings of work and Larry Sherry shut the door over the final two frames for his second save of the series. Brooklyn era hero Carl Furillo's two-run pinch-hit single in the seventh off Sox starter Dick Donovan broke a scoreless tie and proved to be the game winning hit.

Game 4	October 5, 1959
Memorial Coliseum (Los Angeles)	T: 2:30
Los Angeles 5 : Chicago 4	A: 92,650

Trailing 4-0 in the seventh, the White Sox tied it on an RBI single by Ted Kluszewski and a three-run homer by Sherm Lollar. But a leadoff homer by another Brooklyn-era legend, Gil Hodges, in the eighth broke the hearts of the Chicago faithful and pushed the Dodgers to within one win of a World Championship. Larry Sherry pitched a scoreless eighth and ninth and was credited with the victory. Gerry Staley was the loser in relief.

Game 5	October 6, 1959
Memorial Coliseum (Los Angeles)	T: 2:28
Chicago 1 : Los Angeles 0	A: 92,706

Bob Shaw outdueled Sandy Koufax to send the series back to Chicago. Shaw lasted seven and a third innings and Dick Donovan recorded the final five outs for the save. The only run of the game crossed the plate in the fourth on a double play groundball. Koufax, who was saddled with the loss, fanned six in his seven innings of work.

Game 6	October 8, 1959

Comiskey Park (Chicago)	T: 2:33
Los Angeles 9 : Chicago 3	A: 47,653

Larry Sherry hurled 5.2 scoreless innings in relief, picking up his second win of the series to go with two saves as the Dodgers brought Los Angeles its first ever World Championship. Chuck Essegian, Wally Moon and Duke Snider all homered for LA. Ted Kluszewski belted a three-run homer for Chicago to give him a record ten RBI for the series. Early Wynn was saddled with the loss.

1960

Pittsburgh Pirates (4) - NY Yankees (3)
MVP: Bobby Richardson[26]

Pittsburgh second baseman Bill Mazeroski's historic ninth inning homer in Game 7 completes a thrilling upset of the seemingly invincible Yankees.

Game 1	October 5, 1960
Forbes Field (Pittsburgh)	T: 2:29
Pittsburgh 6 : New York 4	A: 36,676

Bill Mazeroski's fourth inning two-run homer proved to be the game winning blow as the Pirates captured the opener. Vern Law got the win and Art Ditmar was saddled with the loss. Roy Face was credited with a save. Elston Howard and Roger Maris homered for the Yankees.

Game 2	October 6, 1960
Forbes Field (Pittsburgh)	T: 3:14
New York 16 : Pittsburgh 3	A: 37,308

Mickey Mantle belted a pair of homers and knocked in five runs as the Yankees clobbered the Pirates to even the series. Bobby Richardson chipped in with three hits and two runs batted in. New York pounded out nineteen hits on the day. Bob Turley got the win and Bob Friend was the loser. Bobby Shantz was credited with a save.

Game 3	October 8, 1960
Yankee Stadium (New York)	T: 2:41
New York 10 : Pittsburgh 0	A: 70,001

The Yankees posted six runs in the bottom of the first and ace lefty Whitey Ford did the rest, turning in his second complete game shutout of the series. Bobby Richardson belted a grand slam homer and finished the day with six runs batted in. Mickey Mantle had four hits, including a homerun. Pittsburgh starter "Vinegar Bend" Mizell lasted just one third of an inning and was saddled with the loss.

Game 4	October 9, 1960
Yankee Stadium (New York)	T: 2:29
Pittsburgh 3 : New York 2	A: 67,812

Vern Law notched his second win of the series and Roy Face his second save as the undaunted Pirates picked themselves up off the deck and evened things up at two-games apiece. Law also singled home a run and scored one as well. Pittsburgh centerfielder Bill Virdon drove home what proved to be the winning run with an RBI single in the fifth and then saved two-runs with a circus catch in the seventh. Ralph Terry suffered the loss. Bill Skowron homered for New York.

Game 5	October 10, 1960
Yankee Stadium (New York)	T: 2:32
Pittsburgh 5 : New York 2	A: 62,753

The Pirates got all the runs they would need when they posted three in the second inning. Bill Mazeroski's two-run homer highlighted the uprising. Harvey Haddix allowed just two runs over 6.1 innings of work and Roy Face shut the door the rest of the way to notch his third save of the series. Art Ditmar suffered the loss. Roger Maris homered for New York.

Game 6	October 12, 1960
Forbes Field (Pittsburgh)	T: 2:38
New York 12 : Pittsburgh 0	A: 38,580

Whitey Ford tossed his second consecutive shutout of the series and Bobby Richardson belted two triples and knocked in three runs to extend his World Series record for RBI in a series to twelve. New York collected seventeen hits on the day including three by Yogi Berra. Pirates' starter Bob Friend lasted just two innings and was handed the loss. Roberto Clemente had two hits for the Pirates.

Game 7	October 13, 1960
Forbes Field (Pittsburgh)	T: 2:36
Pittsburgh 10 : New York 9	A: 36,683

In a seesaw battle for the ages Pittsburgh completed its stunning upset of New York. Leading 4-1 in the sixth, the Pirates asked Roy Face to collect his fourth save of the series. But Face surrendered an RBI single to Mickey Mantle and a three-run homer to Yogi Berra to give the Yankees a 5-4 lead. New York added two more in the eighth to make it a 7-4 game. In the bottom of the frame tragedy struck when Bill Virdon hit what appeared to be a double play grounder to Tony Kubek at shortstop. But the ball took a wicked hop, hitting Kubek in the throat, causing him to collapse.[27] That opened the floodgates as RBI singles by Dick Groate and Roberto Clemente— and a three-run homer off the bat of Hal Smith made it a 9-7 game. Undaunted, the Yankees tied it in the ninth on Yogi Berra's fielder's choice and Mickey Mantle's RBI single, setting the stage for perhaps the most historic homerun in World Series history. Leading off the bottom of the frame Mazeroski launched reliever Ralph Terry's second offering over the left field wall and the Pirates were champions. It was the first time that a World Series ended with a homerun. Harvey Haddix was credited with the victory. Terry was the loser.

1961

NY Yankees (4) - Cincinnati Reds (1)
MVP: Whitey Ford

Roger Maris breaks Babe Ruth's single season homerun record and the Yankee win 109 regular season games en route to their 26th World Series appearance vs. an overwhelmed Cincinnati Reds team.

Game 1	October 4, 1961
Yankee Stadium (New York)	T: 2:11
New York 2 : Cincinnati 0	A: 62,387

Whitey Ford hurled his third consecutive complete game shutout in the World Series and homeruns by Elston Howard and Bill Skowron were all the Yankees needed to capture the opener. Reds' starter Jim O'Toole lasted seven innings but was charged with the loss.

Game 2	October 5, 1961
Yankee Stadium (New York)	T: 2:43
Cincinnati 6 : New York 2	A: 63,083

The Reds evened the series as staff ace Joey Jay scattered four hits and allowed just two runs—each solo homers by Yogi Berra— en route to a complete game victory in his World

Series debut. Gordy Coleman belted a two-run homer and Johnny Edwards had two hits and knocked in two runs as well for Cincinnati. New York starter Ralph Terry suffered the loss.

Game 3	October 7, 1961
Crosley Field (Cincinnati)	T: 2:15
New York 3 : Cincinnati 2	A: 32,589

Roger Maris belted a game-winning homer in the top of the ninth as New York squeaked by Cincinnati. Reds starter Bob Purkey—who also surrendered a game-tying pinch-hit homer to Johnny Blanchard an inning earlier—went the distance but suffered the loss. Reliever Luis Arroyo pitched two scoreless frames and was credited with the victory. Maris's homer was his first hit of the series.

Game 4	October 8, 1961
Crosley Field (Cincinnati)	T: 2:27
New York 7 : Cincinnati 0	A: 32,589

Whitey Ford broke Babe Ruth's World Series record for consecutive scoreless innings, posting six zeroes before being lifted due to an ankle injury.[28] Reliever Jim Coates slammed the door shut the rest of the way as the Yankees cruised to within one victory of another World Championship. Roger Maris crossed the dish with what proved to be the winning run on a double play grounder in the fourth inning. Bobby Richardson and Bill Skowron each had three hits. Reds' starter Jim O'Toole was saddled with his second defeat of the series.

Game 5	October 9, 1961
Crosley Field (Cincinnati)	T: 3:05
New York 13 : Cincinnati 5	A: 32,589

Hector Lopez, substituting for Mickey Mantle,[29] tripled, homered and knocked in five runs as New York completed their conquest of the Reds in decisive fashion. The Yankees tallied five times in the opening frame, sending Cincinnati starter Joey Jay to an early shower. Johnny Blanchard also homered for New York. Bud Daley got the victory in relief and Jay suffered the loss. Frank Robinson and Wally Post homered for Cincinnati.

1962

NY Yankees (4) - San Francisco Giants (3)
MVP: Ralph Terry

Willie Mays and the Giants make their first World Series appearance since moving to San Francisco only to lose to the Yankees in a thrilling seven game series.

Game 1	October 4, 1962
Candlestick Park (San Francisco)	T: 2:43
New York 6 : San Francisco 2	A: 43,852

Whitey Ford's consecutive scoreless innings streak in the World Series was snapped at 33.2 when Willie Mays—who had three hits on the day—scored on Jose Pagan's bunt single in the bottom of the second inning. Pagan also had three hits. Nevertheless, the Yankees' ace allowed just two runs en route to a complete game victory. Clete Boyer's seventh inning homer broke a 2-2 tie and proved to be the game-winner. Giants' starter Billy O'Dell suffered the loss.

Game 2	October 5, 1962
Candlestick Park (San Francisco)	T: 2:11
San Francisco 2 : New York 0	A: 43,910

Giants' ace Jack Stanford pitched a three-hit shutout as San Francisco evened the series. The game winning run crossed the dish in the bottom of the first when Chuck Hiller scored on Matty Alou's grounder. Willie McCovey blasted a gargantuan homer in the eighth to close out the scoring. Ralph Terry suffered the loss despite allowing just two runs in seven innings of work.

Game 3	October 7, 1962
Yankee Stadium (New York)	T: 2:06
New York 3 : San Francisco 2	A: 71,434

Bill Stafford allowed just two runs on four hits en route to a hard fought complete game victory. The Yankees broke a scoreless tie in the bottom of the seventh when Roger Maris singled home two runs and Clete Boyer's fielder's choice forced a third man home. Stafford surrendered a two-run homer to Ed Bailey in the ninth but that was as close as San Francisco would get. Giants' starter Billy Pierce was charged with the loss.

Game 4	October 8, 1962
Yankee Stadium (New York)	T: 2:55
San Francisco 7 : New York 3	A: 66,607

Juan Marichal took a 2-0 lead into the fifth but was knocked out of the series when he was hit by a pitch while attempting to bunt. New York jumped on reliever Bobby Bolin for two in the sixth to tie it up but light-hitting second baseman Chuck Hiller belted a grand slam in the seventh to settle the issue. Former Yankee Don Larsen pitched just one third of an inning but was credited with the victory.[30] Jim Coates was the loser.

Game 5	October 10, 1962
Yankee Stadium (New York)	T: 2:42

| New York 5 : San Francisco 3 | A: 63,165 |

Jack Sanford fanned ten hitters in 7.2 innings of work but suffered the loss as New York moved to within one victory of its twentieth World Series triumph. With the scored knotted at 2-2 in the eighth, rookie slugger Tommy Tresh touched up Sanford for a three-run homer and the Yankees never looked back. Ralph Terry went the distance for the victory. Jose Pagan homered for the Giants.

Game 6	October 15, 1962
Candlestick Park (San Francisco)	T: 2:00
San Francisco 5 : New York 3	A: 43,948

Billy Pierce took a no-hitter into the fifth and wound up allowing just two runs on three hits en route to a complete game victory. Orlando Cepeda singled, doubled and knocked in three runs to pace the Giants' attack. Whitey Ford was saddled with the loss—his first in World Series play since 1958. Roger Maris homered for New York.

Game 7	October 16, 1962
Candlestick Park (San Francisco)	T: 2:29
New York 1 : San Francisco 0	A: 43,948

In one of the most thrilling finishes in World Series history, second baseman Bobby Richardson snared Willie McCovey's screaming liner with two outs and the tying and winning runs at second and third in the bottom of the ninth inning. Bill Skowron scored the only run of the game when Tony Kubek grounded into a double play in the fifth. Ralph Terry tossed a four-hit shutout. Jack Sanford was saddled with the toughest loss of his career. It was Terry's second triumph of the series and Sanford's second defeat.

1963

LA Dodgers (4) - NY Yankees (0)
MVP: Sandy Koufax

Sandy Koufax (25-5, 1.88 ERA, 306 K's) leads Los Angeles to its second Fall Classic in just five seasons and notches two complete game victories as the Dodgers vanquish the Yankees in four straight games.

Game 1	October 2, 1963
Yankee Stadium (New York)	T: 2:09
Los Angeles 5 : New York 2	A: 69,000

Sandy Koufax fanned a World Series record fifteen batters and Johnny Roseboro's second inning three-run homer was all the offense LA would need. Koufax surrendered a two-run homer to Tommy Tresh in the eighth to account for New York's two runs. Whitey Ford, who lasted just five innings, surrendered all five Dodger runs and was saddled with the loss.

Game 2	October 3, 1963
Yankee Stadium (New York)	T: 2:13
Los Angeles 4 : New York 1	A: 66,455

Johnny Podres went 8.2 innings and Ron Perranoski recorded the final out of the game for the save as Los Angeles made it two-straight over New York. Willie Davis's two-run double in the opening frame proved to be the game winning blow. Former Yankee Bill Skowron belted a solo homer and Tommy Davis added an RBI triple to close out the Dodgers' scoring. Al Downing was handed the defeat. Felipe Lopez doubled home a run in the ninth, accounting for New York's only run.

Game 3	October 5, 1963
Dodger Stadium (Los Angeles)	T: 2:05

127

| Los Angeles 1 : New York 0 | A: 55,912 |

In the first World Series game ever played in beautiful Dodger Stadium, Don Drysdale fanned nine and scattered just three hits en route to a complete game shutout. New York starter Jim Bouton, who allowed just one run on four hits in seven innings of work, was saddled with the loss. Tommy Davis singled home the game's only run in the first inning.

Game 4	October 6, 1963
Dodger Stadium (Los Angeles)	T: 1:50
Los Angeles 2 : New York 1	A: 55,912

The Dodgers captured their second World Championship since moving to LA as Sandy Koufax turned in his second complete game victory of the series. Frank Howard's towering homer in the fifth plated the first run of the game. Mickey Mantle homered to tie it up in the seventh, but in the bottom of the frame Jim Gilliam reached on Joe Pepitone's error and scored what proved to be the winning run on Willie Davis' sacrifice fly. Whitey Ford allowed both LA runs and absorbed his second defeat of the series.

1964

St. Louis Cardinals (4) - NY Yankees (3)
MVP: Bob Gibson

The Yankees return to the World Series for the fifth consecutive year and the fifteenth time in eighteen seasons but it's Bob Gibson and the Redbirds' year as St. Louis bags the prize in seven games.

Game 1	October 7, 1964
Busch Stadium (St. Louis)	T: 2:42
St. Louis 9 : New York 5	A: 30,805

The Cardinals wore their hitting shoes to the opener. Mike Shannon belted a two-run homer and Lou Brock had two hits, including an RBI double. Redbirds' starter and winning pitcher Ray Sadecki also knocked in a run with a base hit and battery-mate Tim McCarver chipped in with a double and a triple. Curt Flood also tripled and registered a sacrifice fly. Sadecki went six innings for the victory and Whitey Ford suffered the loss.

Game 2	October 8, 1964
Busch Stadium (St. Louis)	T: 2:29
New York 8 : St. Louis 3	A: 30,805

Rookie right hander Mel Stottlemyre tossed a seven-hit complete game victory in his World Series debut. Bob Gibson, who was saddled with the loss, pitched eight innings, allowing four runs and fanning nine before departing with the game still in question. The Yankees jumped on relievers Barney Schultz and Gordie Richardson for four runs in the ninth to even the series. Phil Linz paced the New York attack with three hits including a solo homerun.

Game 3	October 10, 1964
Yankee Stadium (New York)	T: 2:16
New York 2 : St. Louis 1	A: 30,805

Jim Bouton bested Curt Simmons in a pitching duel that finally ended when Mickey Mantle touched up reliever Barney Schultz for a game winning homer in the bottom of the ninth. Clete Boyer's RBI double in the second gave New York the early lead but Simmons singled home a run in the fifth to tie it. Schultz came on in the ninth and threw just one pitch—to Mantle leading off. "The Mick" deposited the offering into the right field seats to end it.[31]

Game 4	October 11, 1964

Yankee Stadium (New York)	T: 2:18
St. Louis 4 : New York 3	A: 66,312

Ray Sadecki lasted just one third of an inning as the Yankees touched him up for three runs on four hits in the opening frame. Mickey Mantle and Elston Howard had RBI singles in the inning. The lead held up until the sixth when Ken Boyer belted a grand slam off starter Al Downing to close out the day's scoring. Roger Craig pitched 4.2 scoreless innings for the win and Ron Taylor blanked the Bombers over the final four frames for the save.

Game 5	October 12, 1964
Yankee Stadium (New York)	T: 2:37
St. Louis 5 : New York 2 (10)	A: 65,633

Bob Gibson turned in an astonishing performance, fanning thirteen hitters and pitching all ten frames in the Cardinals rollercoaster victory. The flame throwing future Hall of Famer's one mistake came with two outs in the ninth when Tommy Tresh belted a two-run homer to tie it. But battery mate Tim McCarver belted a three-run homer off reliever Pete Mikkelsen in the top of the tenth and the St. Louis ace slammed the door shut in the bottom of the frame for the victory.

Game 6	October 14, 1964
Busch Stadium (St. Louis)	T: 2:37
New York 8 : St. Louis 3	A: 30,805

Jim Bouton collected his second victory of the series, finishing just one out shy of a complete game victory, as the Yankees forced a seventh and deciding game. Joe Pepitone's grand slam off Barney Schultz highlighted a five-run uprising in the eighth. Steve Hamilton got the final out in the ninth and was credited with the save. Mickey Mantle and Roger Maris homered for New York. Lou Brock had three hits for St. Louis. Curt Simmons was the loser.

Game 7	October 15, 1964
Busch Stadium (St. Louis)	T: 2:40
St. Louis 7 : New York 5	A: 30,346

Mel Stottlemyre and Bob Gibson locked horns for the third time in the series—this time on just two days rest. Stottlemyre blinked first, allowing three runs in his fourth and final inning of work.[32] Reliever Al Downing surrendered three more runs in the fifth, without retiring a batter. The Yankees cut the lead in half in the sixth when Mickey Mantle belted a three-run homer but Ken Boyer homered in the Cardinals' half of the seventh to make it 7-3. New York managed two runs in the ninth—one of them coming on a homer by Clete Boyer[33] — but they finished two bucks short and the Cardinals were champions. Gibson went the distance, fanning nine along the way. Stottlemyre was saddled with the loss.[34]

1965

LA Dodgers (4) - Minnesota Twins (3)
MVP: Sandy Koufax

The LA Dodgers return to the Fall Classic for the third time in seven years and lock horns with a Minnesota Twins team making its World Series debut. When the dust finally settles the Dodgers are champions.

Game 1	October 6, 1965
Metropolitan Stadium (Minnesota)	T: 2:29
Minnesota 8 : Los Angeles 2	A: 47,797

There was controversy from the get go in this one as Dodgers' ace Sandy Koufax sat out the opener in observance of the Jewish holiday, Yom Kippur. Don Drysdale lasted just 2.2 innings in Koufax's stead, allowing seven runs—four of them coming on a solo homer by Don Mincher and a three-run blast by Zoilo Versalles. Jim "Mudcat" Grant scattered ten hits en route to a complete game victory. Ron Fairly homered for the Dodgers.

Game 2	October 7, 1965
Metropolitan Stadium (Minnesota)	T: 2:13
Minnesota 5 : Los Angeles 1	A: 48,700

Jim Kaat scattered seven hits and went the distance for the victory as the Twins made it two-straight over LA. Minnesota broke a scoreless tie in the sixth when Tony Oliva singled home a run and Harmon Killebrew followed with what proved to be the game winning hit—an RBI double. Kaat chipped in with the stick as well, singling home two runs in the eighth inning to put the game out of reach. Sandy Koufax, who fanned nine in six innings of work, surrendered just two runs but was saddled with the loss.

Game 3	October 9, 1965
Dodger Stadium (Los Angeles)	T: 2:06
Los Angeles 4 : Minnesota 0	A: 55,934

Claude Osteen got the Dodgers back on track with a desperately needed five-hit shutout. Johnny Roseboro's two-run single in the fourth proved to the game-winning blow. RBI doubles by Lou Johnson and Maury Wills in the fifth and sixth innings respectively, closed out the day's scoring. Minnesota starter Camilo Pascual lasted five innings, allowing three runs on eight hits in a losing effort.

Game 4	October 10, 1965
Dodger Stadium (Los Angeles)	T: 2:15
Los Angeles 7 : Minnesota 2	A: 55,920

Don Drysdale avenged his Game 1 defeat at the hands of "Mudcat" Grant, going the distance to best the Twins' ace. Drysdale

132

allowed just five hits and fanned eleven. Ron Fairly knocked in three runs and Lou Johnson and Wes Parker homered to pace the Dodgers' ten-hit attack. Harmon Killebrew and Tony Oliva homered for the Twins. Grant lasted just five innings, surrendering five runs on five hits.

Game 5	October 11, 1965
Dodger Stadium (Los Angeles)	T: 2:34
Los Angeles 7 : Minnesota 0	A: 55,801

This time it was Sandy Koufax's turn to avenge his defeat at the hand of Jim Kaat, and avenge it he did. The flame throwing lefty turned in a complete game, four-hit, ten-strikeout shutout to leave the Dodgers just one win away from their third Los Angeles World Championship. Maury Wills had four hits and scored twice to pace the LA attack. Kaat, who did not survive the third inning, surrendered four runs in garnering the loss.

Game 6	October 13, 1965
Metropolitan Stadium (Minnesota)	T: 2:16
Minnesota 5 : Los Angeles 1	A: 49,578

The Twins won a game of "long-ball" to stave off elimination and force a seventh and deciding game. "Mudcat" Grant, pitching on just two days' rest, went the distance for the win. Bobby Allison belted what proved to be the game winning blow—a two-run homer in the fourth. Grant blasted a three-run homer in the sixth to end any doubt. Ron Fairly's seventh inning homer accounted for the Dodgers lone run. Claude Osteen lasted five innings and was saddled with the loss.

Game 7	October 14, 1965
Metropolitan Stadium (Minnesota)	T: 2:27
Los Angeles 2 : Minnesota 0	A: 50,596

Sandy Koufax demonstrated the grit and guile of a first-ballot Hall of Famer with a three-hit complete game shutout in the seventh and deciding game of the World Series—all on just two days' rest. The lights out lefty fanned ten along the way. Los Angeles scored the only runs of the game in the fourth on the strength of Lou Johnson's homer and Wes Parker's RBI single. Jim Kaat, who was lifted in the game deciding frame, was saddled with the loss.

1966
Baltimore Orioles (4) - LA Dodgers (0)
MVP: Frank Robinson

In his first season in Baltimore, Frank Robinson posts a Triple Crown season and leads the Orioles to a four-game sweep of the defending World Champion Dodgers.

Game 1	October 5, 1966
Dodger Stadium (Los Angeles)	T: 2:56
Baltimore 5 : Los Angeles 2^{35}	A: 55,941

Frank Robinson belted a two-run homer and Brooks Robinson added a solo blast—all in the very first inning as the Orioles captured the opener in decisive fashion. Don Drysdale lasted just two innings and was saddled with the loss. Moe Drabowsky hurled 6.2 scoreless frames in relief, allowing just one hit and fanning eleven along the way, to post the victory. Jim Lefebvre homered for the Dodgers.

Game 2	October 6, 1966
Dodger Stadium (Los Angeles)	T: 2:26
Baltimore 6 : Los Angeles 0	A: 55,947

Dodgers' centerfielder Willie Davis committed a World Series record three errors in one inning and Los Angeles finished the day with an unprecedented six miscues as Baltimore left town with its second straight road victory. Davis's misfortunes led to three unearned fifth inning runs to break a scoreless tie and send Sandy Koufax home a loser. 20-year old Orioles ace Jim Palmer tossed a four hit shutout, fanning six along the way in his World Series debut.

Game 3	October 8, 1966
Memorial Stadium (Baltimore)	T: 1:55
Baltimore 1 : Los Angeles 0	A: 54,445

21-year old Wally Bunker tossed a six-hit shutout in his World Series debut as the Baltimore Orioles moved to within one victory of their first ever World Championship. Paul Blair's sixth inning homer proved to be the only run of the ballgame. The blast came off Dodgers' starter Claude Osteen who allowed just three hits on the day but was saddled with the loss.

Game 4	October 9, 1966
Memorial Stadium (Baltimore)	T: 1:45
Baltimore 1 : Los Angeles 0	A: 54,458

With their second consecutive 1-0 victory over Los Angeles, Baltimore captured its first World Championship. And for the second day in a row a solo homer—this one by Frank Robinson—was the margin of victory. Dave McNally turned in a four-hit complete game shutout—the third straight complete game shutout by Oriole pitchers. Don Drysdale, who also allowed only four hits, suffered the loss.

1967

St. Louis Cardinals (4) - Boston Red Sox (3)
MVP: Bob Gibson

In a rematch of the 1946 Fall Classic, speedster Lou Brock sets the base paths on fire and flamethrower Bob Gibson notches three victories— including a Game 7 triumph at Fenway Park—as St. Louis outlasts Boston to capture the eighth World Series title in its storied history.

Game 1	October 4, 1967
Fenway Park (Boston)	T: 2:22
St. Louis 2 : Boston 1	A: 34,796

Lou Brock went 4-for-4, stole two bases and scored both Redbird runs and Bob Gibson fanned ten Red Sox hitters en route to a complete game victory in the opener. Roger Maris knocked in both St. Louis runs. Red Sox starter and loser Jose Santiago, who accounted for Boston's lone tally with a third inning homer, was tagged with the loss.

Game 2	October 5, 1967
Fenway Park (Boston)	T: 2:24
Boston 5 : St. Louis 0	A: 35,188

Red Sox ace Jim Lonborg took a perfect game into the seventh inning and a no-hitter into the eighth before settling for a one-hit shutout. Carl Yastrzemski powered the Red Sox offense with two homers and four runs batted in. Dick Hughes lasted 5.1 innings and was saddled with the loss. Julian Javier's eighth inning double was the Redbirds' only hit.

Game 3	October 7, 1967
Busch Stadium (St. Louis)	T: 2:15
St. Louis 5 : Boston 2	A: 54,575

Lou Brock led off the game with a triple and scored its first run and Mike Shannon's two-run homer an inning later proved to be the game deciding blow as the Cardinals flew away with a victory. Nelson Briles went the distance for the win. Sox starter Gary Bell lasted just two innings and suffered the loss. Reggie Smith homered for Boston.

Game 4	October 8, 1967

Busch Stadium (St. Louis)	T: 2:05
St. Louis 6 : Boston 0	A: 54,575

Bob Gibson pitched a complete game shutout to notch his second victory of the series as St. Louis moved to within one win of the ninth World Championship in its proud history. Roger Maris doubled home two runs in a four-run first and the Cardinals never looked back. Gibson scattered five hits and fanned six along the way. Jose Santiago lasted just one third of an inning and was saddled with his second loss of the series.

Game 5	October 9, 1967
Busch Stadium (St. Louis)	T: 2:20
Boston 2 : St. Louis 1	A: 54,575

Jim Lonborg put the Cardinals' celebration on hold with a tough as-nails victory that was even closer than the score might indicate. The Sox ace held St. Louis scoreless until the ninth when Roger Maris belted a solo homer. Cards' lefty Steve Carlton surrendered one unearned run in his six innings of work but was saddled with the loss. Elston Howard's two-run single in the ninth proved to the game winning hit.

Game 6	October 11, 1967
Fenway Park (Boston)	T: 2:48
Boston 8 : St. Louis 4	A: 35,188

Rico Petrocelli belted two homers and Carl Yastrzemski and Reggie Smith joined the homerun parade as well as the Red Sox outslugged the Cardinals to force a seventh and deciding game. Boston pounded out ten hits on the day—including three by Yastrzemski. Lou Brock belted a two-run homer, stole a base and knocked in three runs in a losing cause. Relievers John Wyatt, who won it for the Sox and Jack Lamabe who lost it for the Cards, were the pitchers of record.

Game 7	October 12, 1967

Fenway Park (Boston)	T: 2:23
St. Louis 7 : Boston 2	A: 35,188

In a game that featured each staff's ace, Bob Gibson bested Jim Lonborg and the Cardinals were champions. Gibson, who allowed just three hits, notched his third complete game victory of the series and matched his Game 1 performance with ten strikeouts. The legendary Redbird's ace helped his own cause with a solo homer. Julian Javier also homered and knocked in three runs. Lou Brock had two hits and stole three bases.[36] Lonborg lasted six innings, surrendering all seven St. Louis runs on ten hits.

1968

Detroit Tigers (4) - St. Louis Cardinals (3)
MVP: Mickey Lolich

Unheralded southpaw Mickey Lolich steals the spotlight from thirty-one game winner Denny McLain, notching three victories as the Tigers battle back from a three games to one deficit to win the World Series.

Game 1	October 2, 1968
Busch Stadium (St. Louis)	T: 2:29
St. Louis 4 : Detroit 0	A: 54,692

Bob Gibson set a World Series record fanning seventeen hitters en route to a complete game shutout in the opener. St. Louis pushed three runs across the dish in the fourth on the strength of a two-run single by Julian Javier and Mike Shannon's RBI base hit. Lou Brock's seventh inning homer closed out the day's scoring. Detroit's thirty-one game winner Denny McLain lasted six innings and suffered the loss.

Game 2	October 3, 1968

Busch Stadium (St. Louis)	T: 2:41
Detroit 8 : St. Louis 1	A: 54,692

The Tigers took Cards' pitchers behind the woodshed to the tune of eight runs on thirteen hits to even the series at one apiece. Mickey Lolich scattered six hits and fanned nine en route to a complete game victory. He chipped in at the plate as well, belting the first and only homerun of his Major League career. Norm Cash and Willie Horton also homered for Detroit. Nelson Briles, who allowed seven runs in five innings of work, was saddled with the loss. Lou Brock had two stolen bases.

Game 3	October 5, 1968
Tiger Stadium (Detroit)	T: 3:17
St. Louis 7 : Detroit 3	A: 53,634

Redbird sluggers Tim McCarver and Orlando Cepeda both belted three-run homers as St. Louis caged the Tigers. Lou Brock continued his torrid World Series play, collecting three hits and stealing three bases. Ray Washburn got the win, Earl Wilson took the loss and Joe Hoerner earned the save. Al Kaline and Dick McAuliffe homered for Detroit.

Game 4	October 6, 1968
Tiger Stadium (Detroit)	T: 2:34
St. Louis 10 : Detroit 1	A: 53,634

Bob Gibson notched his second win of the series with a ten strikeout complete game victory. Lou Brock belted an upper deck homerun leading off the game and later tripled and then doubled with the bases loaded to fall just a single short of a cycle. The fleet-footed left fielder finished the day with four runs batted in and also swiped third base to tie the record for stolen bases in a World Series that he'd set the year before. Gibson also homered. Denny McLain did not survive the third inning and suffered the loss. Dick McAuliffe homered for Detroit.

Game 5	October 7, 1968
Tiger Stadium (Detroit)	T: 2:43
Detroit 5 : St. Louis 3	A: 53,634

Orlando Cepeda's two-run homer highlighted St. Louis' three-run first inning but the Tigers pushed two across the dish in the fourth on Willie Horton's sacrifice fly and an RBI single by Jim Northrup and they jumped ahead for good in the seventh on a two-run single by Al Kaline and an RBI base hit by Norm Cash. Mickey Lolich notched his second win of the series. Reliever Joe Hoerner surrendered Detroit's final two runs without retiring a batter and was charged with the defeat.

Game 6	October 9, 1968
Busch Stadium (St. Louis)	T: 2:26
Detroit 13 : St. Louis 1	A: 54,692

The Tigers forced a seventh and deciding game with an absolute mauling of the Cardinals. The onslaught featured a World Series record tying ten runs in the third inning. Jim Northrup's grand slam homerun highlighted the uprising. Al Kaline also homered and finished the day with three hits and four runs batted in. Denny McLain returned to regular season form with a seven strikeout complete game victory. Ray Washburn lasted just two innings and was charged with the loss.

Game 7	October 10, 1968
Busch Stadium (St. Louis)	T: 2:07
Detroit 4 : St. Louis 1	A: 54,692

Mickey Lolich turned in his third complete game victory of the series, allowing just one run on five hits as the Tigers completed their miraculous comeback and captured the third World Championship in their long history. Detroit broke it open in a three-run seventh highlighted by Jim Northrup's two-run triple.[37] Mike

Shannon's solo blast in the bottom of the ninth was all the offense the Cardinals could muster. Bob Gibson went the distance for St. Louis but was saddled with the loss.

1969

New York Mets (4) - Baltimore Orioles (1)
MVP: Donn Clendenon

In what must be considered the most stunning World Series upset of the modern era, the perennial doormat Mets knock off the powerhouse Baltimore Orioles—owners of 109-regular season victories—in five games.

Game 1	October 11, 1969
Memorial Stadium (Baltimore)	T: 2:13
Baltimore 4 : New York 1	A: 50,429

No surprises here. The Orioles jumped out to an early lead when Don Buford took Mets' ace Tom Seaver over the wall in the very first inning. The Birds added three more in the fourth on RBI singles by Mark Belanger, Mike Cuellar and Buford's RBI double. Cuellar went the distance, scattering six hits and fanning eight along the way. Al Weis' seventh inning sacrifice fly accounted for the Mets' only run. Seaver lasted five innings and surrendered all four Baltimore runs.

Game 2	October 12, 1969
Memorial Stadium (Baltimore)	T: 2:20
New York 2 : Baltimore 1	A: 50,850

Jerry Koosman pitched six innings of no-hit ball and came to within one out of a complete game victory as the Mets evened the series. Donn Clendenon took O's starter Dave McNally over the wall in the fourth to make it 1-0. The Orioles tied it in the seventh when Paul Blair singled, stole second and scored on Brooks Robinson's base hit.[38] But the "Amazins" stole the show in the ninth when Al Weis singled home Ed Charles with what proved to be the game winning run. Ron Taylor recorded the last out of the ballgame for the save. McNally went the distance in a losing effort.

Game 3	October 14, 1969
Shea Stadium (New York)	T: 2:23
New York 5 : Baltimore 0	A: 56,335

Tommy Agee belted a leadoff homer and an inning later Mets starter Gary Gentry helped his own cause with a two-run double as New York made it two-straight over Baltimore. Agee was superb in the field as well, making two circus catches—one with two men aboard in the fourth, and the other with the bases loaded in the seventh—probably saving five runs. Gentry went 6.2 innings for the win and a flame throwing twenty-two-year-old right-hander named Nolan Ryan pitched the final 2.1 frames for the save. Ed Kranepool also homered for New York. Jim Palmer was the loser.

Game 4	October 15, 1969
Shea Stadium (New York)	T: 2:33
New York 2 : Baltimore 1 (10)	A: 57,367

Tom Seaver allowed just one run in ten innings of work and the Mets moved to within one victory of the first World Championship in their brief history. Donn Clendenon's second inning solo homer gave New York a lead that lasted until the ninth when Brooks Robinson's sacrifice fly tied the game.[39] But in the bottom of the tenth, Jerry Grote led off with a double, Al Weis was intentionally walked and J. C. Martin laid down a sacrifice bunt. Reliever Pete Richert fielded the ball and fired to first but hit Martin, sending the ball into right field and Grote home with the winning run. Seaver got the win and Dick Hall was the loser.

Game 5	October 16, 1969
Shea Stadium (Shea Stadium)	T: 2:14
New York 5 : Baltimore 3	A: 57,397

It looked like the Orioles would right the ship when they touched up Jerry Koosman for three third inning runs on the strength of a solo homer by Frank Robinson and starter Dave McNally's two run blast. But in the bottom of the sixth Donn Clendenon smashed a two-run homer[4041]—his third round tripper of the series—and an inning later light-hitting infielder Al Weis homered to tie the game. The Mets jumped ahead for good in the eighth when Ron Swoboda doubled home Cleon Jones and scored when Boog Powell booted Jerry Grote's grounder. Koosman went the distance, retiring future Mets manager Davey Johnson on a fly ball to left for the final out of the game. O's ace reliever, Eddie Watt, surrendered the eighth inning runs and was saddled with the loss.

1970

Baltimore Orioles (4) - Cincinnati Reds (1)
MVP: Brooks Robinson

The Baltimore juggernaut wins 108 games and returns to the World Series as prohibitive favorites for the second straight year. This time they take care of business, vanquishing Cincinnati in five games.

Game 1	Oct 10, 1970[41]
Riverfront Stadium (Cincinnati)	T: 2:24

| Baltimore 4 : Cincinnati 3 | A: 51,531 |

Brooks Robinson, whose performance at third base throughout the series was nothing less than legendary, belted a game-winning homer in the seventh and the Orioles captured the opener. Cincinnati took an early three-run lead but a two-run homer by Boog Powell and a solo blast by Elrod Hendricks tied it, setting the stage for Robinson. Jim Palmer went 8.2 innings and Pete Richert recorded the final out for the save. Lee May homered for the Reds. Starter Gary Nolan suffered the loss.

Game 2	October 11, 1970
Riverfront Stadium (Cincinnati)	T: 2:26
Baltimore 6 : Cincinnati 5	A: 51,531

The Orioles erased a four-run deficit—erupting for five runs in the fifth inning to leave the Queen City with a commanding 2-0 series lead. RBI singles by Paul Blair, Boog Powell and Brooks Robinson, and an RBI double by Elrod Hendricks levied the damage. Powell homered earlier in the game as well. Tom Phoebus won it in relief and Dick Hall got the save. Milt Wilcox was the loser. Johnny Bench and Bobby Tolan belted round trippers for the Reds.

Game 3	October 13, 1970
Memorial Stadium (Baltimore)	T: 2:09
Baltimore 9 : Cincinnati 3	A: 51,773

The Orioles pummeled Cincinnati and moved to within one victory of a clean sweep. Don Buford and Frank Robinson homered for the Orioles but the big blow of the game came in the sixth when Dave McNally became the only pitcher ever to hit a grand slam in the World Series. The blast came off Reds' reliever Wayne Granger. McNally got it done on the mound as well, turning in a nine-hit complete game victory. Tony Cloninger was the loser.

Game 4	October 14, 1970

144

Memorial Stadium (Baltimore)	T: 2:26
Cincinnati 6 : Baltimore 5	A: 53,007

The Orioles took a two-run lead into the eighth and it appeared that Cincinnati might be through, but Lee May belted a three-run homer and the Reds lived to fight another day. Clay Carroll won it in relief. Eddie Watt, who came on in the eighth and surrendered the homer to May, was the loser. Pete Rose also homered for the Reds and Brooks Robinson had four hits including a round tripper for Baltimore.

Game 5	October 15, 1970
Memorial Stadium (Baltimore)	T: 2:35
Baltimore 9 : Cincinnati 3	A: 45,341

Mike Cuellar surrendered three first inning runs but slammed the door shut the rest of the way and the Orioles pounded six Reds' pitchers for fifteen hits in the series clinching victory. Paul Blair and Davey Johnson had three hits apiece and Merv Rettenmund and Frank Robinson homered. Jim Merritt, who started it for the Reds and surrendered four runs in just one and two thirds innings of work, was saddled with the loss.

1971

Pittsburgh Pirates (4) - Baltimore Orioles (3)
MVP: Roberto Clemente

The immortal Roberto Clemente's spectacular performance— in all facets of the game—drives the Pirates to a thrilling seven- game triumph over three-time defending AL champion Baltimore.[42]

Game 1	October 9, 1971

Memorial Stadium (Baltimore)	T: 2:06
Baltimore 5 : Pittsburgh 3	A: 53,229

Dave McNally allowed just three hits and three unearned run in a nine-strikeout complete game victory in the opener. All five Baltimore runs came via the long ball. Frank Robinson and Don Buford belted solo homers and Merv Rettenmund launched a three-run blast as well. Dock Ellis suffered the loss. Roberto Clemente had two of Pittsburgh's three hits.

Game 2	October 11, 1971
Memorial Stadium (Baltimore)	T: 2:55
Baltimore 11 : Pittsburgh 3	A: 53,239

The Orioles pounded out fourteen hits including two RBI singles by Brooks Robinson. Davey Johnson and Elrod Hendricks also had two-run singles. Jim Palmer fanned ten in eight innings of work for the win. Dick Hall pitched a scoreless ninth for the save. Starter Bob Johnson was the loser. Richie Hebner's three-run homer encompassed the Pirates' scoring.

Game 3	October 12, 1971
Three Rivers Stadium (Pittsburgh)	T: 2:20
Pittsburgh 5 : Baltimore 1	A: 50,403

Roberto Clemente got it started with an RBI single in the first inning and Bob Robertson belted a three-run homer in the seventh as the Pirates cruised to victory. Steve Blass went the distance, scattering three hits and fanning eight along the way. Mike Cuellar suffered the loss. Frank Robinson homered for the Orioles.

Game 4	Oct 13, 1971[43]
Three Rivers Stadium (Pittsburgh)	T: 2:48

Pittsburgh 4 : Baltimore 3	A: 51,378

Pinch hitter Milt May's RBI single in the bottom of the seventh proved to be the game winning run as the Pirates evened the series at two apiece. Luke Walker lasted just two thirds of an inning, surrendering all three Baltimore runs. Bruce Kison and Dave Giusti held the O's scoreless the rest of the way. Kison notched the victory and Giusti was credited with the save. Eddie Watt was ticketed with the loss.

Game 5	October 14, 1971
Three Rivers Stadium (Pittsburgh)	T: 2:16
Pittsburgh 4 : Baltimore 0	A: 51,377

Nelson Briles tossed a two-hit complete game shutout as the Pirates captured their third straight victory and moved to within one win of a stunning World Series upset. Briles chipped in at the plate with an RBI single in the second inning. Bob Robertson belted a solo homer in that frame as well. Roberto Clemente added a run scoring single later in the ballgame. Dave McNally allowed all four Pittsburgh runs and was charged with the loss.

Game 6	October 16, 1971
Memorial Stadium (Baltimore)	T: 2:59
Baltimore 3 : Pittsburgh 2	A: 44,174

The Orioles won a ten inning thriller to force a seventh and deciding game. Roberto Clemente's second inning homer gave Pittsburgh an early two-run lead but Baltimore tied it on Don Buford's sixth inning homer and Davey Johnson's seventh inning RBI single. Frank Robinson scored on Brooks Robinson's sacrifice fly in the bottom of the frame to end it. Dave McNally won it in relief and Bob Miller lost it in the same capacity. Buford had three hits on the day. Manny Sanguillen had three hits for the Pirates.

Game 7	October 17, 1971
Memorial Stadium (Baltimore)	T: 2:10

Pittsburgh 2 : Baltimore 1	A: 47,291

Roberto Clemente belted a solo homer in the fourth and Jose Pagan doubled home Willie Stargell with what proved to be the winning run in the eighth as the Pirates completed their stunning upset of the Orioles. Steve Blass went the distance for his second victory of the series. Mike Cuellar allowed just two runs on four hits in eight innings of work, but suffered the defeat—his second of the series. Don Buford plated Elrod Hendricks with Baltimore's only run in the eighth inning.

1972
Oakland Athletics (4) - Cincinnati Reds (3)
MVP: Gene Tenace

In a World Series that might have been dubbed, "When Dynasties Collide" the Athletics, capture the first of three consecutive World Championships, defeating a Reds team that would make four Fall Classic appearances in the decade.

Game 1[44]	October 14, 1972
Riverfront Stadium (Cincinnati)	T: 2:18
Oakland 3 : Cincinnati 2[45]	A: 52,918

Gene Tenace became the first player in history to homer in his first two World Series at-bats, belting a two-run homer in the second and a solo blast in the fifth to drive in all three Oakland runs. Ken Holtzman got the win and Vida Blue notched the save. Gary Nolan, who served up both Tenace homers, was charged with the loss.

Game 2	October 15, 1972

Riverfront Stadium (Cincinnati)	T: 2:26
Oakland 2 : Cincinnati 1	A: 53,224

Joe Rudi's sensational catch with two out in the bottom of the ninth—likely the most memorable play of the entire series—saved the day as the A's made it two-straight over Cincinnati. Rudi, who'd homered earlier, raced to the wall and ended the game with a leaping backhand stab of a Dennis Menke blast that would've gone as a game-tying double at least. Jim "Catfish" Hunter finished one out shy of a complete game victory. Rollie Fingers recorded the final out of the ballgame for the save. Ross Grimsley allowed two runs in five innings of work and was saddled with the loss.

Game 3	October 18, 1972
Oakland Coliseum	T: 2:24
Cincinnati 1 : Oakland 0	A: 49,410

Jack Billingham pitched eight innings of shutout ball, allowing just three hits along the way as the Reds climbed back into the series. Cesar Geronimo plated Tony Perez with an RBI single in the seventh for the only run of the game. Clay Carroll pitched a scoreless ninth for the save. John "Blue Moon" Odom, who allowed just the one run on three hits in seven innings of work, was charged with the loss.

Game 4	October 19, 1972
Oakland Coliseum	T: 2:06
Oakland 3 : Cincinnati 2	A: 49,410

Gene Tenace belted a solo blast in the fifth—his third of the series and the run held up until the eighth when Bobby Tolan doubled home two runs to put the Reds in front. But in the bottom of the ninth, pinch-hit singles by Gonzalo Marques, Don Mincher and Angel Mangual led to two Oakland runs and another one-run triumph. Rollie Fingers won it in relief and Clay Carroll lost it in the same capacity.

149

Game 5	October 20, 1972
Oakland Coliseum	T: 2:26
Cincinnati 5 : Oakland 4	A: 49,410

Pete Rose belted Jim "Catfish" Hunter's first pitch of the game over the wall and then drove home what proved to be the winning run with a ninth inning RBI single off Rollie Fingers. Ross Grimsley, who pitched just one third of an inning, was credited with the win. Jack Billingham got the save. Dennis Menke homered for Cincinnati and Bobby Tolan added two RBI singles. Gene Tenace belted a record tying fourth World Series homerun—a three-run blast in the second for the A's.

Game 6	October 21, 1972
Riverfront Stadium (Cincinnati)	T: 2:21
Cincinnati 8 : Oakland 1	A: 52,737

The Reds turned a nail biter into a blowout when they posted five runs in the bottom of the seventh. Bobby Tolan and Cesar Geronimo both had two-run singles to highlight the uprising. Johnny Bench belted a solo homer earlier in the ballgame. Grimsley pitched one scoreless inning in relief and was awarded his second win of the series. Tom Hall notched the save. Vida Blue, who left the game prior to the seventh inning carnage, was saddled with the loss.

Game 7	October 22, 1972
Riverfront Stadium (Cincinnati)	T: 2:50
Oakland 3 : Cincinnati 2	A: 56,040

The A's completed their stunning upset of the Reds with yet another one-run victory. Gene Tenace singled, doubled, knocked in two runs and scored what proved to be the winning run in the sixth on Sal Bando's two-bagger. Jim "Catfish" Hunter got the win in relief of John "Blue Moon" Odom. Rollie Fingers pitched a scoreless eighth and ninth for the save. Pedro Borbon, who surrendered both sixth inning runs, was saddled with the loss. The Reds' runs came on sacrifice flies by Hal McRae and Tony Perez.

1973

Oakland Athletics (4) - New York Mets (3)
MVP: Reggie Jackson

The defending World Champion A's capture the second of three straight World Championships, but the triumph doesn't come easy as the upstart Mets force a seventh and deciding game.

Game 1	October 13, 1973
Oakland Coliseum	T: 2:26
Oakland 2 : New York 1	A: 46,021

Ken Holtzman allowed just one run in five innings of work for the win and he "pitched" in at the plate as well—doubling home the first run of the game and scoring what would prove to be the winning run later in the frame. Rollie Fingers hurled three and a third scoreless innings and Darold Knowles[45] recorded the final two outs for the save. John Matlack surrendered both Oakland runs and took the loss. Cleon Jones doubled home the Mets only run in the fourth.

Game 2	October 14, 1973
Oakland Coliseum	T: 4:13
New York 10 : Oakland 7 (12)	A: 49,151

Oakland tallied twice in the bottom of the ninth, all with two outs, to send the game into extra innings. In the top of the twelfth, Willie Mays broke the tie with an RBI single and one batter later A's second baseman Mike Andrews made the first of two errors in the inning allowing three more runs to cross the dish.[46] Tug McGraw won it in relief and Rollie Fingers was saddled with the loss. Cleon Jones and Wayne Garrett both homered for New York. Reggie Jackson had four hits, including a double and a triple.

Game 3	October 16, 1973
Shea Stadium (New York)	T: 3:15
Oakland 3 : New York 2 (11)	A: 54,817

In a game that featured two of the all-time greatest pitchers— Tom Seaver and Jim "Catfish" Hunter—the A's emerged the victor after a hard-fought eleven inning battle. Bert Campaneris, who had three hits on the day, scored the tying run in the eighth and drove home the winning run with an RBI single in the eleventh. Paul Lindblad won it in relief and Harry Parker lost it in the same capacity. Seaver fanned twelve and allowed just two runs over eight innings. Wayne Garrett belted his second homer of the series leading off the game.

Game 4	October 17, 1973
Shea Stadium (New York)	T: 2:41
New York 6 : Oakland 1	A: 54,817

Rusty Staub belted a three-run homer in the bottom of the first and the Mets never looked back. Staub, who was four-for-four on the night, knocked in five runs. Jon Matlack allowed just one run in eight innings of work and Ray Sadecki pitched a scoreless ninth for the save. Ken Holtzman, who surrendered Staub's first inning blast, lasted just one third of an inning and suffered the defeat.

Game 5	October 18, 1973
Shea Stadium (New York)	T: 2:39
New York 2 : Oakland 0	A: 54,817

Jerry Koosman and Tug McGraw pitched a combined shutout, allowing just three hits along the way, to move to within one win of their second World Championship. Koosman pitched into the seventh before being lifted. McGraw held the fort the rest of the way. John Milner singled home a run in the first and Don Hahn's RBI triple in the sixth closed out the scoring. Vida Blue allowed both Mets' runs and was charged with the loss.

Game 6	October 20, 1973
Oakland Coliseum	T: 2:07
Oakland 3 : New York 1	A: 49,333

Tom Seaver and Jim "Catfish" Hunter locked horns again, but this time it was Hunter and the A's who emerged victorious. Reggie Jackson provided all the runs Hunter would need with an RBI double in the first and a run scoring single in the third. The Mets cut into the lead in the eighth on Felix Millan's RBI base hit. Jesus Alou's sacrifice fly in the bottom of the frame closed out the scoring. Three future Hall of Famers were involved in the decision as Hunter won it, Seaver lost it, and Rollie Fingers picked up the save.

Game 7	October 21, 1973
Oakland Coliseum	T: 2:37
Oakland 5 : New York 2	A: 49,333

Bert Campaneris broke a scoreless tie in the third with a two-run homer and later in the inning Reggie Jackson belted the first World Series round tripper of his Hall of Fame career as the A's outmuscled the Mets to capture their second straight World Championship. Ken Holtzman posted his second win of the series and Rollie Fingers got his second save. Jon Matlack did not survive the A's four-run third and was charged with the defeat.

1974

Oakland Athletics (4) - LA Dodgers (1)
MVP: Rollie Fingers

The A's make it three-straight World Series titles, besting the Dodgers in five games.

Game 1	October 12, 1974
Dodger Stadium (Los Angeles)	T: 2:43
Oakland 3 : Los Angeles 2	A: 55,974

Ron Cey's throwing error in the eighth inning pushed the game winning run across as the A's captured the opener. In a reversal of roles, Rollie Fingers got the win and Jim "Catfish" Hunter notched the save. Andy Messersmith allowed just two earned runs and fanned eight in his eight innings of work, but was saddled with the loss. Reggie Jackson homered for Oakland. Jimmy "Toy Cannon" Wynn homered for the Dodgers.

Game 2	October 13, 1974
Dodger Stadium (Los Angeles)	T: 2:40
Los Angeles 3 : Oakland 2	A: 55,989

Joe Ferguson's sixth inning two-run homer staked the Dodgers to a three-run lead that very nearly crumbled in the ninth when Joe Rudi singled home two runs. But Oakland's designated runner, Herb Washington,[47] sent in to run for Rudi and representing the tying run, was picked off by LA reliever Mike Marshall and the A's ended up a buck short. Don Sutton fanned nine in eight innings of work and was awarded the victory. Marshall garnered the save. Starter Vida Blue was saddled with the loss.

Game 3	October 15, 1974

154

Oakland Coliseum	T: 2:35
Oakland 3 : Los Angeles 2	A: 49,347

An error and an RBI single by Joe Rudi led to two Oakland runs in the third and Bert Campaneris' single drove home what proved to be the winning run an inning later. Jim "Catfish" Hunter allowed just one run in 7.2 innings of work. Rollie Fingers held the fort the rest of the way for the save. Bill Buckner and Willie Crawford belted solo homers in the eighth and ninth respectively, but LA finished a buck short. Al Downing surrendered all three Oakland runs—only one of them earned—and suffered the loss.

Game 4	October 16, 1974
Oakland Coliseum	T: 2:35
Oakland 5 : Los Angeles 2	A: 49,347

Ken Holtzman belted a homer and fanned seven in seven and a third innings of work to claim the victory as the A's moved to within one win of their third consecutive World Championship. Rollie Fingers went the rest of the way for the save. Oakland broke it wide open with a four-run fourth inning highlighted by Jim Holt's two-run pinch-hit single. Andy Messersmith suffered his second loss of the series.

Game 5	October 17, 1974
Oakland Coliseum	T: 2:23
Oakland 3 : Los Angeles 2	A: 49,347

Joe Rudi's seventh inning homer proved to be the game winning run as Oakland captured its third consecutive World Championship. John "Blue Moon" Odom, who pitched just one third of an inning, won it in relief of Vida Blue. Rollie Fingers pitched a scoreless eighth and ninth and was credited with his second save of the series. Ray Fosse also homered for the A's. LA bullpen ace Mike Marshall, who surrendered Rudi's blast, was charged with the defeat.

1975

Cincinnati Reds (4) - Boston Red Sox (3)
MVP: Pete Rose

In a World Series that featured perhaps the most memorable play in modern baseball history—Carlton Fisk's game winning extra-inning homer in Game 6—the Cincinnati Reds defeat the Boston Red Sox in a thrilling seven-game series that is still talked about to this day.

Game 1	October 11, 1975
Fenway Park (Boston)	T: 2:27
Boston 6 : Cincinnati 0	A: 35,205

The Red Sox used six singles a walk and a sacrifice fly to plate six runs in the seventh inning. Luis Tiant hurled a complete game shutout. "El Tiante" ignited the Sox sixth inning fireworks with a leadoff single and he crossed the dish with the first run of the game as well. Rick Burleson and Rico Petrocelli combined for five hits and three runs batted in. Don Gullett allowed four runs on ten hits and was charged with the defeat.

Game 2	October 12, 1975
Fenway Park (Boston)	T: 2:38
Cincinnati 3 : Boston 2	A: 35,205

Bill "Spaceman" Lee took a one-run lead into the ninth inning but Johnny Bench led off with a double and reliever Dick Drago surrendered an RBI single to Dave Concepcion and an RBI double to Ken Griffey later in the frame as the Reds snatched one from the Red Sox to even the series. Rawly Eastwick hurled two scoreless innings in relief and was credited with the victory. Drago was charged with the loss. Johnny Bench and Pete Rose each had two hits.

Game 3	October 14, 1975

Riverfront Stadium (Cincinnati)	T: 3:03
Cincinnati 6 : Boston 5 (10)	A: 55,392

Dwight Evans belted a game-tying two-run homerun in the ninth, sending the affair into extra innings. Cesar Geronimo led off the bottom of the tenth with a single and Ed Armbrister laid down a sacrifice bunt but was so tardy in exiting the batter's box that Carlton Fisk collided with him while attempting to field and throw the ball. When the dust settled Fisk's throw wound up in centerfield, Geronimo was on third and Armbrister took second. The Red Sox argued vehemently for an interference call to no avail. Later in the inning Joe Morgan singled home Geronimo with the game-winning run. Rawly Eastwick won it in relief and Jim Willoughby lost it in the same capacity. Bench, Geronimo and Dave Concepcion homered for the Reds. Fisk and Bernie Carbo also homered for Boston.[48]

Game 4	October 15, 1975
Riverfront Stadium (Cincinnati)	T: 2:52
Boston 5 : Cincinnati 4	A: 55,667

Luis Tiant scattered nine hits en route to his second complete game victory of the series. Dwight Evans tripled home two runs and Rick Burleson added an RBI double in the Sox five-run fourth. Cincinnati took an early two-run lead on RBI two-baggers by Ken Griffey and Johnny Bench in the first inning. The Reds tallied twice in the fourth on another RBI two-bagger—this one by Dave Concepcion—and Cesar Geronimo's RBI triple. Fred Norman, who surrendered four of the Red Sox five runs, was charged with the loss.

Game 5	October 16, 1975
Riverfront Stadium (Cincinnati)	T: 2:23
Cincinnati 6 : Boston 2	A: 56,393

Tony Perez belted two homeruns and knocked in four as the Reds moved to within one win of their first World Championship since 1940. Perez belted a solo blast in the fourth and a three-run missile in the sixth. Don Gullett allowed just two runs in eight and two thirds innings for the win. Rawly Eastwick recorded the final out of the ballgame for the save. Reggie Cleveland allowed five runs in his five innings of work and was saddled with the loss.

Game 6	October 21, 1975
Fenway Park (Boston)	T: 4:01
Boston 7 : Cincinnati 6 (12)	A: 35,205

Carlton Fisk's aforementioned game-winning homerun off the left field foul pole evened the series and forced a seventh and deciding game. Fred Lynn belted a three-run homer in the bottom of the first but the Reds tied it in the fifth when Ken Griffey tripled home two runs and then scored on Johnny Bench's RBI single. The Big Red Machine grinded out three more runs on George Foster's two-run double in the seventh and a solo homer by Cesar Geronimo in the eighth. But in the bottom of the frame Bernie Carbo's pinch-hit three run blast tied the game and Fisk won it in the twelfth with perhaps the most famous homerun in Major League Baseball history. Rick Wise held the Reds scoreless in the top of the frame to notch the victory. Pat Darcy, who will forever be linked with Fisk, was the loser.

Game 7	October 22, 1975
Fenway Park (Boston)	T: 2:52
Cincinnati 4 : Boston 3	A: 35,205

The Red Sox took a three-run lead in the bottom of the third as Carl Yastrzemski singled home a run and Don Gullett issued two bases loaded walks. But the Reds got two back in the sixth when Bill "Spaceman" Lee threw three consecutive "space balls"[49] to Tony Perez. Perez missed the first two but belted the

---

third one over the wall for a two-run homer. Cincinnati tied it an inning later on Pete Rose's RBI single. Joe Morgan's ninth inning two out single plated Ken Griffey with the winning run. Clay Carroll hurled two scoreless innings and was awarded the victory. Will McEnaney retired the side in order in the ninth for the save. Jim Burton surrendered the game deciding run and was saddled with the loss.

1976

Cincinnati Reds (4) - New York Yankees (0)
MVP: Johnny Bench

The Big Red Machine steamrolls the New York Yankees in four straight to capture its second consecutive World Series championship.

Game 1	October 16, 1976
Riverfront Stadium (Cincinnati)	T: 2:18
Cincinnati 5 : New York 1	A: 54,826

Joe Morgan homered in the first inning to give Cincinnati an early lead but the Yankees tied it in the second on Graig Nettles' sacrifice fly. The Reds took the lead for good on Pete Rose's run scoring fly in the third. Tony Perez added an RBI single in the sixth and Johnny Bench closed out the scoring in the seventh when he tripled home a run and scored on a wild pitch later in the inning. Don Gullett pitched into the eighth and picked up the win. Doyle Alexander allowed all five Cincinnati runs in six innings of work and was ticketed with the loss.

Game 2	October 17, 1976
Riverfront Stadium (Cincinnati)	T: 2:33
Cincinnati 4 : New York 3	A: 54,816

The Reds won it in the bottom of the ninth when Fred Stanley— whose RBI double in the seventh inning tied the game— misplayed Ken Griffey's two-out grounder for a two-base error. After an intentional walk to Joe Morgan, Tony Perez singled home Griffey with the winning run. Jack Billingham won it in relief. Catfish Hunter went the distance but suffered the loss.

Game 3	October 19, 1976
Yankee Stadium (New York)	T: 2:40
Cincinnati 6 : New York 2	A: 56,667

The Reds got all the runs they would need in a three-run second inning. George Foster doubled and scored and Cesar Geronimo added an RBI single in the frame. Dan Driessen[50] added a solo homer in the fourth and Joe Morgan doubled and scored on Foster's base hit in the eighth to close out the Reds' scoring. Pat Zachary got the win and Will McEnaney notched the save. Dock Ellis suffered the loss. Jim Mason belted a solo homer for the Yankees in the only World Series at-bat of his career.

Game 4	October 20, 1976
Yankee Stadium (New York)	T: 2:36
Cincinnati 7 : New York 2	A: 56,700

Johnny Bench belted two homeruns and knocked in five as the Big Red Machine completed its demolition of the Yankees. Cincinnati took control in the third when George Foster doubled home a run and Bench followed with the first of his two homers. Thurman Munson's[51] fifth inning RBI single cut the lead to one but Bench connected again—this time with two aboard in a four run ninth to seal the deal with an explanation point. Gary Nolan lasted six and two thirds innings—good enough for the win and Will McEnaney posted his second save of the series. Ed Figueroa took the loss.

1977

NY Yankees (4) - LA Dodgers (2)
MVP: Reggie Jackson

The Yankees and Dodgers renew and old-rivalry, meeting in the World Series for the ninth time. Reggie Jackson's three homeruns in Game 6 catapult him into the stratosphere of legends as the Yankees capture their first World Championship in fifteen years.

Game 1	October 11, 1977
Yankee Stadium (New York)	T: 3:24
New York 4 Los : Angeles 3 (12)	A: 56,668

The matter was finally decided in the twelfth when Willie Randolph— whose sixth inning homer tied the game—led off with a double and scored on Paul Blair's base hit to win it. Sparky Lyle pitched three and a third innings of stellar relief for the win. Rick Rhoden, came on in the final frame, did not retire a single batter, and was charged with the loss.

Game 2	October 12, 1977
Yankee Stadium (New York)	T: 2:27
Los Angeles 6 : New York 1	A: 56,691

The Dodgers had Catfish for lunch—pummeling Yankees' ace Jim "Catfish" Hunter for three homers. Ron Cey got it started with a two run homer in the first and Steve Yeager belted a solo blast in the second. Reggie Smith's two-run shot in the third sent "Catfish" to the showers. Steve Garvey closed out the Dodgers' homerun barrage with a solo homer off Sparky Lyle in the ninth. Burt Hooten scattered five hits and allowed just one run en route to a complete game victory.

Game 3	October 14, 1977
Dodger Stadium (LA)	T: 2:31

161

New York 5 : Los Angeles 3	A: 55,992

The Yankees got three in the first inning when Thurman Munson doubled home a run and Reggie Jackson and Lou Piniella added RBI singles. LA tied it in the third on Dusty Baker's three-run homer. But Mickey Rivers' RBI grounder in the fourth proved to be the game winning run. Mike Torrez turned in a complete game victory, fanning nine along the way. Tommy John surrendered all five New York runs in six innings of work and was charged with the loss.

Game 4	October 15, 1977
Dodger Stadium (LA)	T: 2:07
New York 4 : Los Angeles 2	A: 55,995

RBI singles by Lou Piniella and Bucky Dent highlighted a three-run second—all the offense the Yankees would need to take a commanding lead in the series. Davey Lopes' two-run homer in the bottom of the third was as close as LA would get. Reggie Jackson's solo homer in the sixth accounted for the game's final run. Ron Guidry went the distance for the win. Doug Rau did not survive the second frame and was charged with the loss.

Game 5	October 16, 1977
Dodger Stadium (LA)	T: 2:29
Los Angeles 10 : New York 4	A: 55,995

With their backs to the wall the Dodgers came out swinging. Steve Yeager belted a three-run homer and Reggie Smith added a two-run blast in a lopsided victory that forced the series back to New York. Los Angeles pounded out thirteen hits on the day. Don Sutton went the distance for the victory and Don Gullett was saddled with the loss. Thurman Munson and Reggie Jackson homered for New York.

Game 6	October 18, 1977
Yankee Stadium (New York)	T: 2:18

| New York 8 : Los Angeles 4 | A: 56,407 |

REG-GIE!   REG-GIE!   REG-GIE!   The controversial homerun hitting superstar belted a World Series record tying three homeruns as New York demolished Los Angeles to capture the twenty-first World Championship in its history and the first in fifteen years. Reggie Smith's third inning homer put LA in front but Reggie Jackson's first blast came with a man aboard in the fourth and gave NY a lead they would not relinquish. Reggie smashed his second two-run homer in the fifth and a solo homer in the eighth to complete his night for the ages. Mike Torrez turned in his second complete game victory of the series. Burt Hooten started it for LA but lasted just three innings and was saddled with the loss.

1978

NY Yankees (4) - LA Dodgers (2)
MVP: Bucky Dent

It's New York and Los Angeles again and the Yankees take it in six— again!

Game 1	October 10, 1978
Dodger Stadium (Los Angeles)	T: 2:48
Los Angeles 11 : New York 5	A: 55,997

Davey Lopes belted two homers and knocked in five runs as the Dodgers pummeled the Yankees in the opener. Lopes belted the first of his two round trippers with a man aboard in the second and then launched a three-run blast in the fourth. Tommy John scattered eight hits and surrendered three runs over seven and two thirds innings for the win. Ed Figueroa did not survive the second frame and was tagged with the loss. Dusty Baker also homered for the Dodgers. Reggie Jackson homered for the Yankees.

Game 2	October 11, 1978
Dodger Stadium (Los Angeles)	T: 2:37
Los Angeles 4 : New York 3	A: 55,982

In one of the most memorable showdowns in World Series history, Rookie fireballer Bob Welch fanned "Mr. October", Reggie Jackson, with two out in the bottom of the ninth and the tying and winning runs on base to win it for LA. Ron Cey's sixth inning three-run homer proved to be the game winning blow. Cey knocked in all four LA runs.   Burt Hooten lasted six innings for the win. Jim "Catfish" Hunter was the loser. Welch, who retired both batters he faced in the ninth, was awarded the save.

Game 3	October 13, 1978
Yankee Stadium (New York)	T: 2:27
New York 5 : Los Angeles 1	A: 56,447

Ron Guidry's eight-hit seven-walk complete game victory put the Yankees back in the series. But the real story was the defensive performance of Graig Nettles at third base. Nettles made several sensational diving catches—two with the bases loaded—saving at least five runs from scoring. Don Sutton surrendered all five New York runs and was tagged with the loss. Roy White homered for New York. Thurman Munson and Reggie Jackson had RBI singles. Mickey Rivers had three hits.

Game 4	October 14, 1978
Yankee Stadium (New York)	T: 3:17
New York 4 : Los Angeles 3	A: 56,445

The most memorable play of the entire series unfolded in the bottom of the sixth when Lou Piniella hit a sinking liner to Bill Russell at shortstop. Russell intentionally let the ball hit the ground, stepped on second for the force and then fired to first for a double play. But Reggie Jackson threw his hip into the ball's path and it ricocheted into the outfield allowing Thurman Munson to score from second and Piniella to reach first base safely. Though Dodger manager Tommy Lasorda argued vehemently that Jackson's obstruction was intentional, the ruling stood. Munson tied the game with an RBI double in the eighth and Piniella won it with an RBI single in the tenth. Rich "Goose" Gossage pitched two scoreless innings for the victory. Bob Welch lost it in his third inning of work.

Game 5	October 15, 1978
Yankee Stadium (New York)	T: 2:56
New York 12 : Los Angeles 2	A: 56,448

Los Angeles grabbed an early two run lead but New York jumped ahead for good in the third when they turned four singles and a walk into four runs—and they were only just getting started. RBI doubles by Bucky Dent and Thurman Munson highlighted an eighteen hit attack and by game's end the Dodgers found themselves smothered beneath an avalanche of Yankee offense. Jim Beattie fanned eight en route to a complete game victory. Burt Hooten was ticketed with the loss.

Game 6	October 17, 1978
Dodger Stadium (Los Angeles)	T: 2:34
New York 7 : Los Angeles 2	A: 55,985

Davey Lopes belted a homer leading off the bottom of the first but the Yankees tallied three times in the second and never looked back. Late season call up Brian Doyle and light hitting shortstop Bucky Dent authored the damage with an RBI double and a two-run single respectively. Doyle and Dent singled home runs in the sixth and Reggie Jackson closed out the scoring with a two-run homer in the seventh. Jim "Catfish" Hunter pitched seven solid innings for the win. Rich "Goose" Gossage pitched a scoreless eighth and ninth to end it.[52] Don Sutton suffered the loss.

1979

Pittsburgh Pirates (4) - Baltimore Orioles (3)
MVP: Willie Stargell

Pittsburgh sings "We Are Family" all the way to the World Series where they vanquish Baltimore in seven games for the second time in the decade.

Game 1	October 10, 1979
Memorial Stadium (Baltimore)	T: 3:18
Baltimore 5 : Pittsburgh 4	A: 53,735

Doug DeCinces belted a two-run homer in a five-run first inning and Mike Flanagan fended off the Pirates the rest of the way, allowing four runs en route to a complete game win as the Orioles captured the opener. Baltimore's first two runs crossed the dish on second baseman Phil Garner's throwing error. Bruce Kison, who lasted just one third of an inning and was charged with the loss, wild pitched the third run home and then surrendered DeCinces' two-run blast. Willie Stargell homered and knocked in three runs for the Pirates. Garner's RBI single accounted for Pittsburgh's remaining run.

Game 2	October 11, 1979
Memorial Stadium (Baltimore)	T: 3:13
Pittsburgh 3 : Baltimore 2	A: 53,739

Manny Sanguillen's pinch hit single with two outs in the top of the ninth plated the winning run as the Pirates evened the series. Pittsburgh jumped out to an early lead when Bill Madlock knocked in two runs with a base hit. Orioles' slugger Eddie Murray cut the lead in half in the bottom of the frame with a solo homer and he tied it in the sixth with an RBI double setting the stage for Sanguillen's game-winning hit. Don Robinson pitched two scoreless innings in relief and picked up the win. Kent Tekulve fanned two in a

166

scoreless ninth for the save. O's relief ace Don Stanhouse surrendered the ninth inning run and was charged with the loss.

Game 3	October 12, 1979
Three Rivers Stadium (Pittsburgh)	T: 2:51
Baltimore 8 : Pittsburgh 4	A: 50,848

Dave Parker's first inning sacrifice fly and Phil Garner's third inning two-run double gave Pittsburgh the early lead, but it was all Baltimore the rest of the way. Benny Ayala put the O's on the board with a two-run homer in the third and Kiko Garcia's bases loaded triple highlighted a five-run fourth putting Baltimore in the driver's seat the rest of the way. Scott McGregor went the distance for the win. John Candelaria lasted just three innings, allowed five runs, and suffered the defeat.

Game 4	October 13, 1979
Three Rivers Stadium (Pittsburgh)	T: 3:48
Baltimore 9 : Pittsburgh 6	A: 50,883

The Orioles rallied for six runs in the eighth inning— stunning the Pirates to move to within one win of a World Championship. Back-to-back pinch hit two run doubles by John Lowenstein and Terry Crowley ignited the explosion. Tim Stoddard continued the fireworks with an RBI single and Al Bumbry's run scoring grounder accounted for the final run of the frame. Stoddard pitched three scoreless innings in relief for the win. Pittsburgh relief ace Kent Tekulve, who was rocked for three runs in a disastrous relief appearance, suffered the loss. Willie Stargell homered for the Pirates.

Game 5	October 14, 1979
Three Rivers Stadium (Pittsburgh)	T: 2:54
Pittsburgh 7 : Baltimore 1	A: 50,920

The Orioles broke a scoreless tie in the fifth when a run crossed the dish on a double play grounder but in the sixth Willie

167

Stargell tied it with a sacrifice fly and Bill Madlock singled home what would prove to be the winning run. Madlock was four-for-four on the day. Tim Foli had two hits and knocked in three runs for the Pirates. Bert Blyleven pitched four scoreless innings in relief for the victory. Mike Flanagan lasted six innings and surrendered just two runs in a losing effort.

Game 6	October 16, 1979
Memorial Stadium (Baltimore)	T: 2:30
Pittsburgh 4 : Baltimore 0	A: 53,739

John Candelaria hurled six scoreless innings and Kent Tekulve slammed the door shut over the final three frames as the Pirates forced a seventh and deciding game. Dave Parker's RBI single broke a scoreless tie in the seventh and Willie Stargell plated an insurance run with a sacrifice fly. Pittsburgh added two more in the eighth on a run scoring fly off the bat of Bill Robinson and Omar Moreno's run scoring hit. Candelaria was the winner and Tekulve notched his second save of the series. Jim Palmer allowed all four Pittsburgh runs in eight innings of work.

Game 7	October 17, 1979
Memorial Stadium (Baltimore)	T: 2:54
Pittsburgh 4 : Baltimore 1	A: 53,733

The Pirates became just the fourth team in Major League history to rally from a three-games-to-one deficit to win the World Series. Baltimore plated the first run of the game in the third when Rich Dauer homered off Jim Bibby. The Pirates jumped ahead for good in the sixth when Willie Stargell belted a two-run homer and they sealed the deal in the eighth when Omar Moreno singled home a run and Bill Robinson was hit by a pitch with the bases loaded. Grant Jackson won it in relief and Kent Tekulve notched his third save of the series. Scott McGregor allowed all four runs over eight frames and was saddled with the loss.

168

1980

Philadelphia (4) - Kansas City (2)
MVP: Mike Schmidt

Two future Hall of Fame third baseman—Philadelphia's Mike Schmidt and Kansas City's George Brett—square off in the World Series and when the dust finally settles Schmidt's Phillies defeat Brett's Royals to capture the first World Championship in their long and arduous history.[53]

Game 1	October 14, 1980
Veterans Stadium (Philadelphia)	T: 3:01
Philadelphia 7 : Kansas City 6	A: 65,791

Amos Otis and Willie Mays Aikens both hit two-run homers to give KC a commanding four-run lead. But Bake McBride's three-run homer highlighted a five-run third inning to put Philadelphia in front. The Phillies added two more on Bob Boone's RBI double in the sixth and Garry Maddox's sacrifice fly in the sixth. Aikens connected for his second two-run homer of the game in the eighth but that was as close as KC would get. Bob Walk surrendered all six Royals' runs but picked up the victory. Tug McGraw notched the save. Dennis Leonard did not survive Philly's fifth inning outburst and was awarded the loss.

Game 2	October 15, 1980
Veterans Stadium (Philadelphia)	T: 3:01
Philadelphia 6 : Kansas City 4	A: 65,775

The Phillies erupted for four runs in the eighth inning to end a seesaw battle and fly to Kansas City in the driver's seat. Del Unser and Mike Schmidt had RBI doubles and Keith Moreland and Bake McBride had run scoring singles in the frame. Steve Carlton pitched eight innings for the win. "Lefty" fanned ten along the way. Ron Reed pitched a scoreless ninth for the save. Dan Quisenberry was the loser in relief. Hal McRae had three hits for the Royals. Amos Otis had two, including a two-run double.

Game 3	October 17, 1980
Kaufmann Stadium (Kansas City)	T: 3:19
KC 4 : Philadelphia 3 (10)	A: 42,380

Willie Mays Aikens tenth inning RBI single ended a see-saw battle that put the Royals back in the series. George Brett belted a solo homer in the bottom of the first to give KC an early lead. Mike Schmidt tied the game with a homer in the fifth. Amos Otis's homer put the Royals back in front in the seventh but Pete Rose promptly tied it back up with an RBI single in the eighth setting the stage for Aiken's game winning hit. Dan Quisenberry won it in relief and Tug McGraw lost it in the same capacity.

Game 4	October 18, 1980
Kaufmann Stadium (Kansas City)	T: 2:37
Kansas City 5 : Philadelphia 3	A: 42,363

Willie Mays Aikens belted his third and fourth homers of the series as the Royals evened things up at two apiece. Aikens first homer of the night—a two-run blast—came in a four-run first inning. Aikens launched a solo blast in the second for good measure. Dennis Leonard fended off the Phillies over the first seven innings to pick up the victory. Dan Quisenberry notched the save. Larry Christenson did not survive the first inning and was saddled with the defeat.

Game 5	October 19, 1980
Kaufmann Stadium (Kansas City)	T: 2:51
Philadelphia 4 : Kansas City 3	A: 42,369

Mike Schmidt's fourth inning two-run homer gave the Phillies an early lead but Amos Otis's homer an inning later tied the

170

game. U.L. Washington's sacrifice fly later in the inning gave the Royals their first lead of the day. Philadelphia settled the issue in the ninth when Schmidt singled leading off and scored on Del Unser's double. Manny Trillo's RBI single plated Unser with what proved to be the winning run. Tug McGraw pitched three scoreless innings in relief to pick up the win and Dan Quisenberry was the loser.

Game 6	October 21, 1980
Veterans Stadium (Philadelphia)	T: 3:00
Philadelphia 4 : Kansas City 1	A: 65,838

Steve Carlton allowed just one run on four hits while fanning seven in seven innings of work and Tug McGraw shut the door over the final two frames as the Phillies captured the first World Championship in their long history. Mike Schmidt's two-run single in the third gave Carlton all the runs he would need. Bake McBride added a run scoring fly in the fifth and Bob Boone's RBI single closed out the Phillies scoring in the sixth. Rich Gale, lasted two-plus innings and was saddled with the loss.

1981

LA Dodgers (4) - NY Yankees (2)
Co-MVPs: Cey/Guerrero/Yeager

The Dodgers ride Fernandomania to the World Series where they face the Yankees for the third time in five years. This time it's Los Angeles in six games.

Game 1	October 20, 1981
Yankee Stadium (New York)	T: 2:32
New York 5 : Los Angeles 3	A: 56,470

Bob Watson belted a three-run homer in the bottom of the first and the Yankees added two more later in the game on an RBI

single by Lou Piniella and a bases loaded walk to Dave Winfield—
enough to hold off the Dodgers in the opener. Ron Guidry allowed
just one run in seven innings of work. Rich "Goose" Gossage
notched the save. Jerry Reuss surrendered all five NY runs and
was charged with the loss. Steve Yeager homered for LA.

Game 2	October 21, 1981
Yankee Stadium (New York)	T: 2:29
New York 3 : Los Angeles 0	A: 56,505

Former Dodger Tommy John handcuffed his old mates
over the first seven frames, limiting them to just three hits before
turning the ball over to flame throwing closer Rich "Goose"
Gossage who slammed the door shut over the final two frames for
the save. Larry Milbourne's RBI double broke a scoreless tie in the
fifth and the Yankees added two more in the eighth on Bob
Watson's run scoring single and a sacrifice fly by Willie Randolph.
Burt Hooten allowed one run over six innings but was charged with
the loss.

Game 3	October 23, 1981
Dodger Stadium (Los Angeles)	T: 3:04
Los Angeles 5 : New York 3	A: 56,236

Fernando Valenzuela scattered nine hits, fanned six and
walked seven en route to a 145-pitch complete game victory that
put the Dodgers back in the series. Ron Cey's three-run homer off
Dave Righetti sent the Yankees' rookie ace to an early shower.
New York used the long ball to jump back in front with Bob
Watson's solo homer in the second and Rick Cerrone's two-run
blast in the third spearheading the rally. But the Dodgers regained
the lead for good in the fifth when Pedro Guerrero doubled home a
run to tie it and Mike Scioscia's double-play grounder plated what
proved to be the winning run. George Frazier lost it in relief.

Game 4	October 24, 1981
Dodger Stadium (Los Angeles)	T: 3:32

Los Angeles 8 : New York 7	A: 56,242

The Dodgers and Yankees went toe-to-toe in the middle of the ring and when the fight was over LA was still standing and the series was even. The teams combined for a total of twenty-seven hits on the day. Steve Howe allowed one run—a booming homer by Reggie Jackson—in three innings of relief and was credited with the victory. Jay Johnstone belted a pinch hit two-run homer. Davey Lopes singled home what proved to be the winning run in the seventh. George Frasier suffered his second loss in as many days. Willie Randolph also homered for New York.

Game 5	October 25, 1981
Dodger Stadium (Los Angeles)	T: 2:19
Los Angeles 2 : New York 1	A: 56,115

Pedro Guerrero and Steve Yeager belted back-to-back solo homers in the bottom of the seventh as the Dodgers captured a thriller and made it a clean sweep in LA. Jerry Reuss went the distance for the win. Ron Guidry surrendered both Dodger runs in his seven innings of work. The flame throwing lefty fanned nine in a losing effort. Lou Piniella's second inning single accounted for New York's only run.

Game 6	October 28, 1981
Yankee Stadium (New York)	T: 3:09
Los Angeles 9 : New York 2	A: 56,513

The Dodgers shook the albatross from their neck with a crushing defeat of the Yankees that proclaimed them World Champions. Ron Cey's RBI single in the fifth broke a 1-1 tie and Pedro Guerrero's two-run triple later in the inning gave LA a lead they would not relinquish. Guerrero singled home two more runs in a four-run fifth that put the game out of reach and he added a solo homer in the eighth for good measure. Burt Hooten got the win and Steve Howe notched the save. George Frasier took the loss.

1982

St. L Cardinals (4) - Milwaukee Brewers (3)
MVP: Darrell Porter

The Milwaukee Brewers make their first visit to the Fall Classic where they are vanquished by the St. Louis Cardinals in a thrilling seven-game series.

Game 1	October 12, 1982
Busch Stadium (St. Louis)	T: 2:30
Milwaukee 10 : St. Louis 0	A: 53,723

Former Cardinal Mike Caldwell stifled his former teammates with a complete game three-hit shutout. Paul Molitor had five hits and Robin Yount added four to pace the Brewers attack. Both players knocked in two runs. Ted Simmons belted the only round tripper of the game. Milwaukee registered seventeen hits on the night. Bob Forsch was ticketed with the loss.

Game 2	October 13, 1982
Busch Stadium (St. Louis)	T: 2:54
St. Louis 5 : Milwaukee 4	A: 53,723

Pete Ladd, subbing for injured relief ace Rollie Fingers, walked the first two hitters he faced in the bottom of the eighth inning to force home what proved to be the game-winning run. Ted Simmons' second homer of the series—a solo blast in the third—staked Milwaukee to an early three-run lead but Darrell Porter's two-run double tied it in the sixth setting the stage for Steve Braun's RBI base-on-balls to win it. Bruce Sutter won it in relief. Bob McClure was the loser.

Game 3	October 15, 1982
County Stadium (Milwaukee)	T: 2:53
St. Louis 6 : Milwaukee 2	A: 56,556

Willie McGee's fifth inning three-run homer off AL Cy Young award winner Pete Vuckovich broke a scoreless tie and proved to be the game winning hit. McGee touched up Vuckovich for a solo blast in the seventh as well. Joaquin Andujar held the Brewers scoreless into the seventh and picked up the win. Bruce Sutter held the fort the rest of the way for the save. Cecil Cooper belted a two-run homer in the eighth to account for Milwaukee's runs. Vuckovich pitched into the ninth but was saddled with the loss.

Game 4	October 16, 1982
County Stadium (Milwaukee)	T: 3:04
Milwaukee 7 : St. Louis 5	A: 56,560

George Hendrick's first inning RBI single broke the seal and Cards' speedsters Lonnie Smith and Willie McGee turned on the afterburners in the second as both of them scored on Tommy Herr's second inning sacrifice fly. The clubs exchanged runs in the fifth and sixth but Cards' hurler Dave LaPoint's error opened the floodgates in the seventh as Jim Gantner doubled home a run and Cecil Cooper, Robin Yount and Gorman Thomas added RBI singles. Jim Slaton won it in relief. Bob McClure notched the save. Doug Bair was charged with the loss.

Game 5	October 17, 1982
County Stadium (Milwaukee)	T: 3:02
Milwaukee 6 : St. Louis 4	A: 56,562

Mike Caldwell scattered fourteen hits over eight and a third innings—good enough for his second victory of the series and Bob McClure retired the final two hitters for his second save of the series as the Brewers headed back to St. Louis in the driver's seat. Robin Yount powered Milwaukee's attack with his second four-hit game of the series and his first Fall Classic homer as well. Bob Forsch suffered his second loss.

Game 6	October 19, 1982

Busch Stadium (St. Louis)	T: 2:21
St. Louis 13 : Milwaukee 1	A: 53,723

Facing elimination the Cardinals pummeled the "Brew-Crew" to force a seventh and deciding game. Darrell Porter and Keith Hernandez both belted two-run homers to pace the Redbird's attack. Hernandez also added a two-run single in a six-run sixth inning that erased any doubt. Willie McGee and George Hendrick added RBI singles in the frame, with the final two runs crossing the dish on Jim Gantner's error. John Stuper went the distance for the win. Don Sutton was charged with the loss.

Game 7	October 20, 1982
Busch Stadium (St. Louis)	T: 2:50
St. Louis 6 : Milwaukee 3	A: 53,723

Willie McGee scored the first run of the game on Lonnie Smith's RBI single in the fourth but Brewers' slugger Ben Oglive tied it with a homer in the fifth. A bunt single by Paul Molitor and a sacrifice fly off the bat of Cecil Cooper in the sixth gave Milwaukee a two-run advantage. Keith Hernandez's two-run single in the bottom of the frame tied it and George Hendrick's base hit plated what proved to be the winning run. Joaquin Andujar lasted seven innings and notched his second victory of the series. Bruce Sutter pitched a scoreless eighth and ninth for his second save and the Cardinals' had the ninth World Championship in their proud history.

1983

Baltimore Orioles (4) - Philadelphia Phillies (1)
MVP: Rick Dempsey

Baltimore superstars Eddie Murray and Cal Ripken, Jr. lead the Orioles to the World Series where they vanquish Pete Rose, Joe Morgan and the rest of an aging Phillies team in five games.

Game 1	October 11, 1983
Memorial Stadium (Baltimore)	T: 2:22
Philadelphia 2 : Baltimore 1	A: 52,204

Cy Young award winner John Denny bested Baltimore's eighteen game winner Scott McGregor in the opener, with all three runs coming on solo homeruns. Jim Dwyer got it started with a second inning homer that gave the Orioles the early lead but Joe Morgan put one over the wall in the sixth to tie it. Garry Maddox belted the game winning solo shot in the eighth to win it. Denny got the win and Al Holland the save. McGregor allowed just two runs in eight innings of work but was saddled with the loss.

Game 2	October 12, 1983
Memorial Stadium (Baltimore)	T: 2:27
Baltimore 4 : Philadelphia 1	A: 52,132

The Phillies plated an unearned run in the fourth to break a scoreless tie but the Orioles took the game over with a three-run fifth and never looked back. John Lowenstein's homer and Rick Dempsey's RBI double highlighted the uprising. Cal Ripken Jr. plated the final run of the game with a run scoring single in the seventh. Boddicker went the distance for the win. Charles Hudson was the loser.

Game 3	October 14, 1983
Veterans Stadium (Philadelphia)	T: 2:35
Baltimore 3 : Philadelphia 2	A: 65,792

Early inning homers by Gary Matthews and Joe Morgan staked Steve Carlton to a two-run lead but Dan Ford's sixth inning round tripper cut the lead in half and the O's jumped ahead for good in the seventh when Benny Ayala singled home a run and then scored on shortstop Ivan DeJesus's error. Jim Palmer won it in relief of Mike Flanagan. Tippy Martinez picked up the save. Carlton was saddled with the loss.

177

Game 4	October 15, 1983
Veterans Stadium (Philadelphia)	T: 2:50
Baltimore 5 : Philadelphia 4	A: 66,947

Rich Dauer's fourth inning two-run single gave the Orioles an early advantage but Philadelphia tallied once in the bottom of the frame on an RBI double by Joe Lefebvre and added two more in the fifth when John Denny singled home a run and Pete Rose followed with an RBI two-bagger. Baltimore jumped ahead for good in the sixth when Denny issued a bases loaded walk to Ken Singleton and surrendered a run scoring fly to John Shelby. Storm Davis won it. Tippy Martinez notched his second save of the series. Denny suffered the loss.

Game 5	October 16, 1983
Veterans Stadium (Philadelphia)	T: 2:21
Baltimore 5 : Philadelphia 0	A: 67,064

Scott McGregor pitched a five-hit complete-game shutout and Eddie Murray and Rick Dempsey belted three homeruns between them as the Orioles captured their first World Championship since 1970. Murray opened the scoring with a second inning solo blast and Dempsey launched one an inning later. Murray's second homer came in the fourth with a man aboard. Al Bumbry's sacrifice fly in the fifth closed out the scoring. Charles Hudson surrendered all five O's runs and suffered his second loss of the series.

1984

Detroit Tigers (4) - San Diego Padres (1)
MVP: Alan Trammell

In what must be considered the greatest season in their long and storied history, the Detroit Tigers steamroll through the

American League and then crush the San Diego Padres in the World Series.

Game 1	October 9, 1984
Jack Murphy Stadium (San Diego)	T: 3:18
Detroit 3 : San Diego 2	A: 57,908

Jack Morris survived a rocky opening frame to post an eight hit complete game victory as the Tigers captured the opener. Alan Trammel singled home the first run of the series in the top of the first but Terry Kennedy touched up Morris for a two-run double in the bottom of the frame to put the Padres in front. Larry Herndon's two-run homer in the fifth plated the final two runs of the game. Mark Thurmond allowed all three Detroit runs and was charged with the loss.

Game 2	October 10, 1984
Jack Murphy Stadium (San Diego)	T: 2:44
San Diego 5 : Detroit 3	A: 57,911

Kurt Bevacqua's three-run homer highlighted San Diego's come from behind victory. Detroit scored three in the first but a sacrifice fly by Graig Nettles and Bobby Brown's fielder's choice set the stage for Bevacqua's fifth inning heroics. Andy Hawkins won it in relief of starter Ed Whitson who lasted just one third of an inning. Craig Lefferts pitched three scoreless innings for the save. Dan Petry surrendered all five San Diego runs and was charged with the loss.

Game 3	October 12, 1984
Tiger Stadium (Detroit)	T: 3:11
Detroit 5 : San Diego 2	A: 51,970

The Tigers posted four runs in the second and never looked back. Marty Castillo's two-run homer and Alan Trammell's RBI double highlighted the uprising. Milt Wilcox allowed just one run in his six innings of work and garnered the victory. Willie

179

Hernandez[54] was credited with the save. Tim Lollar did not survive Detroit's second inning fireworks and was saddled with the loss.

Game 4	October 13, 1984
Tiger Stadium (Detroit)	T: 2:20
Detroit 4 : San Diego 2	A: 52,130

Jack Morris turned in his second complete game victory of the series and Alan Trammell belted two two-run homers to account for all four Detroit runs as the Tigers moved to within one victory of a World Championship. Trammell socked the first of his two two-run blasts in the bottom of the first and repeated the feat in the third inning. Eric Show allowed all four runs and suffered the defeat. Terry Kennedy homered for the Padres.

Game 5	October 14, 1984
Tiger Stadium (Detroit)	T: 2:55
Detroit 8 : San Diego 4	A: 51,901

Kirk Gibson belted two homers and knocked in five runs as the Tigers mauled San Diego to cap off an historic season in decisive fashion. Gibson took Padres' starter Mark Thurmond over the wall with a man aboard in the first. Chet Lemmon's RBI single later in the frame sent Thurmond to an early shower. Gibson's second homer of the night—a towering three-run blast into the upper deck off Rich "Goose" Gossage ended any doubt. Aurelio Lopez won it in relief and Willie Hernandez notched his second save of the series. Lance Parrish also homered for Detroit. Kurt Bevacqua homered for the Padres. Andy Hawkins was ticketed with the loss.

1985

KC Royals (4) - St. Louis Cardinals (3)
MVP: Bret Saberhagen

The "Show Me State" hosts the "I-70" Series as St. Louis and Kansas City meet in the Fall Classic. The Royals rally from a three-games-to-one deficit to capture the first World Championship in their history—but a blown call by umpire Don Denkinger is all St. Louis fans remember.

Game 1	October 19, 1985
Kaufmann Stadium (Kansas City)	T: 2:48
St. Louis 4 : Kansas City 1	A: 41,650

Ace lefty John Tudor[55] allowed just one run in 6.2 innings of work and Todd Worrell held the fort the rest of the way as the Cardinals captured the opener. Cesar Cedeno's fourth inning double broke a 1-1 tie and Jack Clark bought the birds some insurance when his two-bagger knocked in a run in the ninth. Danny Jackson, who suffered the loss, allowed just two runs in his seven innings of work.

Game 2	October 20, 1985
Kaufmann Stadium (Kansas City)	T: 2:44
St. Louis 4 : Kansas City 2	A: 41,656

Charlie Liebrandt was just one out away from a 2-0 shutout victory when thunder struck. Jack Clark's two-out single plated Willie McGee. Tito Landrum doubled and after Cesar Cedeno was intentionally walked, Terry Pendleton hit a bases clearing triple to make it 4-2. The stunned Royals went down 1-2-3 in the ninth. Ken Dayley won it in relief and Jeff Lahti notched the save. Back-to-back RBI doubles by George Brett and Frank White in the fourth accounted for the Royals' runs.

Game 3	October 22, 1985
Busch Stadium (St. Louis)	T: 3:00
Kansas City 6 : St. Louis 1	A: 53,634

Bret Saberhagen turned in a desperately needed eight-strikeout complete game victory as the Royals climbed back into the series. Former Cardinal Lonnie Smith's fourth inning two-run double proved to be the game deciding blow. Frank White belted a two-run homer in the fifth and he doubled home a run and scored on Buddy Biancalana's base hit in the seventh to close out the scoring. Joaquin Andujar allowed four runs in four-plus innings of work and suffered the loss. Jack Clark's RBI single in the sixth accounted for the Cardinals only run.

Game 4	October 23, 1985
Busch Stadium (St. Louis)	T: 2:19
St. Louis 3 : Kansas City 0	A: 53,634

John Tudor turned in another gem—a five-hit eight-strikeout complete game victory for his second win of the series. Tito Landrum and Willie McGee belted solo homers in the second and third respectively and Terry Pendleton tripled and scored in the fifth to close out the scoring. Bud Black was charged with the loss. The victory left St. Louis just one win away from the tenth World Championship in their illustrious history.

Game 5	October 24, 1985
Busch Stadium (St. Louis)	T: 2:52
Kansas City 6 : St. Louis 1	A: 53,634

With their backs against the wall the Royals came out swinging and forced the series back to Kansas City with a lopsided victory. Willie Wilson's two-run triple highlighted a three-run second inning and Kansas City never looked back. Danny Jackson went the distance for the victory, scattering five hits and fanning five along the way. Bob Forsch, who did not survive the second, was charged with the loss. Jack Clark's RBI single in the bottom of the first accounted for St. Louis's only run.

Game 6	October 26, 1985
Kaufmann Stadium (Kansas City)	T: 2:48
Kansas City 2 : St. Louis 1	A: 41,628

The Don Denkinger game! Brian Harper's eighth inning two out pinch-hit single broke a scoreless tie setting the stage for one of the greatest controversies in World Series history. With Cards' flame throwing closer Todd Worrell on to close it out, the first batter, pinch-hitter Jorge Orta, grounded to Jack Clark at first base. Clark flipped to Worrell covering and though it was a close play and it appeared that Orta was out, first base umpire Don Denkinger[56] ruled Orta safe. A vehement argument ensued but the call stood and Orta remained at first base. The next batter, Steve Balboni popped up to Clark in foul territory, but Clark misplayed the ball and Balboni promptly singled, sending Orta to second. A passed ball and an intentional walk loaded the bases for pinch hitter Dane Iorg—a former Cardinal—whose base hit scored two runs to win it.

Game 7	October 27, 1985
Kaufmann Stadium (Kansas City)	T: 2:46
Kansas City 11 : St. Louis 0	A: 41,658

The Royals took the Cardinals behind the woodshed in the seventh and deciding game. Darryl Motley's two-run homer in the second proved to be the game winning blow. Steve Balboni's two-run single highlighted a three-run third and KC tallied six more times in the fifth with Motley's RBI single igniting the explosion. Lonnie Smith doubled home two runs and Frank White and Willie Wilson added RBI singles as well. Bret Saberhagen tossed a complete game shutout—his second victory of the series. John Tudor was saddled with the loss.

1986

New York Mets (4) - Boston Red Sox (3)
MVP: Ray Knight

Mookie Wilson's grounder bounces through Bill Buckner's glove and Ray Knight scores the game winning run in one of the most famous plays in baseball history. But it's only one game in a memorable seven game series.

Game 1	October 18, 1986
Shea Stadium (New York)	T: 2:59
Boston 1 : New York 0	A: 55,076

Bruce Hurst and Ron Darling exchanged zeroes over the first six frames but Tim Teufel's seventh inning error led to the game's only run as the Red Sox captured the opener. Darling walked Rice to open the frame and a wild pitch moved him to second base. Then Rich Gedman's routine grounder went through Teufel's legs plating Rice with the game's only run. Hurst lasted eight innings and garnered the win. Calvin Schiraldi pitched a scoreless ninth for the save. Darling was the loser.

Game 2	October 19, 1986
Shea Stadium (New York)	T: 3:36
Boston 9 : New York 3	A: 55,063

The Red Sox pounded out eighteen hits and soundly trounced the Mets to take a commanding series lead. Dave Henderson and Dwight Evans homered for Boston. Wade Boggs had two hits and knocked in two runs. Steve Crawford won it in relief of Roger Clemens. Bob Stanley pitched three scoreless innings and notched the save. Dwight Gooden suffered the loss.

Game 3	October 21, 1986
Fenway Park (Boston)	T: 2:58

New York 7 : Boston 1	A: 33,595

Lenny Dykstra led off the game with a homer and the Mets added three more in the opening frame on Gary Carter's RBI double and a two-run single by Danny Heep. Carter knocked in two more runs with a seventh inning single and Ray Knight chipped in with an RBI two-bagger to close out the Mets' scoring. Marty Barrett's third inning single accounted for Boston's lone run. Former Sox hurler Bob Ojeda lasted seven innings and notched the victory. Dennis "Oil Can" Boyd allowed six runs over seven frames and suffered the loss.

Game 4	October 22, 1986
Fenway Park (Boston)	T: 3:22
New York 6 : Boston 2	A: 33,920

The Mets played power ball to even the series. Gary Carter belted a two-run homer in a three-run third and added a solo blast later in the game as New York trounced Boston. Lenny Dykstra also launched a round tripper with a man aboard for the Mets. Boston plated a pair of runs in the eighth on a single by Dwight Evans and Dave Henderson's sacrifice fly. Ron Darling lasted seven innings and garnered the win. Jesse Orosco notched the save. Al Nipper allowed three runs over six frames and was charged with the loss.

Game 5	October 23, 1986
Fenway Park (Boston)	T: 3:09
Boston 4 : New York 2	A: 34,010

Bruce Hurst notched a complete game victory and the Red Sox moved to within one win of their first World Championship in sixty-eight years. Boston posted a run in the second and third innings on a sacrifice fly by Spike Owen and an RBI single by Dwight Evans respectively. Don Baylor's run scoring single plated what proved to be the winning run in the fifth and Dave Henderson's RBI double later in the frame closed out Beantown's scoring night. Dwight Gooden lasted just four innings and suffered his second loss of the series. Tim Teufel homered for New York.

Game 6	October 25, 1986
Shea Stadium (New York)	T: 4:02
New York 6 : Boston 5 (10)	A: 55,078

The Bill Buckner game! With the score tied in the tenth Dave Henderson belted a leadoff homer. Two outs later Wade Boggs doubled and Marty Barrett singled him home to give Boston a two-run lead. Calvin Schiraldi retired the first two batters in the bottom of the frame but Gary Carter singled to keep hope alive and Kevin Mitchell—pinch hitting for Rick Aguilera—followed with a base hit as well. Then Ray Knight singled,[57] plating Carter, sending Mitchell to third and chasing Schiraldi in favor of Bob Stanley. That brought Mookie Wilson to the plate. With the count 2-2, Wilson fouled off several pitches before Stanley wild pitched Mitchell home with the tying run. Then Wilson rolled one up the first base line. An ailing Bill Buckner[58] raced over to make the play but the ball skipped through his legs for an error, sending Knight home from second base with the winning run and cementing Buckner's place in infamy in the lore of baseball history. Aguilera got the win and Schiraldi took the loss.

Game 7	October 27, 1986
Shea Stadium (New York)	T: 3:11
New York 8 : Boston 5	A: 55,032

The Red Sox took a three-run lead in the second inning when Dwight Evans and Rich Gedman belted back-to-back homers off Ron Darling and Wade Boggs added an RBI single. But it was all Mets from there on out. Keith Hernandez's two-run single highlighted a game tying three-run sixth and the Mets took control in the seventh with Ray Knight's homer highlighting that uprising. Daryl Strawberry's homer and Jesse Orosco's RBI single in the eighth served as icing on the cake. Roger McDowell won it in relief and Orosco collected his second save of the series. Calvin Schiraldi was charged with the loss—his second of the series.

1987

Minnesota Twins (4) - St. Louis Cardinals (3)
MVP: Frank Viola

The Twins, owners of just the fifth-best record in the American League, vanquish the Cardinals in seven games with the Metrodome, aka, the "Homerdome" serving as their greatest weapon.

Game 1	October 17, 1987
Metrodome (Minnesota)	T: 2:39
Minnesota 10 : St. Louis 1	A: 55,171

Dan Gladden's grand slam homer highlighted a seven run fourth inning as the Twins crushed the Cardinals in the opener. Gladden doubled home a run later in the game to close out a five-RBI night. Steve Lombardozzi also homered with a man aboard. Frank Viola scattered five hits and allowed one run in eight innings of work. Joe Magrane allowed five runs over five-plus innings of work and was charged with the loss.

Game 2	October 18, 1987
Metrodome (Minnesota)	T: 2:42
Minnesota 8 : St. Louis 4	A: 55,257

For the second night in a row, the Twins erupted in the fourth inning—this time for six runs—as they re-clobbered the Cardinals. Gary Gaetti's solo homer in the second gave the Twins an early lead. Randy Bush's two-run double and Tim Laudner's two-run single highlighted the fourth inning fireworks. Laudner belted a solo homer later in the ballgame as well. Bert Blyleven fanned eight in seven innings of work to garner the win. Danny Cox was saddled with the loss.

Game 3	October 20, 1987
Busch Stadium (St. Louis)	T: 2:45
St. Louis 3 : Minnesota 1	A: 55,347

Vince Coleman doubled home two runs in the seventh, then stole third and scored on Ozzie Smith's base hit and John Tudor allowed just one run on four hits in seven innings of work as the Cardinals climbed back into the series. Todd Worrell pitched a scoreless eighth and ninth for the save. Les Straker started for the Twins and pitched six scoreless innings. Juan Berenguer lasted just one third of an inning, surrendering all three St. Louis runs in the game-deciding seventh frame.

Game 4	October 21, 1987
Busch Stadium (St. Louis)	T: 3:11
St. Louis 7 : Minnesota 2	A: 55,347

This time it was the Cardinals with the fourth inning explosion as they tallied six times in the frame and flew away with a series tying victory. Tom Lawless, who had one homerun in his entire five-year career, belted a three-run homer to highlight the uprising. Jim Lindeman added an RBI single and Willie McGee added a two-run double to close out the innings activities. Bob Forsch won it in relief. Frank Viola did not survive the fourth inning and was charged with the loss. Gary Gaetti homered for the Twins.

Game 5	October 22, 1987
Busch Stadium (St. Louis)	T: 3:21
St. Louis 4 : Minnesota 2	A: 55,347

Curt Ford singled home two runs to break a scoreless tie in the sixth inning and the game deciding run crossed the plate on an error by Twins' shortstop Greg Gagne later in the frame as the Cardinals doubled up on the Twins to move to within one win of a World Championship. Ozzie Smith's RBI single an inning later closed out St. Louis's scoring night. Minnesota made some noise in the eighth when Gary Gaetti tripled home two runs. Danny Cox pitched into the eighth for the win and Jeff Reardon garnered the save. Bert Blyleven suffered the loss.

Game 6	October 24, 1987
Metrodome (Minnesota)	T: 3:22
Minnesota 11 : St. Louis 5	A: 55,293

The Twins took control of a seesaw battle, scoring four runs in both the fourth and fifth innings to win going away. Gary Gaetti's two-run double and Don Baylor's two-run homer turned a three-run deficit into a one-run advantage in the fifth and Kent Hrbek's grand slam an inning later blew the game wide open. Dan Schatzeder won it in relief. John Tudor surrendered six runs on eleven hits in four-plus innings of work and was charged with the defeat. Tommy Herr homered for St. Louis.

Game 7	October 25, 1987
Metrodome (Minnesota)	T: 3:04
Minnesota 4 : St. Louis 2	A: 55,376

The Twins overcame an early innings deficit to capture the first World Championship in their history. St. Louis tallied twice in the second on RBI singles by Tony Pena and Steve Lake to take the lead but Minnesota answered when Steve Lombardozzi singled home a run in the bottom of the frame. Kirby Puckett's RBI double tied it in the fifth and Greg Gagne's sixth inning single put the Twins ahead for good. Dan Gladden's RBI double plated an insurance run in the eighth. Frank Viola allowed just two runs in eight innings of work to post his second victory of the series. Jeff Reardon retired the side in order in the ninth for the save. Danny Cox was the loser in relief.

1988

LA Dodgers (4) - Oakland Athletics (1)
MVP: Orel Hershiser

The seemingly invincible Oakland Athletics, featuring sluggers Jose Canseco and Mark McGwire, are stunned by a scrappy Los Angeles Dodger team with Kirk Gibson's ninth inning homer in Game 1 setting the stage for the downfall.

Game 1	October 15, 1988
Dodger Stadium (Los Angeles)	T: 3:04
Los Angeles 5 : Oakland 4	A: 55,983

The Kirk Gibson game! Mickey Hatcher belted a two-run homer in the bottom of the first but Jose Canseco's grand slam in the second put the A's back in front. Mike Scioscia's sixth inning RBI single cut the lead to one and set the stage for one of the most famous homers in World Series history. Ace closer and future Hall of Famer Dennis Eckersley retired the first two batters in the ninth and then walked Mike Davis. Kirk Gibson,[59] who was believed to be unavailable due to injury, then hobbled out of the clubhouse and up to the plate to belt a game winning homer to win it for Los Angeles. Alejandro Pena hurled two scoreless innings for the victory.

Game 2	October 16, 1988
Dodger Stadium (Los Angeles)	T: 2:30
Los Angeles 6 : Oakland 0	A: 56,051

Orel Hershiser pitched a complete game shutout as the Dodgers stunned Oakland for the second night in a row to take a commanding series lead. Los Angeles erupted for five runs in the third inning when Franklin Stubbs and Mickey Hatcher hit RBI singles and Mike Marshall belted a three-run homer. Hershiser chipped in at the plate as well with a three-for-three night that featured an RBI double in the fourth. Storm Davis surrendered all six LA runs and was tagged with the loss.

Game 3	October 18, 1988
Oakland Coliseum	T: 3:21
Oakland 2 : Los Angeles 1	A: 49,316

Mark McGwire's game winning solo homer in the bottom of the ninth inning put Oakland back in the series. Ron Hassey singled home the game's first run in the third but the Dodgers tied it in the fifth on Franklin Stubbs's RBI double. McGwire's homer came off Jay Howell who entered the game in the ninth and retired the first batter he faced before the slugging first baseman stepped to the plate to end it. Rick Honeycutt pitched two scoreless innings and was awarded the victory.

Game 4	October 19, 1988
Oakland Coliseum	T: 3:05
Los Angeles 4 : Oakland 3	A: 49,317

The Dodgers moved to within one win of completing their stunning upset of the A's with a hard fought one-run victory. Tracy Woodson's RBI grounder in the seventh proved to be the game winning run but the outcome was in doubt up until the very end when Jay Howell retired Dave Parker with the tying run aboard in the bottom of the ninth. Tim Belcher was credited with the win. Howell garnered the save. Dave Stewart allowed all four Dodger runs and was charged with the loss.

Game 5	October 20, 1988
Oakland Coliseum	T: 2:51
Los Angeles 5 : Oakland 2	A: 49,317

Orel Hershiser turned in his second consecutive complete game victory—fanning nine along the way—as the Dodgers closed out the A's to capture the sixth World Championship in their storied history. Mickey Hatcher belted a two-run homer in the first inning and Mike Davis's two-run blast in the fourth proved to be the game winning blow. Rick Dempsey added an RBI double in the sixth to close out the Dodgers' scoring night. Storm Davis suffered the defeat.

1989
Oakland Athletics (4) – SF Giants (0)
MVP: Dave Stewart

Only an earthquake could stop Oakland's demolition of cross-bay rival San Francisco. But when play resumes nearly two weeks later, the A's finish the job—sweeping the Giants in four straight in the first-ever all Bay Area World Series.

Game 1	October 14, 1989
Oakland Coliseum	T: 2:45
Oakland 5 : San Francisco 0	A: 49,385

The A's made quick work of the Giants in the opener, tallying three times in the second inning and never looking back. RBI singles by Tony Phillips and Rickey Henderson highlighted the attack. Dave Parker and Walt Weiss added solo homers later in the ballgame. Dave Stewart turned in a five-hit complete game shutout, fanning six along the way. Scott Garrelts allowed all five runs in his four-plus innings of work and was charged with the loss.

Game 2	October 15, 1989
Oakland Coliseum	T: 2:47
Oakland 5 : San Francisco 1	A: 49,388

The A's broke it wide open in the fourth when Dave Parker doubled home a run and Terry Steinbach launched a three-run homer. Mike Moore allowed just one run in seven innings of work and was awarded the victory. Rick Reuschel allowed all five runs in his four innings of work and was charged with the loss.

Game 3	October 27, 1989
Candlestick Park (San Francisco)	T: 3:30
Oakland 13 : San Francisco 7	A: 62,038

After a massive earthquake delayed play for nearly two weeks, the teams returned to the diamond and the A's continued their demolition of the NL champs. Dave Henderson doubled home two runs in the very first inning and added two solo homers later in the ballgame to pace Oakland's explosive offensive night. Jose Canseco, Tony Phillips and Carney Lansford also homered for the AL champs. Dave Stewart allowed three runs over seven frames and picked up his second win of the series. Scott Garrelts suffered his second loss of the series. Matt Williams and Bill Bathe homered for the Giants.

Game 4	October 28, 1989
Candlestick Park (San Francisco)	T: 3:07
Oakland 9 : San Francisco 6	A: 62,032

The A's completed a four-game sweep of the Giants to capture their fourth World Championship since moving to Oakland. Rickey Henderson led off the game with a homer and the A's added three more in the second when pitcher Mike Moore doubled home two runs and scored on Henderson's base hit. Terry Steinbach's two-run triple highlighted a three-run fifth that put the game out of reach. Moore allowed two runs in six innings of work— good enough for the victory. Dennis Eckersley hurled a scoreless ninth for the save. Don Robinson did not survive the second innings and was saddled with the loss. Kevin Mitchell and Greg Litton homered for the Giants.

193

1990

Cincinnati Reds (4) - Oakland Athletics (0)
MVP: Jose Rijo

The Cincinnati Reds return to the World Series for the first time in sixteen years and shock the baseball world with a stunning four-game sweep of a seemingly invincible Oakland A's team.

Game 1	October 16, 1990
Riverfront Stadium (Cincinnati)	T: 2:38
Cincinnati 7 : Oakland 0	A: 55,830

Eric Davis belted a two-run homer in the bottom of the first inning and the Reds never looked back. Cincinnati added two more in the third on an RBI double by Billy Hatcher and Paul O'Neill's run scoring grounder and they tallied three more times in the fifth on an RBI single by Davis and a two-run safety off the bat of Chris Sabo. Jose Rijo pitched seven shutout innings. "Nasty Boys" Rob Dibble and Randy Myers pitched a scoreless eighth and ninth respectively. Dave Stewart took the loss.

Game 2	October 17, 1990
Riverfront Stadium (Cincinnati)	T: 3:31
Cincinnati 5 : Oakland 4 (10)	A: 55,832

Joe Oliver's tenth inning RBI single off A's relief ace Dennis Eckersley capped off a thrilling comeback victory and sent the Reds back to Oakland with a commanding series lead. Trailing by a run in the bottom of the eighth, Billy Hatcher tripled[60] and scored the tying run. Eckersley retired the first batter he faced in the tenth, but three consecutive singles—by pinch hitter Billy Bates, Chris Sabo and Oliver amounted to the game winning run. Rob Dibble won it in relief. Jose Canseco homered for Oakland.

194

Game 3	October 19, 1990
Oakland Coliseum	T: 3:01
Cincinnati 8 : Oakland 3	A: 48,269

The Reds blew a close game wide open with a seven-run third inning to move to within one win of a sweep of the mighty A's. Chris Sabo's second inning homer gave Cincinnati an early lead and his two run blast an inning later highlighted the game deciding third. Eric Davis and Mariano Duncan had run scoring singles in the uprising with Joe Oliver and Barry Larkin adding an RBI double and triple respectively. Tom Browning got the win. Mike Moore was the loser. Harold Baines and Rickey Henderson homered for Oakland.

Game 4	October 20, 1990
Oakland Coliseum	T: 2:48
Cincinnati 2 : Oakland 1	A: 48,613

The Reds rallied for two in the eighth to win it. Barry Larkin got it started with a leadoff single and Herm Winningham followed with a bunt hit. Paul O'Neill laid down a sacrifice but Dave Stewart threw wildly to first and the bases were loaded with nobody out. Glenn Braggs pushed the tying run across with a fielder's choice grounder and Hal Morris's sacrifice fly put the Reds in front. Jose Rijo allowed just one run over eight and a third innings to capture his second win of the series. Randy Myers retired the final two batters for the save. Dave Stewart went the distance for the A's but suffered his second loss of the series.

1991

Minnesota Twins (4) - Atlanta Braves (3)
MVP: Jack Morris

In the first ever "Worst-to-First" World Series—two teams that had finished dead last a season earlier—face off in what would go down as one of the greatest World Series of all time.

Game 1	October 19, 1991
Metrodome (Minnesota)	T: 3:00
Minnesota 5 : Atlanta 2	A: 55,108

Greg Gagne's three-run homer in the fifth inning was the game deciding blow as the Twins captured the opener. Kent Hrbek added a solo homer later in the ballgame to close out Minnesota's scoring night. Jack Morris allowed two runs over seven innings to pick up the win. Rick Aguilera notched the save. Charlie Leibrandt allowed four runs in four-plus innings of work and was saddled with the loss. Ron Gant knocked in both Atlanta runs with a pair of RBI singles.

Game 2	October 20, 1991
Metrodome (Minnesota)	T: 2:37
Minnesota 3 : Atlanta 2	A: 51,145

Scott Leius's leadoff homer in the bottom of the eighth proved to be the game winning blow as the Twins made it two-straight over the Braves. Chili Davis belted a two-run homer in the bottom of the first but Atlanta tied it on sacrifice flies by Brian Hunter in the second and Rafael Belliard in the fifth, setting the stage for Leius's game winning blow. Kevin Tapani allowed two runs in eight innings of work to garner the victory. Rick Aguilera posted his second save of the series. Tom Glavine suffered the loss.

Game 3	October 22, 1991
Atlanta-Fulton County Stadium	T: 4:04
Atlanta 5 : Minnesota 4 (12)	A: 50,878

Mark Lemke's RBI single in the bottom of the twelfth ended an extra-innings thriller and put Atlanta back in the series. The Braves carried a three-run lead into the seventh but Kirby Puckett belted a solo homer in that frame and Chili Davis connected for a two-run blast an inning later to tie it. Then in the twelfth, Dave Justice singled, stole second and scored on Lemke's two-out game winning hit. Jim Clancy pitched just one third of an inning and was awarded the victory. Rick Aguilera was charged with the loss.

Game 4	October 23, 1991
Atlanta-Fulton County Stadium	T: 2:57
Atlanta 3 : Minnesota 2	A: 50,878

The Braves captured another thriller in their final at-bat to even the series. Mike Pagliarulo's second inning RBI single gave the Twins the early lead but Terry Pendleton homered to tie it in the third. Pagliarulo struck again in the seventh with a solo homer to put Minnesota back in front and this time Lonnie Smith answered with a game-tying homer. Then in the bottom of the ninth Mark Lemke tripled and scored on Jerry Willard's sacrifice fly to win it. Mike Stanton won it in relief and Mark Guthrie was the loser.

Game 5	October 24, 1991
Atlanta-Fulton County Stadium	T: 2:59
Atlanta 14 : Minnesota 5	A: 50,878

In the only blow out of the series the Braves pummeled the Twins to make it a clean sweep in Atlanta. David Justice's two-run homer highlighted a four-run fourth but Tom Glavine issued two bases loaded walks in Minnesota's three-run sixth to make it interesting. The Braves went on the warpath in the seventh, tallying six times to put it out of reach. Lonnie Smith homered and Mark

197

Lemke belted a two-run triple to highlight the uprising. Glavine picked up the win and Kevin Tapani was the loser. Brian Hunter also homered for the Braves.

Game 6	October 26, 1991
Metrodome (Minnesota)	T: 3:36
Minnesota 4 : Atlanta 3 (11)	A: 55,155

In another thrilling installment of this Fall Classic for the ages, the Twins won an eleven inning marathon to even the series. Kirby Puckett tripled home a run and scored on Shane Mack's single in the bottom of the first to give Minnesota an early advantage. But Atlanta tied it in the fifth when Terry Pendleton belted a two-run homer. Puckett struck again in the bottom of the frame when his sacrifice fly put the Twins back in front. The Braves tied it in the seventh on Ron Gant's fielder's choice grounder. The game remained deadlocked until the eleventh when Puckett homered leading off to end it. Rick Aguilera pitched two scoreless innings and was credited with the victory. Charlie Liebrandt, who faced just one batter—Puckett—was tagged with the defeat.

Game 7	October 27, 1991
Metrodome (Minnesota)	T: 3:23
Minnesota 1 : Atlanta 0 (10)	A: 55,118

Hometown hero Jack Morris pitched a ten inning complete game shutout in the seventh and deciding game to bring Minnesota its second World Championship in five years. The Twins finally broke the scoreless deadlock in the tenth when Dan Gladden doubled leading off, advanced to third on a sacrifice fly by Chuck Knoblauch and scored on pinch-hitter Gene Larkin's base hit to win it. Alejandro Pena was charged with the defeat.

1992

Toronto Blue Jays (4) - Atlanta Braves (2)
MVP: Pat Borders

For the first time in history a World Series game is played outside the United States as the Toronto Blue Jays capture the AL flag and best the Atlanta Braves in six games.

Game 1	October 17, 1992
Atlanta-Fulton County Stadium	T: 2:37
Atlanta 3 : Toronto 1	A: 51,763

Joe Carter's solo homer in the fourth gave Toronto an early lead but Damon Berryhill's three-run blast in the sixth put Atlanta ahead for good as the Braves captured the opener. Tom Glavine went the distance for the win. Jack Morris, who surrendered the Berryhill blast, lasted six innings and was saddled with the loss.

Game 2	October 18, 1992
Atlanta-Fulton County Stadium	T: 3:30
Toronto 5 : Atlanta 4	A: 51,763

The Blue Jays snatched victory from the jaws of defeat when Ed Sprague belted a pinch-hit two-run homer in the ninth to even the series. With the score knotted at two in the fifth, David Justice singled home a run and Brian Hunter launched a sacrifice fly to give the Braves a two-run lead. Sprague's blast came with one out in the ninth and followed a walk to pinch-hitter Derek Bell. Duane Ward won it in relief and Jeff Reardon lost it in the same capacity. Tom Henke notched the save.

Game 3	October 20, 1992
Skydome (Toronto)	T: 2:49
Toronto 3 : Atlanta 2	A: 51,813

Toronto settled the issue in the bottom of the ninth when Candy Maldonado's sacrifice fly plated Roberto Alomar to win it. Duane Ward hurled one scoreless inning and was credited with the win. Steve Avery allowed three runs over eight innings and was charged with the defeat. Joe Carter and Kelly Gruber homered for the Blue Jays. Deion Sanders had three hits for the Braves.

Game 4	October 21, 1992
Skydome (Toronto)	T: 2:21
Toronto 2 : Atlanta 1	A: 52,090

A solo homer by Pat Borders in the third and an RBI single by Devon White in the seventh was all the offense the Blue Jays needed to move to within one win of their first World Championship. Jimmy Key won it and Tom Henke notched his second save of the series. Tom Glavine was the loser.

Game 5	October 22, 1992
Skydome (Toronto)	T: 3:05
Atlanta 7 : Toronto 2	A: 52,268

Lonnie Smith's grand slam homer capped a five-run fifth inning as the Braves averted elimination and sent the series back to Atlanta. David Justice also homered for the Braves. John Smoltz, who allowed both Toronto runs in his six-plus inning stint, garnered the victory. Jack Morris allowed all seven Atlanta runs and was charged with the loss.

Game 6	October 24, 1992
Atlanta-Fulton County Stadium	T: 4:07
Toronto 2 : Atlanta 1	A: 51,763

The Blue Jays captured their first World Championship but the Braves fought tooth and nail until their final breath. Otis Nixon singled home Jeff Blauser with two out in the bottom of the ninth to tie the game but Dave Winfield doubled home two runs in the eleventh to put Toronto back in front. The Braves came storming back in the bottom of the frame, scoring a run and sending Nixon back to the dish with two outs and the tying run just ninety-feet away. But Nixon's surprise bunt was not successful and the Blue Jays were champions.[61] Jimmy Key got the win in relief with Mike Timlin notching the save. Charlie Liebrandt suffered the loss.

1993

Toronto Blue Jays (4) - Philadelphia Phillies (2)
MVP: Paul Molitor

The Blue Jays return to the Fall Classic and face off against a hard nosed and hard fighting Philadelphia Phillies team. Joe Carter's walk off homer in Game 6 closes out the series in dramatic fashion and Toronto is champion for a second straight year.

Game 1	October 16, 1993
Skydome (Toronto)	T: 3:27
Toronto 8 : Philadelphia 5	A: 52,011

The Blue Jays took control of a seesaw battle with a three-run seventh highlighted by Roberto Alomar's two-run double. Al Leiter won it in relief of Juan Guzman. Duane Ward notched the save. Devon White and John Olerud homered for Toronto. Curt Schilling was charged with the loss.

Game 2	October 17, 1993
Skydome (Toronto)	T: 3:35
Philadelphia 6 : Toronto 4	A: 52,062

The Phillies erupted for five runs in the third inning with Jim Eisenreich's three-run homer proving to be the game winning blow. Joe Carter's two-run homer in the fourth and an RBI double by Tony Fernandez made things interesting but Lenny Dykstra answered with a solo homer in the seventh to put it out of reach. Terry Mulholland picked up the win. Mitch Williams notched the save. Dave Stewart was tagged with the loss.

Game 3	October 19, 1993
Veterans Stadium (Philadelphia)	T: 3:16
Toronto 10 : Philadelphia 3	A: 62,689

Paul Molitor tripled home two runs before an out was even recorded and then belted a solo homer when he returned to the plate in the third inning. The future Hall of Famer scored his third run of the night in a three-run seventh that put the game completely out of reach. Pat Hentgen allowed just one run in six innings of work for the win. Danny Jackson allowed four runs in five innings and was charged with the loss. Milt Thompson homered for the Phillies.

Game 4	October 20, 1993
Veterans Stadium (Philadelphia)	T: 4:14
Toronto 15 : Philadelphia 14	A: 62,731

The Blue Jays handed the Phillies a soul-crushing defeat in the highest scoring game in World Series history. After Philadelphia posted five in the sixth—seemingly taking control of the game, Toronto erupted for six in the eighth to fly away with a one-run victory. Tony Castillo won it in relief and Duane Ward notched his second save of the series. Tony Fernandez and Devon White spearheaded the Jays attack with six hits and nine runs batted in between them. Mitch Williams was the loser in relief. Lenny Dykstra homered twice and knocked in five in a losing cause. Darren Daulton also homered for the Phillies.

Game 5	October 21, 1993
Veterans Stadium (Philadelphia)	T: 2:53
Philadelphia 2 : Toronto 0	A: 62,706

Curt Schilling pitched a five-hit complete game shutout as the Phillies averted elimination and forced the series back to Toronto. John Kruk's RBI grounder in the bottom of the first plated Lenny Dykstra with what proved to be the game winning run. Kevin Stocker's run scoring double an inning later closed out the scoring for either side. Juan Guzman surrendered both Philadelphia runs in his seven innings of work and was charged with the defeat.

Game 6	October 23, 1993
Skydome (Toronto)	T: 2:53
Toronto 8 : Philadelphia 6	A: 62,706

Joe Carter's three-run walk off homer in the bottom of the ninth clinched Toronto's second consecutive World Championship. The Jays scored three runs in the first inning, but the Phillies stayed within striking distance and then erupted for five runs in the seventh to take the lead, with Lenny Dykstra's three-run homer highlighting the uprising. The narrow advantage held up until the ninth when Mitch "Wild Thing" Williams surrendered Carter's historic blast. Duane Ward pitched one scoreless inning and was credited with the victory. Paul Molitor also homered for the Jays.

1994

World Series Cancelled

For the first time in ninety years the World Series was cancelled because the players and the owners could not agree on a new labor agreement. The owners wanted a salary cap but the players refused to consent to the idea. The players went on strike on August 12th and on September 14th Commissioner Bud Selig announced that the season was officially cancelled.

1995

Atlanta Braves (4) - Cleveland Indians (2)

203

MVP: Tom Glavine

Cleveland returns to the World Series for the first time in forty-one years but it's another tribe—the Braves—who bring Atlanta its first World Championship.

Game 1	October 21, 1995
Atlanta-Fulton County Stadium	T: 2:37
Atlanta 3 : Cleveland 2	A: 51,876

Greg Maddux's two-hit complete game victory gave Atlanta the early series lead. Kenny Lofton reached on an error leading off the game and scored the first run but Fred McGriff tied it with a homer an inning later. The Braves jumped ahead for good in the seventh when Cleveland pitchers issued three consecutive walks and Luis Polonia and Rafael Belliard plated runs on fielder's choice outs. Cleveland managed another unearned run in the ninth on McGriff's throwing error. Orel Hershiser allowed all three Atlanta runs in his six innings of work and was saddled with the loss.

Game 2	October 22, 1995
Atlanta-Fulton County Stadium	T: 3:17
Atlanta 4 : Cleveland 3	A: 51,877

Cleveland took a two-run lead in the second inning on Eddie Murphy's two-run homer but Chipper Jones's sacrifice fly and Dave Justice's RBI single tied things up in the third. The Braves tallied what proved to be the game winning runs in the sixth when Javier Lopez belted a two-run homer. The Indians managed an unearned run seventh. Tom Glavine posted the victory and Dennis Martinez was the loser. Mark Wohlers notched the save.

Game 3	October 24, 1995
Jacobs Field (Cleveland)	T: 4:09
Cleveland 7 : Atlanta 6 (11)	A: 43,584

Eddie Murray singled home the game winning run in the bottom of the eleventh as the Indians climbed back into the series.

Jose Mesa hurled three scoreless innings in relief to win it. Carlos Baerga had three hits and knocked in three runs. Kenny Lofton had three hits and scored three runs. Alejandro Pena suffered the loss. Ryan Klesko and Fred McGriff homered for Atlanta.

Game 4	October 25, 1995
Jacobs Field (Cleveland)	T: 3:14
Atlanta 5 : Cleveland 2	A: 43,578

Dave Justice's two-run single in the seventh proved to be the game winning blow as the Braves moved to within one win of their first World Championship since moving to Atlanta. Ryan Klesko broke a scoreless tie in the sixth with a solo homer but Albert Belle homered in the bottom of the frame to tie it. Atlanta tallied three times in the seventh with Justice's hit spearheading the uprising. Steve Avery allowed one run in six innings of work for the win. Pedro Borbon pitched a scoreless ninth for the save. Ken Hill was the loser. Manny Ramirez also homered for Cleveland.

Game 5	October 26, 1995
Jacobs Field (Cleveland)	T: 2:33
Cleveland 5 : Atlanta 4	A: 43,595

Albert Belle belted a two-run homer in the first to give Cleveland the early lead. Luis Polonia's fourth inning blast cut the lead in half and Marquis Grissom's RBI single an inning later tied the game. The Indians jumped ahead in the sixth on RBI singles by Jim Thome and Manny Ramirez. Thome closed out the Tribe's scoring night with a solo homer in the eighth. Ryan Klesko's two-run round tripper in the ninth brought the Braves to within one but that was as close as they would get. Orel Hershiser got the win and Jose Mesa posted the save. Greg Maddux took the loss.

Game 6	October 28, 1995
Atlanta-Fulton County Stadium	T: 3:02
Atlanta 1 : Cleveland 0	A: 51,875

Dave Justice's solo homer in the bottom of the sixth proved to be the only run of the game as Atlanta defeated Cleveland to close out the series.[62] Tom Glavine hurled eight scoreless innings, allowing just one hit and fanning eight along the way for his second victory. Mark Wohlers retired the side in order in the ninth for his second save. Jim Poole was the loser.

1996

NY Yankees (4) - Atlanta Braves (2)
MVP: John Wetteland

The Yankees return to the Fall Classic after a fifteen-year absence and vanquish the defending champion Braves with a stirring World Series comeback.

Game 1	October 20, 1996
Yankee Stadium (New York)	T: 3:02
Atlanta 12 : New York 1	A: 56,365

Rookie phenom Andruw Jones[63] belted two homers and knocked in five runs as the Braves mauled the Yankees in the opener. Jones's second homer of the night—a three run blast—came in a six-run third inning that put the game out of reach. Fred McGriff also homered for Atlanta. John Smoltz allowed one run over six frames and picked up the victory. Andy Pettitte was saddled with the loss.

Game 2	October 21, 1996
Yankee Stadium (New York)	T: 2:44

| Atlanta 4 : New York 0 | A: 56,340 |

The Braves returned to Atlanta with a commanding series lead as Greg Maddux blanked the Yankees over the first eight frames and Mark Wohlers struck out the side in the ninth to end it. Fred McGriff's RBI single in the first inning proved to be the game winning hit. McGriff had two singles and knocked in three runs on the night. Jimmy Key surrendered all four Braves' runs and was ticketed with the loss.

Game 3	October 22, 1996
Atlanta-Fulton County Stadium	T: 3:22
New York 5 : Atlanta 2	A: 51,843

Bernie Williams belted a two-run homer and an RBI single to power the Yankees back into the series. David Cone allowed just one run in six innings of work to notch the victory. John Wetteland pitched a scoreless ninth for the save. Tom Glavine allowed two runs (one earned) in seven innings of work and suffered the defeat.

Game 4	October 23, 1996
Atlanta-Fulton County Stadium	T: 4:17
New York 8 : Atlanta 6	A: 51,881

Jim Leyritz belted a game-tying three-run homer in the top of the eighth inning and the Yankees posted two in the tenth on a bases loaded walk and an error to even the series at two-apiece. Graeme Lloyd pitched a scoreless ninth for the win and John Wetteland closed out the tenth for his second save of the series. Mark Wohlers surrendered the Leyritz homer. Steve Avery was the loser in relief. Fred McGriff homered for the Braves.

Game 5	October 24, 1996
Atlanta-Fulton County Stadium	T: 2:54
New York 1 : Atlanta 0	A: 51,881

Andy Pettitte took a shutout into the ninth and John Wetteland recorded the final two outs for the save as the Yankees made it a clean sweep in Atlanta and moved to within one win of the twenty-third World Championship in their storied history. The lone run of the game was plated in the fourth when Marquis Grissom misplayed[64] Charlie Hayes' fly ball and Cecil Fielder followed with an RBI double. Paul O'Neill's ninth inning over the shoulder catch of Luis Polonia's long drive— with the tying run on third and two out—ended the battle in dramatic fashion. John Smoltz fanned ten and allowed just the one unearned run in his eight innings of work but was saddled with the loss.

Game 6	October 26, 1996
Yankee Stadium (New York)	T: 2:53
New York 3 : Atlanta 2	A: 56,375

Joe Girardi's RBI triple broke a scoreless tie in the bottom of the third and Derek Jeter and Bernie Williams added RBI singles—all the runs the Yankees would need to capture their twenty-third World Championship. Jermaine Dye's bases loaded walk in the fourth forced home the Braves' first run. Atlanta managed a run on three hits in the ninth but finished a buck short. Jimmy Key got the win and John Wetteland posted his astounding fourth save of the series. Greg Maddux was charged with the defeat.

1997

Florida Marlins (4) - Cleveland Indians (3)
MVP: Livan Hernandez

Just four years in existence, the Florida Marlins become the first Wild Card team to reach the World Series, and once there, they stun the high powered Cleveland Indians who fail for the second time in three years to capture their first World Championship since 1948.

Game 1	October 18, 1997
Pro Player Stadium (Florida)	T: 3:19
Florida 7 : Cleveland 4	A: 67,245

Moises Alou belted a three-run homer in the bottom of the fourth and Charles Johnson followed with a solo blast as Florida outmuscled Cleveland in the opener. Cuban exile Livan Hernandez allowed three runs in 5.2 innings of work and was credited with the victory. Robb Nen garnered the save. Orel Hershiser took the loss. Manny Ramirez and Jim Thome homered for the Indians.

Game 2	October 19, 1997
Pro Player Stadium (Florida)	T: 2:48
Cleveland 6 : Florida 1	A: 67,025

Bip Roberts two-run single highlighted a three-run fifth and Sandy Alomar Jr. belted a two-run homer in the sixth as the Indians evened the series. Chad Ogea allowed just one run over six and two-thirds innings for the win. Marquis Grissom had three hits for the Tribe. Loser Kevin Brown allowed all six runs on ten hits.

Game 3	October 21, 1997
Jacobs Field (Cleveland)	T: 4:12
Florida 14 : Cleveland 11	A: 44,880

The frigid cold Ohio night made its presence known when the Indians committed three errors and a wild pitch in Florida's game deciding seven-run ninth. Gary Sheffield and Bobby Bonilla had two-run singles in the inning. Dennis Cook pitched just one scoreless frame but was credited with the victory. Darren Daulton, Jim Eisenreich and Sheffield all homered for the Marlins—Sheffield knocked in five runs. Eric Plunk suffered the loss after allowing four runs in just two-thirds of an inning in the final frame. Jim Thome homered for the Indians.

Game 4	October 22, 1997
Jacobs Field (Cleveland)	T: 3:15
Cleveland 10 : Florida 3	A: 44,877

With snow flurries swirling all around and the temperature dipping into the thirties the Indians clobbered the Marlins to even the series. Manny Ramirez and Matt Williams both belted two-run homers. Sandy Alomar had three hits and knocked in three runs. Jaret Wright allowed all three Florida runs over six innings and picked up the win. Brian Anderson pitched three scoreless innings for the save. Tony Saunders lasted just two innings, surrendering seven runs and suffering the loss. Moises Alou homered for the Marlins.

Game 5	October 23, 1997
Jacobs Field (Cleveland)	T: 3:39
Florida 8 : Cleveland 7	A: 44,888

Moises Alou belted his third homerun of the series as the Marlins returned to Florida just one win away from the first World Championship in their short history. Alou's three-run blast came in a four-run sixth. Florida tacked on additional runs in the eighth and ninth on RBI singles by Charles Johnson and Alou respectively. Livan Hernandez posted his second win of the series. Robb Nen garnered his second save. Orel Hershiser suffered the loss. Sandy Alomar homered and knocked in four runs for the Tribe.

Game 6	October 25, 1997
Pro Player Stadium (Florida)	T: 3:15
Florida 4 : Cleveland 1	A: 67,498

Indians starter Chad Ogea, who came into the night's action with a grand total of two Major League at-bats, singled home two runs in the top of the second and added a double later in the game, en route to his second victory of the series. A pair of sacrifice flies by Manny Ramirez accounted for Cleveland's final two runs. Kevin Brown surrendered all four Cleveland runs and was saddled with his second loss of the series. Darren Daulton's sacrifice fly accounted for Florida's lone run.

Game 7	October 26, 1997
Pro Player Stadium (Florida)	T: 4:10
Florida 3 : Cleveland 2 (11)	A: 67,204

Rookie shortstop Edgar Renteria etched his name into World Series lore when he singled home Craig Counsell with the game winning run in the bottom of the eleventh inning to cement Florida's first World Championship.[65] Cleveland jumped out to an early lead on Tony Fernandez's third inning two-run single. Bobby Bonilla's solo homer put the Marlins on the board in the seventh and Craig Counsell's ninth inning sacrifice fly plated Moises Alou with the tying run. Alou singled leading off the eleventh and Counsell reached on an error setting the stage for Renteria's two-out line-drive single up the middle to win it. Jay Powell pitched one scoreless inning and was credited with the win. Charles Nagy was the loser.

1998
NY Yankees (4) - SD Padres (0)
MVP: Scott Brosius

The Yankees win an American League record 114 regular season games and then steamroll the Padres in four-straight games to claim their second World Championship in three years and the twenty-fourth in their astounding history.

Game 1	October 17, 1998
Yankee Stadium (New York)	T: 3:29
New York 9 : San Diego 6	A: 56,712

With the score knotted at two-apiece in the top of the fifth, Tony Gwynn belted a two-run homer and Greg Vaughan followed with a solo blast—his second round tripper of the night—to give the Padres a three-run lead. But the Yankees erupted for seven runs in the seventh when Chuck Knoblauch belted a three-run homer to tie the game and Tino Martinez launched a grand slam to blow it wide open. David Wells got the win. Donne Wall was the loser.

Game 2	October 18, 1998
Yankee Stadium (New York)	T: 3:31
New York 9 : San Diego 3	A: 56,692

Andy Ashby allowed seven runs (four earned) on ten hits as the Yankees crushed the Padres. Ken Caminiti's first inning error plated New York's first run and RBI singles by Chili Davis and Scott Brosius led to two more before the side was retired. Bernie Williams and Jorge Posada belted two-run homers later in the contest. Orlando "El Duque" Hernandez allowed one run in seven innings of work and picked up the win. Quilvio Veras and Ruben Rivera had RBI doubles for the Padres.

Game 3	October 20, 1998
Qualcomm Stadium (San Diego)	T: 3:14
New York 5 : San Diego 4	A: 64,667

Scott Brosius belted two homers in his final two at-bats as the Yankees erased a three-run deficit and moved to within one win of their twenty-fourth World Championship. Brosius's first homer came in the seventh and put New York on the scoreboard for the first time all night. An inning later the unassuming third sacker belted a three-run homer off Trevor Hoffman to put the Yankees ahead for good. The Padres pushed a run across in the eighth to cut the lead to one but Mariano Rivera recorded the final five outs of the contest for the save.

Game 4	October 21, 1998
Qualcomm Stadium (San Diego)	T: 2:58

New York 3 : San Diego 0	A: 65,427

The Yankees completed one of the most dominating seasons in baseball history in fine fashion—shutting out the Padres to complete a four-game World Series sweep. New York broke a scoreless tie in the seventh when Bernie Williams' fielder's choice plated Derek Jeter and they added two more an inning later on an RBI single by Scott Brosius and Ricky Ledee's sacrifice fly. Andy Pettitte took a shutout into the eighth before turning the ball over to Mariano Rivera who notched his third save of the series.

1999

NY Yankees (4) - Atlanta Braves (0)
MVP: Mariano Rivera

In a showdown to determine the "Team of the Decade" the Yankees prove themselves to be the "Team of the Century" as they make quick work of the Braves and capture the twenty-fifth World Championship in their sterling history.

Game 1	October 23, 1999
Turner Field (Atlanta)	T: 2:57
New York 4 : Atlanta 1	A: 51,342

Orlando "El Duque" Hernandez allowed just one run in seven innings of work—fanning ten along the way as the Yankees captured the opener. Chipper Jones's solo homer in the fourth plated the game's only run until New York erupted for four in the eighth. Derek Jeter's single tied it. Paul O'Neill's two-run base hit proved to be the game winning blow. Jim Leyritz walked with the bases loaded to close out the night's scoring. Greg Maddux allowed just two earned runs over seven innings but was charged with the loss. Mariano Rivera notched the save.

Game 2	October 24, 1999

Turner Field (Atlanta)	T: 3:14
New York 7 : Atlanta 2	A: 51,226

First inning RBI singles by Paul O'Neill, Tino Martinez and Scott Brosius were all the runs the Yankees would need as they made it two straight in Atlanta. David Cone pitched seven scoreless innings for the win. Kevin Millwood allowed five runs in just two-plus innings and was saddled with the loss.

Game 3	October 26, 1999
Yankee Stadium (New York)	T: 3:16
New York 6 : Atlanta 5 (10)	A: 55,794

The Yankees overcame a four-run deficit to move to within one win of their second consecutive World Championship; the third in four years and the twenty-fifth in their astounding history. Still trailing by two in the eighth, Chuck Knoblauch belted a two-run homer to tie it and Chad Curtis connected for his second round tripper of the night in the bottom of the tenth to win it. Mariano Rivera pitched two scoreless innings and was awarded the victory. Tino Martinez also homered for New York. Mike Remlinger, who came on in the tenth and faced just one batter—Curtis—was charged with the defeat.

Game 4	October 27, 1999
Yankee Stadium (New York)	T: 2:58
New York 4 : Atlanta 1	A: 56,752

The Yankees not only proclaimed themselves "Team of the Decade" but "Team of the Century" as well as they completed a four game sweep of the Braves for their twenty-fifth World Series title. Tino Martinez's two-run single in the third proved to be all the runs New York would need. Jorge Posada added an RBI single later in the frame and Jim Leyritz belted a solo homer in the eighth to account for the final run. Roger Clemens earned the first World Series victory of his career. Mariano Rivera notched his second save of the series. John Smoltz allowed three runs in seven innings of work and was charged with the loss.

2000
New York Yankees (4) - New York Mets (1)
MVP: Derek Jeter

The Yankees and Mets square off in the first subway series since the Brooklyn Dodgers move to Los Angeles. The Bronx Bombers make quick work of their cross-town rivals en route to their third consecutive World Championship and the twenty-sixth in their incredible history.

Game 1	October 21, 2000
Yankee Stadium	T: 4:51
NY Yankees 4 : NY Mets 3 (12)	A: 55,913

David Justice's sixth inning two-run two-bagger broke a scoreless tie but the Mets jumped ahead in the seventh on Bubba Trammell's two-run single and Edgardo Alfonzo's RBI base hit. The lead lasted until the ninth when Chuck Knoblauch's sacrifice fly tied the game. Jose Vizcaino's RBI single ended it in the twelfth. Mike Stanton hurled two scoreless innings for the win. Turk Wendell was the loser.

Game 2	October 22, 2000
Yankee Stadium	T: 3:30
NY Yankees 6 : NY Mets 5	A: 55,069

It was all Yankees until the ninth when Mike Piazza belted a two-run homer, and two outs and two singles later, Jay Payton launched a three-run blast, cutting the lead to just one run. But that was as close as the Mets would get as Mariano Rivera fanned Kurt Abbott to end it. Roger Clemens pitched eight scoreless innings and fanned nine en route to the victory. Scott Brosius homered for

215

the Yankees. Mike Hampton allowed all four Yankee runs and was charged with the loss.

Game 3	October 24, 2000
Shea Stadium	T: 3:39
NY Mets 4 : NY Yankees 2	A: 55,299

The Mets snapped the Yankees World Series winning streak at fourteen, but the win was anything but easy. Todd Zeile doubled home the tying run in the sixth and scored the go-ahead run in the eighth on a two-bagger off the bat of Bennie Agbayani. John Franco won it in relief and Armando Benitez posted the save. Orlando "El Duque" Hernandez fanned twelve in a losing effort. Scott Brosius homered for the Yankees.

Game 4	October 25, 2000
Shea Stadium	T: 3:20
NY Yankees 3 : NY Mets 2	A: 55,290

Derek Jeter hit the first pitch of the game over the wall and the Yankees added runs in the second and third on a sacrifice fly by Scott Brosius and a fielder's choice grounder off the bat of Luis Sojo respectively. Mike Piazza's third inning two-run homer closed out the scoring for either side as the Bronx Bombers held on for the victory. Jeff Nelson got the win in relief and Mariano Rivera notched the save. Bobby Jones allowed all three Yankee runs over five innings and was charged with the loss.

Game 5	October 26, 2000
Shea Stadium	T: 3:32
NY Yankees 4 : NY Mets 2	A: 55,292

The Yankees closed out the final Fall Classic of the century to capture an unprecedented twenty-sixth World Series title. Bernie Williams' second inning solo homer opened the scoring but the Mets tallied twice in the bottom of the frame on Jorge Posada's throwing error and an RBI single off the bat of Benny

Agbayani. Derek Jeter's solo homer in the sixth tied the game and Luis Sojo's two-out two-run single in the ninth proved to be the game winning blow. Mike Stanton posted his second win of the series and Mariano Rivera posted his second save. Al Leiter was saddled with the loss.

2001

Arizona Diamondbacks (4) NY Yankees (3)
Co-MVPs: Randy Johnson/Curt Schilling

In the first Fall Classic of the new century, with the nation reeling from the tragic events of 9/11, the upstart Diamondbacks stage an upset of epic proportion, vanquishing the three-time champion Yankees in the bottom of the ninth inning of the seventh and deciding game.

Game 1	October 27, 2001
Bank One Ballpark (Arizona)	T: 2:44
Arizona 9 : New York 1	A: 49,646

It was all Arizona in the opener as the Diamondbacks pounded out ten hits including a solo homer by Craig Counsell, a two-run homer by Luis Gonzalez and a two-run double by Mark Grace. Curt Schilling held the Yankees to just one run on three hits in seven innings of work and fanned eight along the way for the win. Mike Mussina lasted just three innings and was charged with the loss.

Game 2	October 28, 2001
Bank One Ballpark (Arizona)	T: 2:35
Arizona 4 : New York 0	A: 49,646

Randy Johnson turned in a gem of a performance— allowing just three hits and striking out eleven en route to a complete game shutout. Danny Bautista's run scoring double in the bottom of the second proved to be the game winning run. Matt

Williams belted a three-run homer in the seventh to end any doubt. Andy Pettitte allowed all four Diamondback runs and was ticketed with the loss.

Game 3	October 30, 2001
Yankee Stadium (New York)	T: 3:26
New York 2 : Arizona 1	A: 55,820

Roger Clemens struck out nine and allowed just one run over seven innings and Mariano Rivera pitched a perfect eighth and ninth for the save as the Yankees squeaked past Arizona to climb back into the series. Jorge Posada's solo homer in the second gave New York the early lead but the Diamondbacks tied it on Matt Williams' sacrifice fly in the fourth. Scott Brosius plated what proved to be the game winning run in the sixth with a run scoring fly. Brian Anderson suffered the loss.

Game 4	October 31, 2001
Yankee Stadium (New York)	T: 3:31
New York 4 : Arizona 3 (10)	A: 55,863

Curt Schilling and Orlando "El Duque" Hernandez hooked up in a pitcher's duel with each hurler allowing just one run over seven innings of work. The Diamondbacks tallied twice off reliever Mike Stanton in the eighth and were just one out away from victory when Tino Martinez belted a game tying two-run homer off Byung-Hyun Kim to force the game into extra innings. Derek Jeter took Kim over the wall with two out in the tenth to win it.[67] Mariano Rivera pitched one scoreless inning and was credited with the victory.

Game 5	November 1, 2001[68]
Yankee Stadium (New York)	T: 4:15
New York 3 : Arizona 2 (12)	A: 56,018

For the second night in a row the Yankees pulled a rabbit out of the hat when Scott Brosius belted a two-out two-run game tying homer in the bottom of the ninth inning. Arizona took a two-run lead in the fifth when Mike Mussina surrendered solo homers to Steve Finley and Ron Barajas. The lead held up until Brosius took Byung-Hyun Kim over the left field wall with a man aboard to tie it. The winning run finally crossed the dish in the bottom of the twelfth when Brosius singled, moved to second on a sacrifice bunt and scored on Alfonso Soriano's RBI single. Sterling Hitchcock won it in relief and Albie Lopez was the loser.

Game 6	November 3, 2001
Bank One Ballpark (Arizona)	T: 3:33
Arizona 15 : New York 2	A: 49,707

The Diamondbacks pounded out twenty-two hits and clobbered the Yankees to force a seventh and deciding game. Danny Bautista had three hits and knocked in five runs to pace the Arizona attack. An eight run third inning that featured six singles and two doubles blew the game wide open. Randy Johnson lasted seven innings and was credited with the victory. Andy Pettitte did not survive the third inning and was saddled with the loss.

Game 7	November 4, 2001
Bank One Ballpark (Arizona)	T: 3:20
Arizona 3 : New York 2	A: 49,589

Trailing by one run in the bottom of the ninth of the seventh game of the World Series the Diamondbacks pulled a rabbit of their own out of the hat to claim their first World Championship. Mark Grace led off the fateful frame with a single and Mariano Rivera's wild throw to second on Damian Miller's sacrifice bunt attempt put runners on first and second with nobody out. One out later Tony Womack ripped a double down the right field line to tie it and after Craig Counsell was hit by a pitch, Luis Gonzales blooped a single into short left centerfield to plate the winning run. Randy Johnson won it in relief to post his third victory of the series. Alfonso Soriano homered for New York.

2002

Anaheim Angels (4) - SF Giants (3)
MVP: Troy Glaus

In an All-California World Series that featured four one-run victories, two blowouts and one three-run win, the upstart Angels defeat Barry Bonds and the Giants in seven games.

Game 1	October 19, 2002
Edison Field (Anaheim)	T: 3:43
San Francisco 4 : Anaheim 2	A: 44,603

The Giants out-homered the Angels to capture the opener. Barry Bonds and Reggie Sanders homered in the top of the second and Troy Glaus launched a solo blast in the bottom of the frame for Anaheim. The "power-ball" continued in the sixth when J.T. Snow hit a two-run homer and Glaus answered with a solo round tripper in the home half. Adam Kennedy's RBI single two outs later cut the lead to one but that was as close as the "Halos" would get. Jason Schmidt was the winner. Jarrod Washburn suffered the loss.

Game 2	October 20, 2002
Edison Field (Anaheim)	T: 3:57
Anaheim 11 : San Francisco (10)	A: 44,584

Tim Salmon was 4-for-4 with two homers and four runs batted in as the Angels outslugged the Giants to even the series. Reggie Sanders, David Bell, Jeff Kent and Barry Bonds all homered for San Francisco. Sanders's blast came with two men aboard. Salmon's second homer of the night—a two-run job—came in the eighth and put the Halos ahead to stay. Rookie reliever Francisco Rodriguez pitched three scoreless innings for the win. Troy Percival notched the save. Felix Rodriguez was the loser in relief.

Game 3	October 22, 2002

Pac Bell Park (San Francisco)	T: 3:37
Anaheim 10 : San Francisco 4	A: 42,707

Scott Spezio's two-run triple highlighted a four-run third inning and RBI singles by Adam Kennedy and Bengie Molina highlighted a four run fourth as the Angels trounced the Giants. Ramon Ortiz allowed four runs in five innings of work for the win. Livan Hernandez allowed six run over three and two thirds innings and was charged with the loss. Rich Aurilia and Barry Bonds homered for San Francisco.

Game 4	October 23, 2002
Pac Bell Park (San Francisco)	T: 3:02
San Francisco 4 : Anaheim 3	A: 42,703

A sacrifice fly by David Eckstein and a two-run homer by Troy Glaus gave the Angels an early lead but the Giants tied it in the sixth on RBI singles by Rich Aurilia and Benito Santiago with a sacrifice fly by Jeff Kent mixed in between. David Bell singled home J.T. Snow with what proved to be the winning run in the eighth. Tim Worrell won it in relief and Robb Nen notched the save. Francisco Rodriguez allowed an unearned run and was tagged with the loss.

Game 5	October 24, 2002
Pac Bell Park (San Francisco)	T: 3:53
San Francisco 16 : Anaheim 4	A: 42,713

Jeff Kent belted two two-run homers to pace a sixteen-hit attack as the Giants steamrolled the Angels. Rich Aurilia and Kenny Lofton joined the fireworks with a three-run homer and a two-run triple respectively. Chad Zerbe won it and Jarrod Washburn was the loser.

Game 6	October 26, 2002
Edison Field (Anaheim)	T: 3:48
Anaheim 6 : San Francisco 5	A: 44,506

Shawon Dunston's two-run homer highlighted a three-run fifth inning and the Giants added runs in the sixth and seventh on a solo homer by Barry Bonds and an RBI single by Jeff Kent to take a commanding lead. But Scott Spiezio drilled a three-run homer in the Halo's half of the seventh and the fireworks continued in the eighth when Darin Erstad homered and Troy Glaus's two run double plated what proved to be the winning run. Brandon Donnelly won it in relief and Tim Worrell lost it in the same capacity.

Game 7	October 27, 2002
Edison Field (Anaheim)	T: 3:16
Anaheim 4 : San Francisco 1	A: 44,598

Garrett Anderson's third inning bases loaded triple was the deciding factor as the Angels captured the first World Championship in their history. Rookie right hander John Lackey allowed just one run in five innings of work and was credited with his second win of the series. Troy Percival pitched a scoreless ninth to post his second save of the series. Livan Hernandez allowed all four Angel runs in just two-plus innings and was charged with his second loss of the series.

2003

Florida Marlins (4) – New York Yankees (2)
MVP: Josh Beckett

The Florida Marlins captured the second World Championship in their brief history with a stunning six-game triumph over the heavily favored New York Yankees.

Game 1	October 18, 2003
Yankee Stadium (New York)	T: 3:43
Florida 3 : New York 2	A: 55,769

222

Juan Pierre's bunt single got it started in the top of the first as the speedy centerfielder came around to score the first run of the game on Ivan "Pudge" Rodriguez's sacrifice fly. Derek Jeter's RBI single tied things up in the third but Pierre came through with a two-run single in the fifth to put the Marlins ahead for good. Bernie Williams belted a solo homer in the sixth but that was as close as New York would get. Brad Penny picked up the win and Ugueth Urbina notched the save. David Wells was the loser.

Game 2	October 19, 2003
Yankee Stadium (New York)	T: 2:56
New York 6 : Florida 1	A: 55,750

Hideki Matsui belted a three-run homer in the bottom of the first and the Yankees never looked back. Juan Rivera doubled home a run in the second and Alfonso Soriano hit a two-run homer in the fourth to close out New York's scoring night. Andy Pettitte finished just one out shy of a shutout but did garner the victory. Mark Redman was the loser.

Game 3	October 21, 2003
Pro Player Stadium (Florida)	T: 3:21
New York 6 : Florida 1	A: 65,731

Florida took a first inning lead when Juan Pierre doubled leading off and Miguel Cabrera singled him home. New York tied it in the fourth when Josh Beckett walked Derek Jeter with the bases loaded. Jeter scored the go-ahead run in the eighth on Hideki Matsui's single. The Yankees blew it wide open in the ninth when Aaron Boone hit a solo homer and Bernie Williams launched a three run blast to put it totally out of reach. Mike Mussina fanned nine over seven frames for the victory. Josh Beckett allowed two runs and struck out ten in just over seven innings of work, but was tagged with the loss.

Game 4	October 22, 2003
Pro Player Stadium (Florida)	A: 4:03

Florida 4 : New York 3 (12)	T: 65,934

The Marlins touched up Roger Clemens for three runs in the opening frame with Miguel Cabrera's two-run homer highlighting the outburst. Aaron Boone's sacrifice fly in the second cut the lead in half and the Yankees were down to their last out when Ruben Sierra tripled home two runs to tie it in the ninth. Alex Gonzalez finally settled the issue when he led off the bottom of the twelfth with a homer to win it. Braden Looper picked up the victory. Jeff Weaver was the loser.

Game 5	October 23, 2003
Pro Player Stadium (Florida)	T: 3:05
Florida 6 : New York 4	A: 65,975

Brad Penny notched his second victory of the series and the Marlins moved to within one win of a stunning upset of the Yankees. Penny helped his own cause when he singled home two runs in a three run second inning. Florida added three more runs on an RBI double by Juan Pierre and Mike Lowell's two-run single later in the game. Ugueth Urbina was summoned from the bullpen to record the final two outs of the ballgame. Jose Contreras allowed four runs in three innings of work and was charged with the defeat.

Game 6	October 25, 2003
Yankee Stadium (New York)	T: 2:57
Florida 2 : New York 0	A: 55,773

Josh Beckett, pitching on just three days rest, turned in a five hit, nine-strikeout, complete game victory as the Marlins completed their stunning upset of the Yankees. Luis Castillo plated what proved to be the game winning run with an RBI single to break a scoreless tie in the sixth. Juan Encarnacion's sacrifice fly an inning later scored the final run of the ballgame. Beckett's mound-rival, Andy Pettitte, allowed just two runs in seven innings of work, but was charged with the defeat.

2004

Boston Red Sox (4) - St. Louis Cardinals (0)
MVP: Manny Ramirez

Fresh off the greatest comeback in MLB playoff history[66], the Red Hot Red Sox make quick work of the Cardinals to lift "The Curse of the Babe" and claim their first World Championship in eighty-six years.

Game 1	October 23, 2004
Fenway Park (Boston)	T: 4:00
Boston 11 : St. Louis 9	A: 35,035

David Ortiz belted a three-run homer in a four-run first inning and the Red Sox outlasted the Cardinals in a slugfest that featured twenty runs and twenty-four hits. Back-to-back RBI doubles by Edgar Renteria and Larry Walker—who'd homered earlier—tied the game in the sixth. Boston reclaimed the lead in the seventh on RBI singles by Manny Ramirez and Ortiz. Back came the Cards in the eighth, tying it on another RBI single by Renteria and Boston's fourth and final error of the night. Mark Bellhorn's two-run homer in the bottom of the frame finally settled the issue. Keith Foulke won it in relief and Julian Tavarez lost it in the same capacity.

Game 2	October 24, 2004
Fenway Park (Boston)	T: 3:20
Boston 6 : St. Louis 2	A: 35,001

Mark Bellhorn's two-run double in the bottom of the fourth proved to be the game winning blow as the Red Sox made it two in a row over the Cardinals. Jason Varitek's first inning two-run triple gave Boston a lead they would never surrender. Orlando Cabrera's two run single in the sixth accounted for the Sox final two runs. St.

225

Louis managed an unearned run in the fourth, with Scott Rolen's sacrifice fly in the eighth accounting for their final run. Curt Schilling won it and Matt Morris suffered the loss.

Game 3	October 26, 2004
Busch Stadium (St. Louis)	T: 2:58
Boston 4 : St. Louis 1	A: 52,015

Manny Ramirez belted a solo homer in the top of the first and added an RBI single later in the game as the Red Sox moved to within one win of a clean sweep of St. Louis. Pedro Martinez pitched seven scoreless innings for the victory. Bill Mueller and Trot Nixon had RBI singles as well. The Cardinals tallied their only run of the game when Larry Walker homered in the ninth. Jeff Suppan surrendered all four Boston runs and was saddled with the loss.

Game 4	October 27, 2004
Busch Stadium (St. Louis)	T: 3:14
Boston 3 : St. Louis 0	A: 52,037

Derek Lowe hurled seven scoreless innings, allowing just three hits along the way and Johnny Damon's leadoff homer proved to be all the runs the Red Sox would need to capture their first World Championship in eighty-six years. Trot Nixon's third inning two-run double closed out the scoring for either side. Keith Foulke pitched a scoreless ninth for the save. Jason Marquis allowed all three Boston runs and was charged with the loss.

2005

Chicago White Sox (4) - Houston Astros (0)
MVP: Jermaine Dye

The White Sox capture their first World Championship since 1917 with a four-game sweep of the Houston Astros—a team making the first World Series appearance in its forty-four year history.

Game 1	October 22, 2005
U.S. Cellular Field (Chicago)	T: 3:13
Chicago 5 : Houston 3	A: 42,479

Joe Crede's solo homer in the bottom of the fourth proved to be the game winning blow as the White Sox captured the opener. Jose Contreras went seven innings to garner the win with flame throwing closer Bobby Jenks posting the save. Jermaine Dye also homered for Chicago. Roger Clemens allowed three runs in just two innings of work and was saddled with the loss. Mike Lamb homered for Houston.

Game 2	October 23, 2005
U.S. Cellular Field (Chicago)	T: 3:11
Chicago 7 : Houston 6	A: 41,432

Paul Konerko's grand slam homer in the bottom of the seventh gave the White Sox a two-run lead but Jose Vizcaino's two-out two run ninth inning single tied the game. Scott Podsednik—who had not homered in the regular season—belted a game winning round tripper leading off the bottom of the ninth to win it. Neal Cotts, who faced just one batter, was credited with the win. Brad Lidge, who also faced only one batter—Podsednik—suffered the loss. Morgan Ensberg homered for the Astros.

Game 3	October 25, 2005
Minute Maid Park (Houston)	T: 5:41
Chicago 7 : Houston 5 (14)	A: 42,848

In the longest World Series game ever played the White Sox tallied twice in the fourteenth inning to capture a marathon victory. Chicago took a one-run lead into the eighth inning when Jason Lane's run scoring double tied the game. The Astros squandered several opportunities to win it in extra innings before Chicago's light hitting utility infielder Jeff Blum homered in the fourteenth to break the deadlock. A bases loaded walk to Chris

Widger later in the frame plated the final run of the contest. Damaso Marte was credited with the victory and Ezequiel Astacio took the loss.

Game 4	October 26, 2005
Minute Maid Park (Houston)	T: 3:20
Chicago 1 : Houston 0	A: 42,936

Jermaine Dye singled home the game's only run in the eighth inning as the White Sox completed their sweep of the Astros to capture their first World Championship since 1917. Former Houston farmhand Freddy Garcia pitched seven scoreless innings and picked up the win. Bobby Jenks pitched a scoreless ninth for the save. Brad Lidge suffered the loss—his second of the series.

2006

St. Louis Cardinals (4) - Detroit Tigers (1)
MVP: David Eckstein

The Cardinals and Tigers square off for the third time in World Series history and when it's all said and done St. Louis fans are dancing in the streets.

Game 1	October 21, 2006
Comerica Park (Detroit)	T: 2:54
St. Louis 7 : Detroit 2	A: 42,479

For the first time in World Series history two rookie pitchers locked horns in the opener. Anthony Reyes allowed just two runs over eight-plus innings for the win while highly touted flame thrower Justin Verlander allowed six runs in five-plus innings and suffered the loss. The Cardinals tallied three times in the third and never looked back. Albert Pujols's two-run homer highlighted the attack. Scott Rolen also homered for St. Louis. Craig Monroe homered for Detroit.

Game 2	October 22, 2006
Comerica Park (Detroit)	T: 2:55
Detroit 3 : St. Louis 1	A: 42,533

The Tigers scored all the runs they would need in the very first inning when Craig Monroe belted his second homer of the series and Carlos Guillen drilled an RBI double. Guillen scored Detroit's third and final run of the game in the fifth when Sean Casey singled him home. The Cardinals pushed a run across in the ninth and had the tying and go-ahead runs on base as well, but Doug Jones retired the dangerous Yadier Molina to end it. Kenny Rogers pitched eight scoreless innings for the win. Jones was awarded the save. Jeff Weaver was saddled with the loss.

Game 3	October 24, 2006
Busch Stadium (St. Louis)	T: 3:03
St. Louis 5 : Detroit 0	A: 46,513

Cardinals' ace Chris Carpenter pitched eight innings of scoreless baseball, allowing just three hits and fanning six along the way to tame the Tigers. Jim Edmonds' two-run double in the bottom of the fourth proved to be the game winning blow. Detroit reliever Joel Zumaya's crucial two-run throwing error in the seventh ended any doubt.   Nate Robertson allowed two runs over five innings and was ticketed with the loss.

Game 4	October 26, 2006
Busch Stadium (St. Louis)	T: 3:35
St. Louis 5 : Detroit 4	A: 46,470

A torrid rainstorm postponed the series for a day and made its presence felt when the teams returned to the diamond. David Eckstein's seventh inning drive to centerfield went for a double instead of an out when Curtis Granderson slipped on the still-slick grass. Then Fernando Rodney fielded So Taguchi's sacrifice bunt attempt and threw wildly to first allowing Eckstein to score the tying run. In the eighth inning Eckstein—baseball's smallest player—proved himself a giant when his second double of the game plated Aaron Miles with what proved to be the winning run. Adam Wainwright won it in relief and Joel Zumaya lost it in the same capacity.

Game 5	October 27, 2006
Busch Stadium (St. Louis)	T: 2:56
St. Louis 4 : Detroit 2	A: 46,638

David Eckstein continued his hot hitting with an RBI single in the second that plated the first run of the game. Detroit took its only lead on Sean Casey's two-run homer in the fourth but in the bottom of the frame Justin Verlander committed a throwing error on a sacrifice bunt—the third such error by Tiger pitchers in the series—allowing Yadier Molina to race home from second with the tying run. Eckstein promptly singled home the go-ahead run. Jeff Weaver fanned nine of his former teammates in a masterful eight inning performance. Adam Wainwright pitched a scoreless ninth for the save. Verlander was charged with the loss.

2007

Boston Red Sox (4) - Colorado Rockies (0)
MVP: Mike Lowell

The Boston Red Sox return to the World Series for the second time in three years and vanquish a red-hot Colorado Rockies team—cooled off only by a weeklong layoff—in four games.

Game 1	October 24, 2007
Fenway Park (Boston)	T: 3:30
Boston 13 : Colorado 1	A: 36,733

The Red Sox jumped on the Rockies in the very first inning and never let up. Dustin Pedroia homered leading off, Manny

Ramirez singled home a run and J.D. Drew doubled in two more. The Sox exploded for eight more runs in the fifth with RBI doubles by Kevin Youkillis and David Ortiz highlighting the uprising. Rockies' reliever Ryan Speier added insult to injury when he walked three consecutive batters with the bases loaded. Josh Beckett struck out nine over seven innings to pick up the win. Jeff Francis lasted four rocky innings and was ticketed with the loss.

Game 2	October 25, 2007
Fenway Park (Boston)	T: 2:56
Boston 2 : Colorado 1	A: 36,370

The Rockies took a first inning lead when leadoff hitter Willy Taveras was hit by a pitch and scored on Todd Helton's fielder's choice grounder. The Red Sox tied it in the fourth on Jason Varitek's sacrifice fly and they took the lead for good an inning later on Mike Lowell's run scoring double. Curt Schilling pitched into the sixth inning and was credited with the victory. Hideki Okijima[67] held the Rockies hitless and fanned four before turning the ball over to Jonathan Papelbon who notched the save. Ubaldo Jimenez allowed both Boston runs and was charged with the loss.

Game 3	October 27, 2007
Coors Field (Colorado)	T: 4:19
Boston 13 : Colorado 1	A: 49,983

David Ortiz doubled home a run and Mike Lowell and Daisuke Matsuzaka chipped in with two-run singles as the Red Sox crushed the Rockies. Jacoby Ellsbury's RBI double closed out the inning's fireworks. RBI singles by Brad Hawpe and Yorvit Torrealba in the sixth and a three-run homer by Matt Holliday in the seventh made it a one-run game. But the Red Sox answered with three in the eighth on an RBI double by Dustin Pedroia and a two run two-bagger by Ellsbury. Jason Varitek's ninth inning sacrifice fly plated the final run of the game. Matsuzaka was credited with the victory. Josh Fogg was charged with the loss.

Game 4	October 28, 2007
Coors Field (Colorado)	T: 3:35
Boston 4 : Colorado 3	A: 50,041

The Red Sox took a three-run lead into the eighth inning but Garrett Atkins belted a two-run homer to cut the lead to one, and in the bottom of the ninth, with flame throwing closer Jonathan Papelbon on to close it out, Jamie Carroll missed tying the game with a homer by little more than a foot. Papelbon then fanned pinch-hitter Seth Smith to end it and the Red Sox were champions. John Lester, whose recent battle with cancer had placed his career—if not his very life in jeopardy— lasted 5.1 innings and picked up one of the most inspirational victories in baseball history. Aaron Cook allowed three runs over six innings and was charged with the defeat.

2008

Philadelphia Phillies (4) - TB Rays (1)
MVP: Cole Hamels

The worst-to-first Rays shock the baseball world by capturing the AL pennant only to fall to the Phillies in five games.

Game 1	October 22, 2008
Tropicana Field (Tampa Bay)	T: 3:23
Philadelphia 3 : Tampa Bay 2	A: 40,783

Chase Utley's two-run homer in the top of the first got the Phillies off to a flying start and Carlos Ruiz's fourth inning fielder's choice plated what proved to be the game winning run as Philadelphia captured the opener. Carl Crawford's fourth inning solo homer and Akinori Iwamura's fifth inning RBI double pulled the

Rays to within one run but that was as close as they would get. Cole Hamels pitched seven solid innings and was credited with the victory. Brad Lidge notched the save. Scott Kazmir suffered the loss.

Game 2	October 23, 2008
Tropicana Field (Tampa Bay)	T: 3:05
Tampa Bay 4 : Philadelphia 2	A: 40,843

B.J. Upton's second inning RBI single proved to be the game winning run as the Rays double up on the Phillies to even the series. James Shields, who took a shutout into the sixth before being lifted, was credited with the win. Brett Myers allowed three runs over seven innings and was charged with the loss. Eric Bruntlett homered for Philadelphia.

Game 3	October 25, 2008
Citizens Bank Park (Philadelphia)	T: 3:41
Philadelphia 5 : Tampa Bay 4	A: 45,900

Carlos Ruiz's rollercoaster night ended on a high note as the Phillies edged the Rays. Ruiz homered in the second inning to give Philadelphia an early lead. Chase Utley and Ryan Howard hit back-to-back solo homers in the sixth to make it a three-run ballgame. But Tampa Bay tallied twice in the seventh on a pair of fielder's choice grounders and then tied it in the eighth when B.J. Upton stole third and came home on Ruiz's wild throw. The steady backstop did not miss his chance at redemption when he singled with the bases loaded and nobody out in the bottom of the ninth to end it. J.C. Romero won it in relief and J.P. Howell lost it in the same capacity.

Game 4	October 26, 2008
Citizens Bank Park (Philadelphia)	T: 3:08
Philadelphia 10 : Tampa Bay 2	A: 45,903

The Phillies clobbered the Rays to move to within one win of a World Championship. Ryan Howard had three hits including a two-run homer and a three-run homer. Jason Werth connected for a two-run blast and pitcher Joe Blanton got into the act with a solo round tripper as well. Blanton allowed two runs over six innings and was awarded the victory. Andy Sonnanstine allowed five runs in just four innings of work and was tagged with the loss. Carl Crawford and Eric Hinske homered for Tampa Bay.

Game 5	October 27+29
Citizens Bank Park (Philadelphia)	T: 3:28
Philadelphia 4 : Tampa Bay 3	A: 45,940

In a game that took nearly fifty-hours to complete, the Phillies finished off the Rays and captured the second World Championship in their long history. Shane Victorino's two-run single gave Philadelphia an early lead but RBI singles by Evan Longoria and Carlos Pena tied the game. After a rain delay that lasted nearly two days, play resumed and Jason Werth put Philadelphia back in the driver's seat with an RBI single. The lead was short lived as Rocco Baldelli launched a solo homer in the seventh to restore the deadlock. But in the bottom of the frame Pedro Feliz plated what proved to be the winning run with an RBI single. J.C. Romero picked up his second win of the series in relief. Brad Lidge posted his second save. J.P. Howell suffered his third loss of the series—all in relief.

2009
New York Yankees (4) Philadelphia Phillies (2)
MVP: Hideki Matsui

The Yankees christen the third edition of "The House That Ruth Built" with the 27th World Championship in their spectacular history.

Game 1	October 28, 2009
Yankee Stadium (New York)	T: 3:27
Philadelphia 6 : New York 1	A: 50,207

Phillies' late season acquisition, lefty ace Cliff Lee, scattered six hits and fanned ten en route to a complete game victory over the Yankees in the opener. Chase Utley belted two solo homers off New York's burly southpaw, C.C. Sabathia, to power the Philadelphia attack. Lee lost a shutout bid in the ninth when Mark Teixeira's ground ball out plated Derek Jeter.

Game 2	October 29, 2009
Yankee Stadium (New York)	T: 3:25
New York 3 : Philadelphia 1	A: 50,181

Solo homers by Mark Teixeira and Hideki Matsui powered the Yankees to a series tying victory over the Phillies. Teixeira's blast tied the game in the fourth and Matsui's, later in the inning, put New York ahead for good. Jorge Posada's RBI single in the seventh closed out the scoring. A.J. Burnett allowed just four hits and fanned nine over seven innings of work for the win. Pedro Martinez allowed all three Yankee runs in his six inning stint. Matt Stairs singled home the Phillies only run in the second. Mariano Rivera pitched two scoreless innings and was credited with the save.

Game 3	October 31, 2009
Citizens Bank Park (Philadelphia)	T: 3:25
New York 8 : Philadelphia 5	A: 46,061

New York's veteran southpaw Andy Pettitte posted the fourth win of his World Series career, allowing four runs over six innings of work before calling it a day. Nick Swisher's sixth inning solo homer off A.J. Happ proved to be the game winning blow. Alex Rodriguez also homered for the Yankees. The Phillies' Jayson

Werth belted two homers and Carlos Ruiz launched a round tripper as well in a losing effort.

Game 4	November 1, 2009
Citizens Bank Park (Philadelphia)	T: 3:25
New York 7 : Philadelphia 4	A: 46,415

The Yankees erupted for three runs in the ninth inning to break a 4-4 deadlock and move to within one win of their twenty-seventh World Championship. Alex Rodriguez's RBI double proved to be the game-winning blow. Jorge Posada followed with a two run single and Mariano Rivera slammed the door shut in the bottom of the frame for his second save of the series. Joba Chamberlain won it in relief. Brad Lidge lost it in the same capacity. Pedro Feliz had three hits and knocked in two runs for the Phillies in a losing effort.

Game 5	November 2, 2009
Citizens Bank Park (Philadelphia)	T: 3:26
Philadelphia 8 : New York 6	A: 46,178

The Phillies staved off elimination and sent the series back to New York as Cliff Lee posted his second win of the series. Chase Utley belted two homers including a three-run blast in the bottom of the first to power the Philadelphia attack. Raul Ibanez added a pair of solo round trippers as well. A.J. Burnett lasted just two innings and was saddled with the loss. Ryan Madson notched the save.

Game 6	November 4, 2009
Yankee Stadium (New York)	T: 3:52
New York 7 : Philadelphia 3	A: 50,135

Hideki Matsui tied a single-game World Series record[68] with six runs batted in as the Yankees clinched their twenty-seventh World Championship. Matsui had three hits including a two-run homer. Derek Jeter had three hits and scored two runs. Andy Pettitte posted his second win of the series and the fifth of his career. Pedro Martinez allowed four runs in four innings of work and was charged with the loss. Ryan Howard belted a two run homer for the Phillies.

2010

San Francisco Giants (4) Texas Rangers (1)
MVP: Edgar Renteria

After more than half a century the Giants bring a World Championship to the city by the bay.

Game 1	October 27, 2010
AT&T Park (San Francisco)	T: 3:36
San Francisco 11 : Texas 7	A:43,601

Juan Uribe's three-run homer highlighted a six-run fifth inning that broke a 2-2 tie and the Giants never looked back. San Francisco pounded out fourteen hits on the day, Freddy Sanchez had four—three of them doubles—and also knocked in three runs. Texas ace lefty, Cliff Lee, took a 2-0 lead into the third but the Giants tied things up in that frame and jumped ahead for good in the fifth with Uribe's homer—off reliever Darren O'Day—highlighting the uprising. Giants' ace, Tim Lincecum, was far from dominant, allowing four runs on eight hits and walking two in 5.2 innings of work—good enough for the victory. Lee was saddled with the loss.

Game 2	October 28, 2010
AT&T Park (San Francisco)	T: 3:17
San Francisco 9 : Texas 0	A: 43,622

The Giants erupted for seven runs in the bottom of the eighth inning to turn a nail biter into a blow out and take a commanding 2-0 lead in the series. Edgar Renteria's fifth inning solo homer broke a scoreless tie and the Giants added another run in the seventh on an RBI single by Juan Uribe. Then in the eighth, the flood gates opened, all with two out. A Buster Posey single, four straight walks by the Rangers bullpen, a two-run single by Renteria, a two-run triple by Aaron Rowan and an RBI double by Andres Torres left Texas crushed beneath an avalanche of runs. Matt Cain earned the victory, scattering four hits over 7.2 innings, he walked two and fanned two along the way. C.J. Wilson allowed just two earned runs in six innings of work but was ticketed with the defeat.

Game 3	October 30, 2010
Rangers Ballpark in Arlington	T: 2:51
Texas 4 : San Francisco 2	A: 52,419

Matt Moreland's three-run homer in the bottom of the second inning, off Jonathan Sanchez, proved to be the game-winning blow as Texas climbed back into the series. Josh Hamilton touched up Sanchez for a solo round tripper in the fifth to make it 4-0. The Giants made things interesting when Cody Ross and Andres Torres belted solo homers in the seventh and eighth innings respectively off Rangers starter Colby Lewis. But that was as close as they would get. Neftali Feliz pitched a scoreless ninth to cement the victory and garner the save. Lewis lasted 7.2 innings. He fanned six and walked two en route to the victory. Sanchez was ticketed with the loss.

Game 4	October 31, 2010
Rangers Ballpark in Arlington	T: 3:09
San Francisco 4 : Texas 0	A: 51,920

Rookie southpaw Madison Bumgarner hurled eight innings of scoreless baseball, allowing just three hits and fanning six along the way as the Giants moved to within one victory of their first World Championship since moving to San Francisco. Aubrey Huff's two-run homer in the third inning proved to be the game winning blow. An RBI double by Andres Torres in the seventh, and a solo round tripper by Buster Posey an inning later, closed out the scoring. Giants' closer Brian Wilson pitched a 1-2-3 ninth to notch the save. Rangers' starter Tommy Hunter allowed two runs over four innings of work and was saddled with the loss.

Game 5	November 1, 2010
Rangers Ballpark in Arlington	T: 2:32
San Francisco 3 : Texas 1	A: 52,045

Edgar Renteria's three-run homer in the top of the seventh broke a scoreless tie and proved to be the game-winning blow as the Giants captured their first World Championship since 1954—and the first in their San Francisco history. Nelson Cruz's solo blast in the bottom of the frame was all the offense the Rangers would muster. Tim Lincecum notched his second win of the series. The Giants' ace scattered just three hits over eight innings of work, fanning ten along the way. Cliff Lee was ticketed with his second defeat of the series. The heralded southpaw lasted seven innings, scattering six hits and fanning six as well. Brian Wilson slammed the door shut in the ninth, notching his second save of the series.

2011
St. Louis Cardinals (4) – Texas Rangers (3)
MVP: David Freese

The St. Louis Cardinals fly to the World Series for the eighteenth time in their illustrious history, capturing their eleventh World Championship, and sending the Texas Rangers back to the range as runners up for the second year in a row.

Game 1	October 19, 2011
Busch Stadium III (St. Louis)	T: 3:06
St. Louis 3 : Texas 2	A: 46,406

Lance Berkman singled home two runs in the bottom of the fourth to break a scoreless tie, but Mike Napoli's two-run homer in the fifth tied it. The Cardinals took the lead for good in the sixth when David Freese doubled off Rangers' starter CJ Wilson and scored on Allen Craig's single off Alexi Ogando who came on in relief later in the frame. Chris Carpenter scattered six hits in six innings of work and fanned four en route to the victory. Wilson was ticketed with the loss and Jason Motte pitched a scoreless ninth for the save.

Game 2	October 20, 2011
Busch Stadium III (St. Louis)	T: 3:04
Texas 2 : St. Louis 1	A: 47,288

Allen Craig broke a scoreless tie in the bottom of the seventh with a two-out single that plated David Freese but in the top of the ninth sacrifice flies by Josh Hamilton and Michael Young plated Ian Kinsler and Elvis Andrus respectively, allowing the Rangers to take the lead. Rangers' closer Neftali Feliz walked Yadier Molina leading off the bottom of the ninth, but retired the next three batters, two via the K, to notch the save and even the series. Mike Adams pitched a scoreless seventh and got the win. Jason Motte allowed both Rangers' runs in the ninth and was saddled with the loss. Jaime Garcia pitched seven scoreless innings for the Cardinals but did not figure in the decision.

Game 3	October 22, 2011
Rangers Ballpark in Arlington	T: 4:04
St. Louis 16 : Texas 7	A: 51,462

Albert Pujols became only the third player in World Series history to homer three times in one game and the Cardinals proved themselves rude guests, burying the Rangers beneath an avalanche of runs. Pujols had five hits and knocked in six runs in what will unquestionably go down as the greatest game of his stellar career. After singling his first two times up, the Hall of Fame bound slugger hit a three-run homer, a two-run homer, and a solo homer, in that order. Allen Craig also homered for the Cardinals. Michael Young and Nelson Cruz homered for the Rangers. Lance Lynn won it in relief. Rangers' starter Matt Harrison allowed five runs in 3.2 innings of work and was saddled with the loss.

Game 4	October 23, 2011
Rangers Ballpark in Arlington	T: 3:07
Texas 4 : St. Louis 0	A: 51,539

Derek Holland took a shutout into the ninth inning before surrendering the ball to closer Neftali Feliz who recorded the final two outs for the save as the Rangers evened the series. The Rangers jumped out to an early lead in the very first frame when speedster Elvis Andrus singled and scored on Josh Hamilton's double. Mike Napoli's three-run homer in the sixth proved to be icing on the cake. Holland allowed just two hits, while walking two and fanning seven. Cardinals' starter Edwin Jackson allowed three runs in his 5.1 innings of work and suffered the loss.

Game 5	October 24, 2011
Rangers Ballpark in Arlington	T: 3:31
Texas 4 : St. Louis 2	A: 51,459

Mike Napoli belted a two-run double to break a 2-2 tie in the bottom of the eighth and Neftali Feliz pitched a scoreless ninth to cement the victory and leave the Rangers just one win shy of their first ever world championship. The Cardinals touched up Rangers' starter CJ Wilson for two runs in the second on Yadier Molina's RBI single and a run scoring fielder's choice off the bat of Skip Schumaker. The Rangers tied it on solo homers by Mitch Moreland and Adrian Beltre in the third and sixth innings respectively, setting the stage for Napoli's heroics. Darrin Oliver pitched a scoreless eighth and was credited with the win. Chris Carpenter allowed two runs in seven innings of work but did not figure in the decision. Octavio Dotel was the loser.

Game 6	October 26, 2011

Busch Stadium III (St. Louis)	T: 4:33
St. Louis 10 : Texas 9 (11)	A: 47,325

The Cardinals outlasted the Rangers in a thrilling seesaw battle that saw the emergence of Missouri native David Freese onto the national stage. With two on and two out in the bottom of the ninth and the Cardinals down by two runs, Freese belted a two-strike, two run double to tie the game. The rollercoaster ride continued in the tenth when Josh Hamilton belted a two-run homer that seemed to cinch the Rangers' first World Championship. But in the bottom of the frame an RBI fielder's choice grounder off the bat of Ryan Theriot and a two-out running scoring infield single by Lance Berkman tied the game. Jake Westbrook held the Rangers scoreless in the eleventh and Freese entered Cardinal immortality in the bottom of the frame when he greeted Rangers' reliever Mark Lowe with a solo homer to force a seventh and deciding game. Westbrook was credited with the win and Lowe took the loss.

Game 7	October 27, 2011
Busch Stadium III (St. Louis)	T: 3:17
St. Louis 6 : Texas 2	A: 47,399

The Rangers tallied twice in the opening frame on RBI doubles by Michael Young and Josh Hamilton but David Freese's World Series heroics continued when he doubled home two runs in the bottom of the frame to tie it. Allen Craig's solo homer two innings later proved to be the game deciding blow. The Cardinals added two runs in the fifth on the strength of three walks and two hit batters and nary a base hit. An RBI single by Yadier Molina plated Lance Berkman with the game's final run in the seventh. Chris Carpenter pitched six plus innings, allowing both Rangers' runs on six hits for his second victory of the series. Rangers' starter Matt Harrison surrendered three runs in four innings of work and was saddled with the defeat.

2012

San Francisco Giants (4) – Detroit Tigers (0)
MVP: Pedro Sandoval

The San Francisco Giants capture their second World Championship in three seasons, taming the Detroit Tigers in four straight.

Game 1	October 24, 2012
AT&T Park (San Francisco)	T: 3:26
San Francisco 8 : Detroit 3	A: 42,855

Pablo Sandoval became the fourth player in World Series history to homer three times in one game as the Giants captured the opener. Sandoval began the fireworks early, homering off Tigers' starter Justin Verlander in his first two plate appearances and then taking reliever Al Albuquerque over the wall in his next at-bat. The slugging third baseman had the chance to become the first player ever in World Series history to hit four homers in one game, but had to settle for a single in his final trip to the dish. Barry Zito pitched into the sixth inning and was credited with the victory. Verlander was tagged with the defeat. Jhonny Peralta homered for Detroit.

Game 2	October 25, 2012
AT&T Park (San Francisco)	T: 3:05
San Francisco 2 : Detroit 0	A: 42,982

Madison Bumgarner pitched seven scoreless innings, allowing just two hits and striking out seven as the Giants made it two-straight over the Tigers. The game remained scoreless until the seventh when the Giants loaded the bases with nobody out. Drew Smyly came on in relief of starter Doug Fister and induced Brandon Crawford to bounce into a 4-6-3 double play. But Hunter Pence crossed the dish, breaking the deadlock. Then in the eighth, Pence's sacrifice fly off Octavio Dotel plated Angel Pagan with the game's final run. Sergio Romo pitched a scoreless ninth and was credited with the save.

Game 3	October 27, 2012
Comerica Park (Detroit)	T: 3:25
San Francisco 2 : Detroit 0	A: 42,262

Ryan Vogelsong and Tim Lincecum held the Tigers scoreless over the first eight frames and Sergio Romo pitched a scoreless ninth as the Giants moved to within one victory of their second World Championship in three seasons, blanking the Tigers 2-0 for the second time in as many contests. The Giants got all the runs they would need in the second inning when Gregor Blanco tripled home Hunter Pence who'd walked leading off. Blanco crossed the dish later in the frame on a base hit by Brandon Crawford. Vogelson pitched into the sixth and was credited with the victory. Anabel Sanchez was ticketed with the loss.

Game 4	October 28, 2012
Comerica Park (Detroit)	T: 3:34
San Francisco 4 : Detroit 3 (10 inn)	A: 42,152

Max Scherzer surrendered a run in the second when Hunter Pence doubled and Brandon Belt tripled him home. The Tigers jumped in front when Miguel Cabrera belted a two-run homer off Matt Cain in the third. Buster Posey's two-run homer off Scherzer in the sixth put the Giants back in the driver's seat but Delmon Young's solo homer off Cain in the bottom of the frame tied the game. The score remained knotted until the tenth when Ryan Theriot singled off Phil Coke leading off. Theriot was sacrificed to second by Brandon Crawford and scored what proved to be the championship clinching run on a base hit by Marco Scutaro. Sergio Romo struck out the side in the bottom of the tenth and the Giants were World Champs. Santiago Casilla pitched one-third of an inning and was awarded the victory. Coke took the loss.

2013

Boston Red Sox (4) – St. Louis Cardinals (2)
MVP: David Ortiz

After an eighty-six year championship drought, the Red Sox capture their third Fall Classic in ten years. Boston's beloved slugger, David "Big Papi" Ortiz, leads the way with an historic World Series performance that completes an already legendary post season legacy.

Game 1:	October 23, 2013
Fenway Park (Boston)	T: 3:17
Boston 8 : St. Louis 1	A: 38,345

Mike Napoli doubled home three runs in the first inning off Cardinals' ace Adam Wainwright and the Red Sox never looked back. David Ortiz homered and knocked in three runs. Jon Lester scattered five hits and fanned eight in 7.2 innings of work to earn the victory. Matt Holliday homered for the Cardinals. Wainwright allowed five runs in five innings of work and was ticketed with the loss.

Game 2:	October 24, 2013
Fenway Park (Boston)	T: 3:05
St. Louis 4 : Boston 2	A: 38,436

The Cardinals evened the series, outlasting the Red Sox in a seesaw battle that sent the Beantown faithful home in silence. Yadier Molina's RBI fielder's choice broke a scoreless tie in the fourth but the Red Sox jumped ahead in the sixth when David Ortiz belted a two-run homer off Cardinals' starter Michael Wacha. The Cardinals jumped back in front in the seventh and entered the World Series record books in the process, as Matt Carpenter's sacrifice fly plated both Dave Kozma and John Jay. Carlos Beltran's RBI single later in the frame closed out the night's scoring. Wacha lasted six innings and was credited with the victory.

245

Red Sox starter John Lackey left with the lead but was ticketed with the loss. Trevor Rosenthal notched the save.

Game 3:	October 26, 2013
Busch Stadium III (St. Louis)	T: 3:54
St. Louis 5 : Boston 4	A: 47,432

First inning RBI singles by Matt Holliday and Yadier Molina gave the Cardinals the early lead. The Red Sox tied it on a fielder's choice grounder by Mike Carp in the fifth and an RBI single by Daniel Nava an inning later. Holliday struck again in the seventh when he doubled home two runs to put the Cardinals back in front. The Red Sox came right back in the eight, tying it on Nava's fielder's choice grounder and an RBI single by Xander Bogaerts. The game came to a raucous close in the ninth when, with runners on second and third and one out, John Jay smacked a grounder back up the middle that Dustin Pedroia backhanded and threw home to get Molina at the plate. Catcher Jarred Saltalamachia then fired to third base to throw out Allen Craig. The ball got past Will Middlebrooks and Craig took off for home but was thrown out. Umpire Jim Joyce ruled that Middlebrooks tripped Craig, who was then ruled safe at home and the game was over.

Game 4:	October 27, 2013
Busch Stadium (St. Louis)	T: 3:34
Boston 4 : St. Louis 2	A: 47,469

Carlos Beltran's RBI single in the bottom of the third gave the Cardinals the early lead but Steven Drew's sacrifice fly in the fifth tied it and Johnny Gomes's three-run homer off Seth Maness an inning later put the game out of reach. The Cardinals managed a run in the seventh on an RBI single by Matt Carpenter but that was as close as they would get. Felix Doubront won it in relief and Kenji Uehara notched the save. Lance Lynn lasted into the sixth, was charged with three runs and was ticketed with the defeat.

Game 5:	October 28, 2013

Busch Stadium (St. Louis)	T: 2:52
Boston 3 : St. Louis 1	A: 47,436

Adam Wainwright and Jon Lester locked horns in a pitcher's duel but when the dust settled the Red Sox were victors. Back-to-back doubles by Dustin Pedroia and David Ortiz in the opening frame gave Boston the early lead. The Cardinals tied it in the fourth on a solo homer by Matt Holliday. Then in the seventh an RBI double by David Ross and an RBI single by Jacoby Ellsbury plated what proved to be the game's final runs. Lester scattered four hits and fanned seven in his 7.2 innings of work. Koji Uehara slammed the door shut the rest of the way and was credited with the save. Wainwright went seven and fanned ten along the way in a losing effort.

Game 6:	October 30, 2013
Fenway Park (Boston)	T: 38,447
Boston 6 : St. Louis 1	A: 3:15

Shane Victorino's three-run double in the third broke a scoreless tie and the Red Sox tacked on three more an inning later to clinch the eighth World Championship in their history. Steven Drew homered and Mike Napoli and Victorino had RBI singles in the fourth inning uprising that erased any doubt. Carlos Beltran's RBI single in the seventh accounted for the Cardinals' only run. John Lackey scattered nine hits in 6.2 innings of work for the win. Michael Wacha surrendered all six Red Sox runs in a rocky 3.2 inning outing that garnered him the loss.

2014

SF Giants (4) – KC Royals (3)
MVP: Madison Bumgarner

Madison Bumgarner's historic performance staves off the Kansas City Royals whose Cinderella season comes to an end with the tying run on third in the bottom of the ninth of the seventh game.

Game 1:	October 21, 2014
Kauffman Stadium (Kansas City)	T: 3:32
San Francisco 7 : Kansas City 1	A: 40,459

Pablo Sandoval doubled home the game's first run in the opening frame and Hunter Pence followed with a two-run homer that proved to be all the offense the Giants would need. Madison Bumgarner pitched six shutout innings, allowing just three hits en route to the victory. James Shields lasted three innings, surrendered five runs and was saddled with the loss. Salvador Perez's seventh inning solo homer accounted for the Royals only run.

Game 2:	October 22, 2014
Kaufmann Stadium (Kansas City)	T: 3:24
Kansas City 7 : San Francisco 2	A: 40,446

The Royals erupted for five runs in the sixth inning, breaking a 2-2 tie and never looking back. A two-run double by Salvador Perez and a two-run homer by Omar Infante highlighted the uprising. Billy Butler had two RBI singles on the night and Alcides Escobar chipped in with a run-scoring double as well. Kelvin Herrera won it in relief. Gregor Blanco homered leading off the game for the Giants. Brandon Belt's RBI double accounted for their only other run. Jake Peavy allowed four runs in five plus innings of work and was ticketed with the defeat.

Game 3:	October 24, 2014
AT&T Park (San Francisco)	T: 3:15
Kansas City 3 : San Francisco 2	A: 43,020

Lorenzo Cain's first inning fielder's choice RBI grounder gave the Royals the early lead and they tacked on two more in the sixth when Alex Gordon doubled home Alcides Escobar and then scored what proved to be the game-winning run on a base-hit by Eric Hosmer. The Giants tallied twice in the bottom of the frame on an RBI double by Mike Morse and Buster Posey's run scoring fielder's choice but that was as close as they would get. The Royals' lights-out bullpen slammed the door shut the rest of the way to cement the victory. Jeremy Guthrie pitched into the sixth inning and was credited with the win. Wade Davis pitched a scoreless ninth and was awarded the save. Tim Hudson allowed three runs in 5.2 innings of work and suffered the loss.

Game 4:	October 25, 2014
AT&T Park (San Francisco)	T: 4:00
San Francisco 11 : Kansas City 4	A: 43,066

Despite the lopsided final score, the win did not come easy for the Giants. The Royals erupted for four runs in the third inning but the Giants chipped away, tying it in the fifth, adding three more in the sixth and ending any doubt with a four-run seventh. Hunter Pence had three hits and knocked in three runs to pace the sixteen-hit attack. Yesmeiro Petit, pitched three scoreless innings in relief and got the win. Brandon Finnegan allowed five runs in just one inning of relief and was tagged with the loss. Eric Hosmer and Salvador Perez each had three hits for the Royals who pounded out sixteen hits on the night.

Game 5:	October 26, 2014
AT&T Park (San Francisco)	T: 3:09
San Francisco 5 : Kansas City 0	A: 43,087

Madison Bumgarner turned in yet another post season gem, scattering four hits en route to a complete game shutout victory. The otherworldly southpaw, struck out eight and did not walk a batter. The Giants got all the runs they would need in the second when Hunter Pence singled and later crossed the dish on Brandon Crawford's RBI fielder's choice. Crawford singled home a run an inning later. The Giants blew it open in the eighth when Juan Perez doubled home two runs and then scored on yet another

RBI single from Crawford to close out the scoring. James Shields allowed just two runs in six innings of work but was ticketed with the loss.

Game 6:	October 28, 2014
Kaufmann Stadium (Kansas City)	T: 3:21
Kansas City 10 : San Francisco 0	A: 40,372

The Royals forced a seventh and deciding game, erupting for seven runs in the second inning and pounding out fifteen hits on the night. Mike Moustakas, Eric Hosmer and Billy Butler all had RBI doubles in the game-deciding frame. Lorenzo Cain chipped in with a two-run single as well. Cain had three hits to pace the Royals attack. Yordano Ventura allowed just three hits in his seven innings of work. The rookie right hander fanned four and walked five—good enough for the victory. Giants' starter Jake Peavy did not survive the second inning. The veteran righty, allowed five runs and was tagged with the defeat.

Game 7:	October 29, 2014
Kaufmann Stadium (Kansas City)	T: 3:10
San Francisco 3 : Kansas City 2	A: 40,345

The Giants touched up Royals' starter Jeremy Guthrie for two runs on sacrifice flies by Mike Morse and Brandon Crawford in the second inning. But the Royals came right back in the bottom of the frame, touching up Tim Hudson for two runs to tie it when Alex Gordon doubled home Billy Butler and then scored on a sacrifice fly by Omar Infante. The Giants plated what proved to be the winning run in the fourth when Guthrie surrendered an RBI single to Morse. Madison Bumgarner came on in relief in the fifth and slammed the door shut the rest of the way, allowing just two hits in five innings of work. Things got interesting in the ninth when Gregor Blanco's error put the tying run on third base with two outs, but Bumgarner induced Salvador Perez to pop out meekly to end it. Jeremy Affeldt pitched 2.1 scoreless innings and was credited with the victory. Bumgarner was awarded the save. Guthrie took the loss.

2015

Kansas City Royals (4) – New York Mets (1)
MVP: Salvador Perez

The Royals return to the Fall Classic for the second consecutive year and gain redemption, demolishing the Mets in five games and capturing their first World Championship in thirty years.

Game 1:	October 27, 2015
Kaufmann Stadium (Kansas City)	T: 5:09
Kansas City 5 : New York 4 (14)	A: 40,320

The Royals captured the opener in signature comeback fashion. Trailing by a run in the bottom of the ninth, Alex Gordon belted a solo homer off Mets' closer, Jeurys Familia. The score remained tied until the fourteenth when Alcides Escobar reached on an error and moved to third on a base hit by Ben Zobrist. After Lorenzo Cain was intentionally walked to load the bases, Eric Hosmer delivered a sacrifice fly, plating Escobar to win it. Chris Young pitched three scoreless inning in relief and was credited with the victory. Bartolo Colon suffered the loss despite not allowing an earned run in three innings of work. Escobar homered for the Royals. Curtis Granderson homered for the Mets.

Game 2:	October 28, 2015
Kaufmann Stadium (Kansas City)	T: 2:54
Kansas City 7 : New York 1	A: 40,410

The Mets plated their only run of the game in the fourth when Lucas Duda singled home Daniel Murphy, but it was all Royals from there. Kansas City tallied four times in the sixth on the strength of RBI singles by Alcides Escobar and Mike Moustakas and a two-run single by Eric Hosmer. They added three more in the eighth to end any doubt. An RBI double by Alex Gordon, a sacrifice fly by Paulo Orlando, and an RBI triple by Escobar accounted for the additional onslaught. Johnny Cueto went the distance for the

Royals, allowing just two hits along the way Jacob DeGrom allowed four runs in five innings of work and was ticketed with the loss.

Game 3	October 30, 2015
Citi Field (New York)	T: 3:22
New York 9 : Kansas City 3	A: 44,781

David Wright and Curtis Granderson each belted two-run homers and the Mets banged out twelve hits on the night to climb back into the series. A seesaw battle turned into a route when the Mets touched up reliever Franklin Morales for four runs in the sixth. Wright added a two run single to highlight the uprising. Noah Syndergaard allowed all three Royals' runs in six innings of work and was credited with the victory. Yordano Ventura started for the Royals but did not survive the fourth inning. He was charged with five runs and ticketed with the loss. Raul Mondesi, Jr. became the first player to make his Major League debut in a World Series game. He struck out as a pinch hitter leading off the fifth inning.

Game 4	October 31, 2015
Citi Field (New York)	T: 3:29
Kansas City 5: New York 3	A: 44,815

Trailing by one run in the eighth inning, the Royals turned two walks, a run scoring error, and rbi singles by Matt Moustakas and Salvador Perez into a three-run rally that put them in the driver's seat for good. Lights out closer Wade Davis retired the side in the bottom of the frame but things got interesting in the Mets' final at-bat. After striking out David Wright leading off, Davis surrendered singles to David Murphy and Yoenis Cespedes to put runners on the corners for Lucas Duda. Duda hit a soft line drive to Moustakas at third. Cespedes inexplicably took off for second and was easily doubled off to end the game. Ryan Madson pitched one scoreless inning in relief and was credited with the win. Davis notched the save. Taylor Clippard allowed two runs and lasted just one third on an inning to garner the defeat. Michael Conforto belted two solo homeruns for the Mets.

Game 5	Nov 1, 2015
Citi Field (New York)	T: 4:15
Kansas City 7 : New York 2	A: 44,859

Mets' ace Matt Harvey took a shutout into the ninth inning, but once again late inning Royals' magic stole the show. Trailing by two, Lorenzo Cain walked to open the frame and after swiping second base, came home on a double off the bat of Eric Hosmer. Hosmer scored to tie the game on a fielder's choice grounder by Salvador Perez. The game remained tied until the twelfth when the Royals erupted for five runs. Cain's three-run double highlighted the uprising. Wade Davis struck out the side in the bottom of the frame and the Royals were World Champions. Luke Hochevar pitched two scoreless innings and was credited with the victory. Addison Lee was charged with all five twelfth inning runs and was saddled with the defeat.

2016

Chicago Cubs (4) – Cleveland Indians (3)
MVP: Ben Zobrist

The lame walk, the blind see—and the Cubs are World Champs for the first time in over a century.

Game 1:	October 25, 2016
Progressive Field, (Cleveland)	T: 3:37
Cleveland 6 : Chicago 0	A: 38,091

Roberto Perez belted a solo homer in the fourth and a three run blast in the eighth as the Indians scalped the Cubs in the opener. The Tribe touched up Cubs starter Jon Lester for a pair of runs in the first inning on the strength of an RBI single by Jose Ramirez, and a hit batsman (Brandon Guyer) with the bases loaded. Corey Kluber fanned nine in six innings of work and was awarded the victory.

Game 2:	October 26, 2016
Progressive Field, (Cleveland)	T: 4:04
Chicago 5 : Cleveland 1	A: 38,172

253

Anthony Rizzo doubled home a run in the first, and scored what proved to be the winning run on Kyle Schwarber's RBI single in the third. The Cubs broke it open in the fifth on the strength of an RBI triple by Ben Zobrist, an RBI single by Schwarber and Addison Russell's bases loaded walk. Cleveland managed a run in the sixth when Jason Kipnis crossed the dish on Jake Arietta's wild pitch. Arietta went 5.2 innings and was credited with the win. He fanned six and walked four. Trevor Bauer allowed two runs in 3.2 innings of work and was tagged with the loss.

Game 3:	October 28, 2016
Wrigley Field (Chicago)	T: 3:33
Cleveland 1 : Chicago 0	A: 41,703

Coco Crisp's seventh inning pinch hit single plated pinch-runner Michael Martinez with what proved to be the game's only run as Cleveland took a 2-1 lead in the series. Kyle Hendricks struck out six in 4.2 innings of work but was not involved in the decision. Andrew Miller pitched 1.1 innings of scoreless relief and was credited with the victory. Cody Allen notched 1.1 scoreless innings and was credited with the save. Carl Williams suffered the loss.

Game 4:	October 29, 2016
Wrigley Field (Chicago)	T: 3:16
Cleveland 7 : Chicago 2	A: 41,706

Anthony Rizzo's first inning RBI single gave the Cubs the early lead but it was all Indians from there. The Tribe took the lead in the second on a solo homer by Carlos Santana and an RBI single by Corey Kluber. Francisco Lindor plated Jason Kipnis in the third with what proved to be the winning run. Lonnie Chisenhall added a sacrifice fly in the sixth and Kipnis busted it wide open with a three-run homer in the seventh. Kluber scattered five hits and fanned six in six innings of work. Good enough for the victory. John Lackey allowed three runs in five innings of work and was ticketed with the loss. Dexter Fowler belted a solo homer for the Cubs.

Game 5:	October 30, 2016
Wrigley Field (Chicago)	T: 3:27
Chicago 3 : Cleveland 2	A: 41,711

The Cubs scored all three of their runs in the fourth inning and fended off the Indians to send the series back to Cleveland. Jose Ramirez belted a solo homer in the second inning to break a scoreless tie but Kris Bryant's solo homer, an RBI single by Addison Russell and David Ross's sacrifice fly proved to be all Cubs would need. Francisco Lindor's RBI single in the sixth was as close as the Tribe would get. Jon Lester went six innings, scattering four hits and fanning five for the win. Aroldis Chapman shut the door over the final 2.2 frames and was awarded the save, fanning four along the way. Trevor Bauer allowed all three Chicago runs in four innings of work and was saddled with the loss.

Game 6:	Nov 1, 2016
Progressive Field (Cleveland)	T: 3:29
Chicago 9 : Cleveland 3	A: 38,116

Kris Bryant belted a first inning solo homer to highlight a three-run uprising and Addison Russell belted a grand slam in the third as the Cubs mauled the Indians to force a seventh and deciding game. Russell belted a two-run double earlier in the contest and finished the night with six RBI. Anthony Rizzo chipped in with a two-run homer as well. Jake Arietta fanned nine in 5.2 innings of work en route to the victory. Mike Napoli and Roberto Hernandez had RBI singles, and Jason Kipnis belted a solo homer, accounting for Cleveland's runs. Josh Tomlin allowed six runs in 2.1 innings of work and was saddled with the defeat.

Game 7:	Nov 2, 2016
Progressive Field (Cleveland)	T: 4: 28
Chicago 8 : Cleveland 7 (10)	A: 38,104

In one of the most exciting seventh games in the Fall Classic's storied history, the Cubs fended off a late-innings charge by the Indians and proclaimed themselves World Champions for the first time in 108 years. Dexter Fowler led off the game with a homerun but Carlos Santana's RBI single in the third tied it. The Cubs jumped back in front in the fourth on RBI singles by Addison Russell and Willson Contreras. In the fifth, Javier Baez belted a solo homer and Anthony Rizzo singled home a run putting the Cubs in the driver's seat. But the Indians would not go quietly scoring two runs on a wild pitch by Jon Lester that saw Jason Kipnis score from second base. David Ross's solo homer an inning later seemed to quell the Indians hopes but in the eighth, Brandon Guyer belted an RBI double and Rajai Davis a game-tying two-run homer. In the tenth, Ben Zobrist's RBI double broke the tie, and Miguel Montero followed with an RBI single. The Indians pulled themselves off the deck just one more time in the bottom of the frame. After two were out, Brandon

Guyer walked, stole second and scored on Davis's RBI single, but Davis was left stranded at first as pinch-hitter Michael Martinez grounded out to end it. Aroldis Chapman won it in relief and Mike Montgomery, who retired Martinez for the final out, garnered the save. Bryan Shaw was the loser.

2017

Houston Astros (4) – LA Dodgers (3)
MVP: George Springer

In a thrilling seven-game series, Houston captures its first World Series title and the Dodgers championship drought reaches thirty years.

Game 1:	October 24, 2017
Dodger Stadium, (Los Angeles)	T: 2:28
Los Angeles 3: Houston 1	A: 54,253

Chris Taylor led off the bottom of the first with a solo homer off Astros' ace Dallas Keutchel but Alex Bregman's solo bomb in the fourth off Dodgers' ace Clayton Kershaw tied it. The matter was settled in the sixth when with two out, Taylor walked and Justin Turner launched a two-run roundtripper that closed out the night's scoring. Kershaw was magnificent, fanning eleven in seven innings of work without walking a batter. Brandon Morrow pitched a scoreless eighth and Kenley Jansen slammed the door shut in the ninth for the save. Keutchel allowed all three Dodger runs and was ticketed with the loss.

Game 2:	October 25, 2017
Dodger Stadium (Los Angeles)	T: 4:19
Houston 7: Los Angeles 6	A: 54,293

The Astros evened the series, vanquishing the Dodgers in an eleven inning seesaw battle for the ages. Alex Bregman's rbi single off Rich Hill in the third broke a scoreless tie but Joc Pedersen homered off Justin Verlander in the fifth to tie it and an inning later a two-run homer off the bat of Corey Seager put the Dodgers in the driver's seat. The Astros cut the lead to one in the eighth, touching up closer Kenley Jansen for a run on an rbi single by Carlos Correa. Then in the ninth, Marwin Gonzalez belted a solo homer leading off and the game was tied. The Astros grabbed the lead in the tenth when reliever Josh Fields surrendered back-to-back solo homers to Jose Altuve and Correa. The Dodgers answered the bell in the bottom of the frame when Yasiel Puig homered leading off and two outs later Logan Forsythe walked, moved to second on a wild pitch and scored on Kike Hernandez's clutch base hit to tie it. But in the eleventh George Springer belted a two-run homer and the Dodgers came up a buck short in the bottom of the frame on the strength of Charlie Culberson's solo homerun. Chris Devenski won it in relief and Brandon McCarthy was the loser.

Game 3:	October 27, 2017
Minute Maid Park (Houston)	T: 3:46
Houston 5 : Los Angeles 3	A: 43,282

The Astros punished Yu Darvish for four runs on five hits in the second inning and never looked back. Yuli Gurriel got it started with a solo homer leading off and Marwin Gonzalez and Brian McCann added rbi singles with Alex Bregman's rbi sac fly closing out the frame's fireworks. Things got interesting in the third when starter Lance McCullers walked the first three Dodger batters but Corey Seager bounced into a run scoring 3-6-1 double play. The Astros were gifted their final run of the game in the fifth on a throwing error by reliever Tony Watson. The Dodgers scored their final two runs of the contest in the fifth on a fielder's choice rbi grounder by Yasiel Puig and a wild pitch by reliever Brad Peacock that plated Justin Turner. McCullers was credited with the win and Peacock notched the save. Darvish was the loser.

Game 4:	October 28, 2017
Minute Maid Park (Houston)	T: 3:06
Los Angeles 6 : Houston 2	A: 43,322

George Springer's solo homer broke a scoreless tie in the bottom of the sixth but in the top of the seventh, Cody Bellinger doubled and Logan Forsythe singled him home to tie it. The score remained deadlocked until the ninth when the Dodgers erupted for five runs. Bellinger's second double of the game plated Corey Seager and after Austin Barnes's sacrifice fly plated Charlie Culberson, Joc Pedersen belted a three-run homer. Alex Bregman's solo homer in the bottom of the frame accounted for the Astros final run. Tony Watson won it in relief and Ken Giles was ticketed with the loss.

Game 5:	October 29, 2017
Minute Maid Park (Houston)	T: 5:17

Houston 13 : Los Angeles 12   A: 43,300

In yet another see-saw battle for the ages, the Astros rallied twice and ultimately fended off the relentless Dodgers to take a 3-2 series lead. Logan Forsythe's two-run single highlighted a three-run first inning, and in the fourth, Forsythe doubled and scored on Austin Barnes' single giving Dodgers ace Clayton Kershaw a four-run cushion. But in the bottom of that frame a Carlos Correa rbi double and Yuli Gurriel's three-run homer tied the game. Then in the fifth, Cody Bellinger's three-run homer gave Kershaw a three-run lead but Kershaw walked two batters and Jose Altuve belted a three-run homer off Kenta Maeda to tie it up all over again. The Dodgers took the lead in the seventh when Bellinger tripled Kike Hernandez home. But the Astros charged right back, touching up Brandon Morrow for four runs on the strength of a solo homer by George Springer, an rbi double by Altuve and a two-run homer by Correa. Corey Seager doubled home a run in the top of the eighth but Brian McCann belted a solo homer in the bottom of the frame and the Dodgers found themselves down three runs going into the ninth. Facing reliever, Chris Devinski, Yasiel Puig belted a two-run homer and Chris Taylor touched Devisnki up for a clutch two-out rbi single to tie the game. The Astros won it in the tenth when Kenley Jansen hit McCann, walked Springer and surrendered an rbi single to Alex Bregman to end it. Joe Musgrove pitched a scoreless tenth for the Astros and was credited with the victory.

Game 6:   October 31, 2017
Dodger Stadium (Los Angeles)   T: 3:22
Los Angeles 3 : Houston 1   A: 54,128

George Springer belted a solo homer off Rich Hill in the third to break a scoreless tie but the Dodgers took the lead in the sixth on an rbi double by Chris Taylor and a sacrifice fly off the bat of Corey Seager. Joc Pedersen belted a solo homer off Joe Musgrove in the seventh to close out the scoring and force a seventh and deciding game. Tony Watson retired just one batter yet was credited with the win. Kenley Jansen pitched a 1-2-3 ninth, fanning two, for the save. Justin Verlander allowed two runs in six innings of work and was ticketed with the loss.

Game 7:   November 1, 2017
Dodger Stadium (Los Angeles)   T: 3:37
Houston 5: Los Angeles 1   A: 54,124

For the second time in the series, the Astros demolished Yu Darvish, pulverizing the Dodgers high-priced late season acquisition to clinch the first World Championship in their long history. George Springer doubled off the wall leading off the game as the Astros tallied twice in the opening frame. Then in the second Darvish walked Brian McCann leading off and surrendered a booming double to Marwin Gonzalez. After Lance McCullers' rbi fielder's choice grounder, Springer struck again, touching up Darvish for a two-run homer. The Dodgers managed their only run in the sixth on Andre Ethier's pinch-hit rbi single. Charlie Morton got the win in relief of McCullers. Darvish did not survive the second inning, surrendering all five Houston runs in the crushing defeat.

2018
Boston Red Sox (4) – LA Dodgers (1)
MVP: Steve Pearce

Curse of the... WHO?! The Boston Red Sox post a franchise record 108 wins en route to their fourth World Championship in fourteen years, steamrolling the Los Angeles Dodgers in five games and cementing their place in baseball history as one of the greatest teams of all time.

Game 1:	October 23, 2018
Fenway Park (Boston)	T: 3:52
Boston 8: Los Angeles 4	A: 38,454

Eduardo Nunez's pinch hit three run homer in the seventh put what was a nip and tuck battle out of reach as Boston captured the opener. The Red Sox wasted little time, tallying twice in the first on rbi singles by Andrew Benintendi and J.D. Martinez. Matt Kemp's solo homer in the second and an rbi single by Manny Machado in the third tied the game. Martinez doubled home another run in the bottom of the frame but Machado's rbi fielder's choice grounder in the fifth tied it up again. The Red Sox took the lead for good in their half of the fifth on an rbi fielder's choice grounder by Xander Bogaerts and Rafael Devers' rbi single. Machado's sac fly in the seventh cut the lead to one but Nunez's blast off reliever Alex Wood put the game out of reach. Benintendi had four hits and scored three runs. Matt Barnes got the win in relief of Chris Sale and Clayton Kershaw was tagged with the loss.

Game 2:   October 24, 2018
Fenway Park (Boston)   T: 3:12
Boston 4: Los Angeles 2   A: 38,644

Ian Kinsler singled home Xander Bogaerts in the second to give the Red Sox the early lead but the Dodgers gained their first lead of the series in the fourth, tallying twice on an rbi sacrifice fly by Matt Kemp and Yasiel Puig's rbi single. The Red Sox scored what proved to be the game deciding runs in the fifth when Dodgers reliever Ryan Madson walked Steve Pearce with the bases loaded and then surrendered a two-run single to J.D. Martinez. Los Angeles could not manage a single base runner over the final five and a third frames as starter David Price and relievers Joe Kelly, Nathan Eovaldi and Craig Kimbrel retired the final sixteen batters. Price went six innings and got the win, Kimbrel was credited with the save and Dodgers starter Hyun-Jin Ryu was tagged with the loss.

Game 3:   October 26, 2018
Dodger Stadium (Los Angeles)   T: 7:20
Boston 2: Los Angeles 1 (18)   A: 53,114

Max Muncy's leadoff homer in the bottom of the eighteenth inning ended the longest game in World Series history as the Dodgers beat the Red Sox to climb back into the series. Joc Pedersen's third inning solo homer staked rookie ace Walker Buehler to a 1-0 lead but Dodger skipper ₇₂Dave Roberts elected to lift Buehler in the eighth, (even though the flame throwing righty had retired the side in order in the seventh--fanning Mitch Moreland and J.D. Martinez--the last two batters he'd faced) asking closer Kenley Jansen to turn in a two-inning save. Jansen retired the first two batters he faced but then surrendered a game-tying homer to Jackie Bradley, Jr., and the stage was set for the marathon of historic proportion that followed. In the thirteenth, the Red Sox took the lead when Dodger reliever Scott Alexander walked Brock Holt leading off, and later in the inning Eduardo Nunez's infield single and a throwing error by Alexander allowed Holt to cross the dish with the go ahead run. The Dodgers tied it in the bottom of the frame when Muncy led off with a walk, advanced to second when Nunez made a sensational diving catch into the seats along the third base line, and scored on an infield single by Yasiel Puig and a throwing error by Ian Kinsler. The score remained tied until the eighteenth when Muncy homered off Nathan Eovaldi leading off to end it. In a bitter twist of statistical irony, Alex Wood pitched a scoreless eighteenth and was credited with the victory while Eovaldi, who pitched six scoreless innings before surrendering Muncy's game winning blast, was tagged with the defeat.

Game 4:   October 27, 2018
Dodger Stadium (Los Angeles)   T: 3:57
Boston 2: Los Angeles 1   A: 54,400

In what will go down as one of the most devastating losses in Dodger history, manager Dave Roberts, with one on and one out and the Dodgers leading 4-0 in the seventh, removed starter Rich Hill who was pitching a two-hit shutout and watched the lead and the Dodgers season quickly go up in smoke. Though Hill struck out Eduardo Nunez, the last batter he would face, Roberts brought in Scott Alexander who walked Brock Holt (the only batter he would face) on four pitches. Roberts then called on Ryan Madson even though Madson had allowed all five runners he'd inherited in the first two games to score. Madson promptly surrendered a pinch hit three run homer to Mitch Moreland to make it a 4-3 game. Roberts then called on closer Kenley Jansen in the eighth, for the second night in a row, and for the second night in a row Jansen surrendered a game-tying homer--this time to Steve Pearce. The Red Sox kicked the door open in the ninth, touching up three Dodger relievers for five runs with Pearce's three-run double highlighting the uprising. Kike Hernandez's two-run homer in the bottom of the frame was too little too late and the Red Sox left the field one win shy of their fourth world championship in fourteen years and the ninth in their storied history. Joe Kelly pitched two scoreless innings and was credited with the victory. Dylan Floro was tagged with the defeat. Yasiel Puig belted a three-run homer in the Dodgers four-run sixth.

Game 5:   October 28, 2018
Dodger Stadium (Los Angeles)   T: 3:00
Boston 5: Los Angeles 1   A: 54,367

In a fitting finish to their storied season, the Red Sox dominated the Dodgers from the get-go and cruised to a World Series clinching victory. Steve Pearce's two-run homer off Clayton Kershaw in the first inning proved to be all the runs the Bostons would need. David Freeze's homer in the bottom of the frame would account for LA's lone run. Mookie Betts and J.D. Martinez belted solo homers off Kershaw in the sixth and seventh respectively, and Pearce belted another two-run homer off Pedro Baez in the eighth to close out the scoring. David Price allowed one run

261

and scattered three hits in seven innings of work and was credited with his second victory of the series. Kershaw was saddled with his second defeat.

2019

Washington Nationals 4

Houston Astros 3

First series in which both sides in the first six ties won away

2020

Season postponed because of coronavirus
until: curtailed season

World Series   Dodgers   Rays
October 20 Globe Life Field, Arlington
Dodgers 8 Rays 3
WP: Kershaw

Game 2: Rays 6 Dodgers 4
Brandon Lowe 2 homers
Brandon Snell pitched well

Game 3 Dodgers 6 Rays 2
Turner & Barnes. homers
Walker Buehler pitcher allowed 1 run!

Game 4 Dodgers 7 Rays 8

Game 5 Dodgers 4 Rays 2

Joc Pederson max muncy homers
Clayton Kershaw starred
13th post season win

Game 6 Dodgers WIN!! First World Series for
Corey Seager (MVP)   262   32 years
Won 3.1
Seager gave LA the lead whilst
Mookie Betts hit a homer in the 8th.

+1 Red Sox first team in postseason history to hit 3 Grand Slams in 1st 3 innings 1st 3 games
+2 Astros 7 runs top/9th second team after marlins 1997.
+3 Chris Taylor (LA) first to hit 3 HR in post season game (1st time in career)
+4 First time in MLB history lead off batter hit HR in WS - Jorge Soler (Atl.)

Hope you enjoyed and will continue to enjoy The World Series: A Game By Game History. I'll do my best to keep it up to date. On that note, in the opening pages I stated that I put the footnotes at the bottom of the page where they occur for the reader's convenience, and in earlier editions of this book I did so. But due to formatting issues that I just have not been able to make my way past, I am going to have to place them at the end of the book. I regret the inconvenience. Thanks again, for including The World Series: A Game By Game History in your collection of baseball memorabilia. Touch 'Em All!

Your Friend,

Douglas Mallon

Alvarez (h) Astros
L. Garcia (p) Astros
+1 +2

2021 ALCS Red Sox
NLCS Dodgers

Astros (4·5) (9·5) (12·3)(2·9)(1·9)(0·5)
        Hou   Hou Bos. Bos. Bos. Hou
Braves (2·3)(4·5)(6·5)(2·9)(11·2)(2·4)
        Atl. Atl. LA   LA   +3   Atl.

Astros win AL pennant!
Braves win NL pennant!

WORLD SERIES: 2021

ASTROs: BRAVEs:

+4 Game 1: Houston: Braves 6:2 Soler hr. Duvall 2 run hr.
Game 2: Houston: Astros 7:2 Jose Urquidy (p Astros) W Fried L
Game 3: Atlanta: Braves 2:0 Travis d'Arnaud (c) hr Anderson (p WP / Garcia LP)
Game 4: Atlanta: Braves 3:2 Braves 0·2 in 6th. Back to back homers in 7th 3:2 Swanson a Soler (hr) after Riley batted in single to make it 1:2

Game 5: Atlanta: Astros 9·5 Grand Slam Braves 1st. inn Duval Astros rally nine runs, no homers!!

Game 6. Houston Braves: 7·0 Soler & Swanson HR double act again Max Fried (Braves pitcher) 6 inns O run
BRAVES 4:2 !! Freeman HR 4 hits

263

Matt Snikker (Braves. manager)
Dusty Baker (Astros)

WS MVP. Jorge Soler (Cuban 2nd a. after L. Hernan (Florid

Footnotes

1. T = Time of Game   A = Attendance

2. McGraw brazenly sent his team onto the field in black jerseys with World Champions emblazoned across the chest.

3. Schmidt, who was playing with a broken throwing hand, allowed two passed balls, committed two throwing errors, and allowed a World Series record seven stolen bases.

4. This is the smallest crowd in World Series history.

5. Cobb travelled separately from the team to avoid arrest in Ohio where he was wanted in connection with a stabbing incident.

6. Mack, who managed the A's for fifty seasons, holds the Major League record for both wins (3,766) and losses (4,025) as a manager.

7. Merkle's rbi single in the top of the frame gave NY the lead, and Snodgrass, after his error, made a sensational over the shoulder catch that likely would've gone for a run scoring triple.

8. Hooper's theft of home came on the front end of a double-steal. Tris Speaker was out at second and Hooper was safe on catcher Ed Hooper's error. He was not credited with a steal of home.

9. Ruth's World Series record 29.2 scoreless innings streak came to an end when Chicago scored two in the eighth.

10. The players went on strike before the game, demanding a bigger share of the gate receipts, but laid down their picket signs less than an hour later.

11. On August 16, 1920, Chapman was hit in the head by a pitch and died the next day.

12. In Peckinpaugh's defense, there were torrential rainstorms all afternoon long and the playing field was, by all accounts, unplayable. In the sixth inning Commissioner Landis declared the game over and the Senators (who were leading at that point) champions. But owner Calvin Griffith would not accept a tainted victory and insisted the game be completed.

13. Suspicion bordered on certainty that Alexander, the chronic alcoholic, was drunk during this stint on the mound. Said opposing pitcher Pipgras, "...I put my hand out for him to shake and I swear he missed it by a foot, he was so drunk..."

14. Martin had a cup of coffee with the Cardinals in '28 & '30, but '31 was his first full season.

15. Navin Field was renamed Briggs Stadium in 1938 and became Tiger Stadium in 1961.

16. Walters won twenty-two games and Derringer twenty games in 1940.

17. Johnny Vander Meer, the only Major Leaguer ever to hurl two consecutive no-hitters, pitched three scoreless innings for Cincinnati in the lone World Series appearance of his career.

18. Due to wartime travel restrictions, the first three games were played in Detroit, and the final four contests staged in Chicago.

19. Satchel Paige, the AL's first African-American pitcher, joined the team in midseason.

20. Konstanty, the NL's MVP, made seventy-four relief appearances. His start in Game 1 of the World Series was his first of the season.

21. This is the earliest date that a World Series game has been started. The record was matched in the following year as well.

22. Amoros, who enjoyed a solid seven year career, will always be remembered for this sensational, momentum shifting, and series deciding play.

23. Larsen's gem was also the first and only no-hitter in World Series history.

24. It was the second year in a row that Burdette started the seventh game of the World Series on two days rest.

25. The record was shattered in Game 4 when 92,650 were in attendance, and again in Game 5 when 92,706 fans passed through the turnstiles.

264

26. Bobby Richardson became the first player from a losing team to be named World Series MVP.

27. Kubek, who coughed up blood and couldn't breathe, was rushed to a hospital and made a full recovery. He played five more seasons and went on to enjoy a long career as a broadcaster on NBC'S Game of the Week.

28. Ford left with thirty-two consecutive scoreless innings, exceeding Ruth's standard by three.

29. Mantle missed the entire World Series due to an abscess on his hip.

30. Larsen's victory came six years to the day that he tossed his perfect game for New York vs. Brooklyn in the 1956 Fall Classic.

31. Mantle's homer was the sixteenth of his World Series career, surpassing Babe Ruth for the all-time leader.

32. The fourth inning uprising included a steal of home by Tim McCarver.

33. Clete Boyer's ninth inning solo homer marked the first time that two brothers homered in the same World Series, let alone the same game.

34. Gibson's thirty-one strikeouts set the standard for punch-outs by a pitcher in a World Series.

35. Lou Johnson crossed the plate in the bottom of the third inning with what proved to be the final run the Dodgers would score in the 1966 World Series.

36. Brock's seven steals set a World Series record.

37. In one of the most memorable plays of the 1968 World Series, Cards' centerfielder, Curt Flood misjudged Northrup's fly ball and then slipped while in pursuit of it. After the game the sure-handed Flood remarked, "I screwed it up. I don't want to make any alibis about it."

38. Blair and Robinson's seventh inning singles were the only two hits Baltimore would manage all afternoon.

39. Ron Swoboda made a diving catch of Brooks Robinson's sinking liner and Frank Robinson scored on the play. Swoboda made another sensational catch for the final out of the inning.

40. The previous batter, Cleon Jones, insisted that a low and inside pitch had actually hit his foot. Initially, home plate umpire, Lou DiMuro disagreed. But Jones pointed to the black shoe polish on the ball, was awarded first base and scored on Clendenon's blast.

41. Game 1 of the 1970 World Series was the first ever played on artificial turf.

42. The 1971 Orioles are the only team to feature four twenty-game winning pitchers: Mike Cuellar, Pat Dobson, Jim Palmer, Dave McNally.

43. Game 4 of the 1971 World Series was the first ever World Series game played at night.

44. The A's played the entire 1972 World Series without the services of Reggie Jackson who was injured.

45. Six of the seven games were decided by one run.

46. Knowles would go on to appear in all seven games of the 1972 World Series.

47. A's owner Charlie Finley was so incensed by Andrew's errors that he removed him from the roster after the game. Oakland's fans and players alike were outraged. So was Commissioner Bowie Kuhn who fined Finley for his actions and ordered Andrews immediately reinstated.

48. One of A's owner Charlie Finley's many "innovations" to baseball was the Designated Runner. Washington, a Michigan State track star with no baseball experience, appeared in ninety-two games during the 1974 season, all as a pinch-runner. Also, quite interestingly, Marshall was a professor at MSU whilst Washington was a student there.

49. Carbo's homer came as a pinch-hitter, the first of two pinch-hit homers he would hit in the 1975 World Series.

50. A slowly lobbed novelty pitch better suited for spring training then Game 7 of the World Series.

51. Driessen became the first National Leaguer to bat as a DH.

52. Munson finished the series with a .529 batting average. The highest for a player on a losing team in World Series history.

53. It was the tenth time in their storied history that New York won back-to-back World Championships.

54. In 2007 the Phillies became the first professional sports team in American history to lose 10,000 games.

55. Hernandez, who was 9-3 with 32 saves and a 1.92 ERA, was named both AL Cy Young award winner and regular season MVP.

56. Both Tudor and Joaquin Andujar notched twenty-one victories for the Cards in 1985.

57. Denkinger, who readily admits that he blew the call, received death threats from irate Cardinals' fans for many years. Though he enjoyed an otherwise unblemished thirty-one year career as a Major League umpire, he will always be remembered for this incident.

58. Knight's bloop single came on an 0-2 count, putting Boston just one strike away from a long awaited World Championship.

59. In his twenty-two year career, Buckner collected 2,715 hits and was a career .289 hitter. Yet he will always be remembered for this one regrettable moment.

60. It was Gibson's only appearance in the 1988 World Series.

61. It was Hatcher's seventh straight hit in as many at-bats in the 1990 World Series.

62. The Blue Jays became the first non-American franchise to win the World Series.

63. The Braves became the first Major League franchise to win a World Championship for three different cities: (Boston 1914, Milwaukee 1957, Atlanta 1995)

64. Jones became only the second player (Gene Tenace) in World Series history to homer in his first two at-bats.

65. The smooth fielding Grissom was distracted and nearly collided with right fielder Jermaine Dye on the play.

66. The Marlins became the youngest franchise (four years in existence) to win the World Series.

67. Jeter's homer came after the midnight hour constituting the first time a World Series homerun had been hit in the month of November.

68. Game 5 was the first World Series game to be started in November.

69. The Red Sox became the first team in MLB history to win a league championship series after trailing three-games-to-none. (vs. New York Yankees)

70. Okijima became the first Japanese born player to appear in a World Series game.

71. Bobby Richardson, also of the Yankees, set the bar in the 1960 World Series.

72. Many informed baseball minds believe that Roberts' marriage to analytics as the guiding force in in-game decision making proved catastrophic for the Dodgers in both the 2017 & 2018 World Series.

"High fly ball into right field...SHE IS...GONE!"
-Vin Scully, Dodger Stadium, October 15, 1988

Bill 'Moose' pg.111
Skowron? (Yankees) Grand Slam to win W/S 1956
Duvall (Braves) 2021 Braves lost!

Printed in Great Britain
by Amazon